Uses of the Other

BORDERLINES

Uses of the Other

"The East" in European Identity Formation

IVER B. NEUMANN

BORDERLINES, VOLUME 9

University of Minnesota Press

Minneapolis

Chapter 1 originally appeared as "Self and Other in International Relations," *European Journal of International Relations* 2, no. 2 (1996): 139–74; reprinted with the permission of Sage Publications. Portions of chapter 2 originally appeared as Iver B. Neumann and Jennifer M. Welsh, "The Other in European Self-Definition: An Addendum to the Literature on International Society," *Review of International Studies* 17, no. 4 (October 1991): 327–46; reprinted with the permission of Cambridge University Press. Chapter 4 originally appeared as "A Region-Building Approach to Northern Europe," *Review of International Studies* 20, no. 1 (January 1994): 53–74; reprinted with the permission of Cambridge University Press. Chapter 5 originally appeared as "Russia as Central Europe's Constituting Other," *East European Politics and Society* 7, no. 2 (1993). Chapter 6 originally appeared as "Russian Identity in the European Mirror," *European Security* 3, no. 2 (summer 1994); reprinted with permission from *European Security,* published by Frank Cass and Company, Ltd., 900 Eastern Avenue, Ilford, Essex, England.

Published by the University of Minnesota Press
111 Third Avenue South, Suite 290
Minneapolis, MN 55401-2520
http://www.upress.umn.edu

Printed in the United States of America on acid-free paper

Library of Congress Cataloging-in-Publication Data

Neumann, Iver B.
    Uses of the other : "The East" in European identity formation / Iver B. Neumann.
      p.   cm. — (Borderlines ; v. 9)
    Includes bibliographical references and index.
    ISBN 0-8166-3082-8 (hc : alk. paper). — ISBN 0-8166-3083-6 (pb : alk. paper)
    1. World politics—1989– 2. Europe—Civilization—1945– 3. Nationalism—Europe. 4. Regionalism—Europe. I. Title. II. Series: Borderlines (Minneapolis, Minn.) ; v. 9.
D860.N388   1998
327.1′094′09049 — dc21   98-11627
                                      CIP

10 09 08 07 06 05 04 03 02 01 00 99   10 9 8 7 6 5 4 3 2 1

To Jennifer Welsh: collaborator, companion, confidante

There are, it may be, so many kinds of voices in the world, and none of them is without signification. Therefore if I know not the meaning of the voice, I shall be unto him that speaketh a barbarian, and he that speaketh shall be a barbarian unto me.

— 1 CORINTHIANS 14:10–11

Contents

Preface

Of what life would be like without shackles or wounds, the Grand Idea of Emancipation tells little and knows less still. That life after emancipation has been lodged, after all, in the future—the absolute Other, the ungraspable and ineffable. — Zygmunt Bauman 1992: 225

This book presents the archeology, uses, and limitations of the self/other dichotomy in the study of world politics, and so it falls into three parts. The introduction traces thinking about self and other along four paths—the ethnographic, psychological, and Continental philosophical paths as well as what I call the "Eastern excursion"— and their convergence in the discipline of international relations (IR). The bulk of the book analyzes the identity formation of some European and territorially bounded human collectives: There are two chapters on how European identities have emerged in relation to Turkish and Russian others, two chapters on the subregions Central Europe and Northern Europe, and two chapters on the nations of Russia and Bashkortostan, focusing on their European and Russian and Tatar others, respectively. The conclusion draws on those six analyses to summarize how the self/other dichotomy can aid the understanding of collective identities, but it also points out that its use may be reifying and that we consequently need to destabilize and move beyond it.

I first became concerned with these issues in 1989, when I was a doctoral student in one of the nodes of what has been called the English school of international relations, at Oxford University. One of the canonical texts of that school is a book called *The Expansion of International Society,* and my doctorate was about how Russians had come to terms with being expanded upon by that alleged society. (A spinoff of that project surfaced in *European Security* 3, no. 2 [1994] and appears here as Chapter 6.) Of course, there was a flip side to this process, namely, how "international society," with its strong European historicity, had negotiated its own identity partly by differentiating itself from what it deemed to be its outside. As I discussed these matters with my friend and fellow student Jennifer Welsh, who was writing a doctorate about Edmund Burke and the idea of culture in international relations, we decided to write an article together about Turkey as Europe's other. It appeared in *Review of International Studies* 17, no. 4 (1991). Parts of the article have been reworked and expanded as Chapter 2, and the book is dedicated to Jennifer in gratitude for our collaboration and companionship on that first leg of the journey the fruit of which is this book.

The setting for our work was nothing less than the end of the Cold War. In the summer of 1989, I had taken up work with the Norwegian Institute of International Affairs (NUPI) as a Russianist. This was the time when, in a small country like Norway, anyone who knew how to spell Bulgaria in Bulgarian and say "put your finger down your throat" in Czech was considered an Eastern European specialist. Actually, by an extension that seemed to come unsettlingly naturally to the Norwegian press, being a Russianist with an interest in what was then known as the "Soviet Union" *meant* that you were already a specialist on Eastern Europe. This made me think about the importance of regional taxonomy for international relations. The first result of this thinking was an article about representations of a Central European regional self published in *East European Politics and Society* 7, no. 2 (1993), the predecessor of Chapter 5. It was as I finished the first draft for that article, in the spring of 1991, that I decided to investigate more systematically the uses to which the self/other nexus could be put, with a view to writing a book about European identities.

I spotted the next chance to pursue this goal right away. One of the regional results of the end of the Cold War was that, with a knowledge of what was now emerging as "Russia" and "the Baltic states," during the autumn of 1991 one was invited to conferences on themes such as "A Region in the Making?" (Tallinn), "Scandinavia in a Future European Security Arrangement" (Oslo), and "The Baltic Sea Region: Cooperation or Conflict?" (Kiel). My conference papers for these region-building activities were all metareflections about region building. At all these occasions, one of the fellow participants, who happened to work in the Norwegian Ministry of Foreign Affairs, was particularly taken by my hypothesis that all political actors would try to place themselves as centrally as possible in region-building activities. I was of course flattered by his interest—and not a little surprised when he showed me a paper he had written arguing that one should construct a "Region North" with the tiny northern Norwegian city of Kirkenes as its center. This idea went on to become one of the beginnings of what is now the institutional fact of the Barents Euro-Arctic Region in the high north, and to me, at least, there is a lesson here about intertextuality and about the fact that any intellectual, regardless of critical intent, may end up as an organic intellectual for the bearers of the state. The ideas on region building in Northern Europe eventually resulted in another article in *Review of International Studies* 20, no. 1 (1994), which appears here as Chapter 4.

Another result of this region-building activity was scholarly exchange, and together with a Russian colleague who visited NUPI, Mikhail Kryukov, I wrote a long report on whether the Russian federation would go the way of the Soviet Union, a much shortened version of which appeared in *National and Ethnic Politics* 1, no. 2 (1995). I have radically rewritten parts of this work, and it appears here as Chapter 7.

As these texts took shape under my hands, I continued to read texts on personal and collective identity formation, and I began to see the small IR literature on the issue begin to mushroom. I presented papers on this issue at seminars in Oxford, Kiev, Copenhagen, and Oslo and to meetings of the International Studies Association and the Nordic International Studies Association in 1994. Every time I was struck by how little those IR specialists who did not see the issue of identity as relevant to their research actually knew about the theorizing that I found to be most interesting and relevant, and so I decided to rewrite this material as an introduction to the study of collective identity by dint of fastening onto the self/other nexus. The result appeared in *European Journal of International Relations* 2, no. 2 (1996), and once again here in this book, as Chapter 1.

At this stage, in the summer of 1995, the book project had taken on the approximate shape in which it appears here, with the main portion consisting of two chapters on the making of Europe, two on the making of regions, and two on the making of nations. In the autumn of that year I took up a Jean Monnet Fellowship at the European University Institute, which gave me ample opportunity to write. I drafted what is now Chapter 3, on Russia as Europe's other, and really experienced "myself as another" in doing so, since it involved returning to the Europe/Russia nexus that had been the topic of my doctorate, but from a fresh perspective. I took the draft on the road and presented it in Paris, Florence, and Geneva. Geneva turned out to be a bit of a crossroads. Before Geneva, the self/other perspective had almost invariably proven unsettling to IR audiences. In Geneva, however, it came in for some rather hefty criticism for still being structuralist and dialogical when what was wanted was something poststructuralist and heterological. And, one notes, the criticism hailed from a select band of IR scholars with ties to the University of Minnesota: Karin Fierke, Keith Krause, Jennifer Milliken, and David Sylvan. So I went back and reread Derrida on binary oppositions, and I reread my own work with all that fresh in my mind, and sure enough, the tendency toward reification was certainly there. So in addition to going over all the texts again, I set myself to thinking about the limits of self/other perspectives, as well as about ways to soften the reifying tendencies of applying self/other perspectives. I presented a paper on this at the 1997 annual conference of the International Studies Association in Toronto. This paper and a paper written for a conference at the Copenhagen Peace Research Institute that same spring formed the basis for the Conclusion. It is offered as a reflective comment on the strengths and weaknesses of self/other perspectives themselves: This is what I think they can be used for. Self/other perspectives have their limits, but they also have a place inasmuch as they may fruitfully explore a dimension of *all* writings on world politics. If one is serious about approaching world politics from the margins, however, then that must also mean moving on when the margin one has temporarily chosen to occupy becomes more and more incorporated into the general text. As the self/other perspective is finding its place in so many analyses of world politics, marginals may like to contemplate whether it is not time to move elsewhere.

Given the long gestation of the book, the heterologue from which it has taken shape has consisted of many voices. Some have already been mentioned. Some have been there all along: Tim Dunne, Thomas Hylland Eriksen, Pertti Joenniemi, Ola Tunander, Ole Wæver. Some were very helpful at particular times: Andreas Behnke, Peter Burgess, David Campbell, Walter Carlsnaes, James Der Derian, Espen Barth Eide, Richard Little, Lene Hansen, Pål Kolstø, Heikki Patomäki, Ying-hsien Pi, Erik Ringmar, Adam Roberts, Alexander Wendt, Marlene Wind, Geoffrey Wiseman, and many more. And some were not helpful at all. Let me extend a word of thanks to those who assisted me in enhancing the cohesion of the book: Mathias Albert, David Campbell again, Kathy Delfosse, Karsten Friis, Carrie Mullen, Tor-Arne Rysstad, Michael Shapiro, Eilert Struksnes, Henrik Thune, to the Norwegian Non-Fiction Writers and Translators Association and the Norwegian Ministry of Defense for small grants, and to the aforementioned professional journals, whose custodians have granted me permission to reprint material.

It would of course have been nice to call this book *Care of the Other*. Given its content, however, *Uses of the Other* is definitely a more apt title. That observation should, of course, first and foremost be read as an exhortation for us to take more care when *we* tell our stories about our others.

1

Uses of the Other in World Politics

Choisir le dialogue, cela veut dire aussi éviter les deux extrêmes que sont le monologue et la guerre. —TZVETAN TODOROV 1989: 15

The discipline of international relations (IR) is witnessing a surge of interest in identity and identity formation.[1] This development has definitely been permitted and facilitated by the general uncertainty of a discipline that feels itself to have spent the 1980s barking up the wrong trees. A lack of faith in the old has made it easier for the new to break through. And yet because identity formation has been foremost among the common concerns of social theory for years and years, it is hardly coincidental that "the new" happened to take the study of identity formation as one of its major shapes. In this chapter I trace ideas about identity formation as they have evolved around the conceptual pair self/other down four different paths. This entails a good deal of rummaging in the broader field of social theory. I then examine how the interest in identity formation entered the IR discipline in full force in the late 1980s and early 1990s. In conclusion, I suggest that by drawing on the literature on collective identity formation, the discipline may not only arrive at a fuller understanding of the international system of states, but it may also finally give an ontological status to the sundry subjects or "actors" in world politics.

IDENTITY FORMATION IN SOCIAL THEORY

Tracy B. Strong, in the introduction to a reader on the self and the political order, wrote:

> Theoretical reflection on the relation of the self and the order begins in the city-states of the Eastern Mediterranean some time after around 1000 BC. It corresponds to the human understanding that there is a choice to be made as to with whom and how one will live—that humans and human lives are and can be shaped by humans themselves. (1992a: 9)

Those working outside Western philosophy may like to trace that relation back to India (Mauss [1938] 1985: 13). Anthropologists like Clifford Geertz (1979; see also Sampson 1989) repeatedly warn against treating Western ideas about the self as somehow "natural": "The [modern] Western conception of the person as a bounded, unique, more or less integrated motivational and cognitive universe . . . is, however incorrigible it may seem to us, a rather peculiar idea within the context of the world's cultures." (Geertz 1979: 229). Nonetheless, the rest of this chapter will concentrate on "Western" ideas of the self, the other, and identity formation for two reasons: First, in Erik Ringmar's (1996b) lovely phrase, modern European man and the modern state were born at the same time, and they grew up together. Almost the entire social theory literature on collective identity formation depends on an anthropomorphization of human collectives, and the human being that is being emulated is very much Renaissance Man. Second, because of the continued pertinence of its European cultural roots to international society and the continued pertinence of international society to world politics, "the Western conception of the person" continues to exert its influence on world politics everywhere, for better or worse (Bull and Watson 1984).

The history of the Western self stretches back to the Roman idea that a *persona* could have general rights and duties by dint of the idea of an inner life. In a sweeping generalization, Martin Hollis identifies basically two orientations, the Humean and the Hobbesian:

> Hobbes and Hume differ over the concept of a person. Hume . . . can find nothing but a bundle of perceptions from which to compose the self. Social theorists descended from him treat an agent as a set of ordered preferences, which action aims to satisfy. Those of Hobbesian

persuasion add a presocial atom, whose preferences they are. (Hollis 1985: 226)

The theorist who specifically relates the question of identity formation to the conceptual pair of self/other, however, is Hegel. He refines the idea that by knowing the other, the self has the power to give or withhold recognition, so as to be constituted as self at the same time:

> Each is for the other the middle term through which each mediates itself; and each is for himself, and for the other, an immediate being on its own accord, which at the same time is such only through this mediation. They recognize themselves as mutually recognizing one another. (Hegel 1977: 112)

Marx incorporated this idea in his reformulation of Hegelian dialectics, notably when he grappled with the idea of self-alienation in the 1844 Paris Notebooks (Marx 1994: 83–93). Whereas Hegel offered himself readily to what I shall later contrast as dialogical and dialectical readings of identity formation, Marx insisted much more strongly on the dialectical principle. In the end, it was Marx's version of a dialectical identity formation that became the dominant version in twentieth-century social theory; most readings of collective identity formations still tend to be dialectical, not dialogical: "The theme of 'the Other'—and specially what constitutes the otherness of 'the Other'—has been at the very heart of the work of every major twentieth-century Continental philosopher," wrote Richard Bernstein (1991: 68). Rodolphe Gasché (1986: 101) even insisted that "Western philosophy is in essence the attempt to domesticate Otherness, since what we understand by thought is nothing but such a project." One could add that it has also been central to at least one social discipline, namely, social anthropology, and that there has been a good deal of interest in other fields such as psychology, sociology, and literary theory. It is, therefore, only with considerable trepidation that I venture to suggest that this theorizing has taken four different paths. These are what may be called *the ethnographic path, the psychological path, the Continental philosophical path,* and *the "Eastern excursion."* Whereas the first three paths are institutionalized forms of knowledge production, the fourth path has unfolded on the margins of academia; it has been a chain of activity that has unfolded in sites that have been marginal in many ways:

marginal because excluded from the center of academic disciplines and so thriving in those spaces where those disciplines overlapped one another; marginal because characterized by the double-voicedness to be found in milieus of exile; marginal, also, because it has questioned the very possibility of centers and unequivocal production of knowledge; marginal, that is, to the academic, national, and political archives of modernity. But perhaps exactly for this reason, the, as it were, subterranean theorizing that has taken place along this path has over the last thirty years descended on the other three paths and proved to be the main catalyst for change. This path is, for all these reasons, the most interesting path of the four and is therefore to be presented last.

THE ETHNOGRAPHIC PATH

The ethnographic path has been trodden by those international relations scholars who have done work on nationalism and may therefore be, as it were, closest to home. The basic insight of this literature goes back to Emile Durkheim's theory of the social division of labor: The lineation of an "in-group" must necessarily entail its demarcation from a number of "out-groups," and that demarcation is an *active* and ongoing part of identity formation. The creation of social boundaries is not a consequence of integration; rather, it is one of its necessary a priori ingredients (Durkheim 1964: 115–22; Lévi-Strauss [1973] 1978).

In the postwar period, it was mainly left to social anthropology to carry out a range of studies of self/other relations whose sophistication far surpassed what had been done in the other social sciences (see, for example, Epstein 1978). In the classic *Ethnic Groups and Boundaries* (1969b), Fredrik Barth et al. proposed that ethnicity (and, one could argue by extension, collective identity formation generally) could most fruitfully be studied by taking the boundaries of ethnic groups as a point of departure. Until then, studies tended to draw up unsystematic catalogues of cultural traits that seemed to be endogenous. Barth moved the focus by demonstrating that ethnic groups were reproduced by the very maintenance of the boundaries that separate them from other groups, who were seen to be constituted as other by their lack of this or that trait. In other words, he proposed that the self/other nexus be studied, as it were, from the slash outward, in terms of the boundary markers of identity, which he calls "diacritica." Thus, when studying the self/other nexus, the starting point should be to identify the slash and how it is maintained. It is the great merit of this move that it wrests identity formation from the psychological path, which will be discussed later, and places it firmly in the sphere of social interaction. From the standpoint of world politics, however, one must warn against the bias inculcated by the subject matter of ethnography: When ethnographers set out to study collective identity formation, they will immediately settle for the study of ethnic groups, subcultures, villages, and other small-scale collectives. And yet, although the lingering hegemony of nationalism makes ethnically based collective identities particularly prone to being inscribed with political meaning, there are also republicanism (Mouritsen 1995), gender (Olesen 1994), and class (see the discussion of the Continental philosophical path). For our purposes, a scale upgrade is needed.

Ethnography's break with psychological conjecture does not mean that psychological insights lose their relevance altogether. An anthropologist like Jonathan Friedman may still refer to early socialization processes and argue that otherness "begins at home, with our primary others. We become egos, it is said, via the internalisation of significant others' objectification of ourselves. Our unity is located in the *regard de l'autre*" (1991: 99). It means, however, that there is no excuse for simply postulating this or that psychological mechanism—the other as a "looking-glass self," for example—and neglecting the actual research that it takes to analyze the formation of particular self/other nexuses. For example, it is easy to follow theorists of nationalism like Benedict Anderson (1983; compare Gellner 1983) in asserting that the nation is an "imagined community." This, however, is only a starting point. It is a research question, and not a question of conjecture, to decide which diacritica mark a particular self/other nexus, between nations as well as between other human collectives.

Barth has recently remarked casually that "the selection of such diacritica is far less haphazard than I may have indicated in 1969" (1994: 179). But which are they? If one takes into consideration the effects of globalization (Robertson 1992)—of a "world time" to which more and more collective identity formation sequences have to relate—and if one still grants hegemonic force to the idea of the nation, then language may be expected to be a crucial marker. As suggested by, among others, Benedict Anderson's (1983) and Thomas Eriksen's (1993) studies of nationalism, for example, nationalism tends to have a "modular quality" whereby the imagining of each new nation tends to draw on some of the diacritica evolved in earlier imaginings of nations.[2] Of course, as pointed out by Partha Chatterjee (1986, 1993), this insight must not get in the way of representing each specific nationalism as being also unique. The cost of such an assimilating perspective would be very high indeed:

> The shift from a focus on the *productivist* and *aesthetic* underpin-nings of the emergence of the national form to an emphasis on the *circulationist* character of the national idea paradoxically results in the removal of *all* imagination from the process of imagining community. At an even more elementary level, while Anderson's initial discussion of nationalism involves a metaphysics of *becoming*, sensitive to the effect of spatio-temporal change upon the imagination, by the end of the book, his discussion of nationalism is imbued with a metaphysics of *being*, incapable of recognising how recent changes in communica-tion and transportation technology might impact upon processes cen-tral to imagining community. (Ullock 1996: 427–28)

Barth's insistence on a certain regularity where boundary markers are concerned does not of course ipso facto rule out any phenomena; *anything* may be inscribed with meaning as a politically relevant boundary marker. Although in the analyses to follow most of the diacritica discussed will turn on matters of language, history, reli-gion, and so on, there are two lessons here that should indeed be heeded: Certain diacritica will be highly culture specific, and other diacritica may be made crucial by interpretations that may strike the outside observer as highly esoteric. Two preliminary examples will suffice. Most international relations scholars (but not most anthro-pologists) were surprised that song festivals were among the key dia-critica when the Baltic states inscribed their collective identities with ever more political meaning; in this case, human collectives actually sang themselves toward sovereignty. Language has been a crucial marker of national identity. (Even if only inversely so: In Arab-speaking countries, there exist strong sanctions against making spo-ken forms relevant for written ones, since this is held to constitute an onslaught on the commonly held Arab identity, which is in all these countries one of the overlapping political identities.) What makes language an important bearer of national identity, however, is not necessarily its distance to other languages relevant to the social setting in question. To take but one example: In terms of etymology, syntax, and pronunciation, the distances between Croatian and Serbian or Russian and Ukrainian are negligible compared to the distance between Finnish and Swedish or Hungarian and Romanian. This, however, does not seem to disqualify Croatian and Ukrainian as markers of national identity. (Yet nation builders seem to feel a certain unease about the affinities: Ongoing attempts at standardizing written Croatian and Ukrainian generally imply privileging those variants of vocabulary and syntax whose distance from Serbian and Russian are deemed the greater.) The pervasiveness of the view that these things are of political importance means that even states that profess to having the same state language will make linguistic differences a matter of political identity. To give a lexical example: Austria's recent protocol of accession to the European Union (EU) included a list of twenty-three objects for which one word (for example, *Kartoffel*) is used in Germany and another (for example, *Erdapfel*) is used in Austria. When potatoes are referred to in an EU document, the protocol states that both words must be given in the German text. Thus every time an EU document involving one of these word pairs is published, it will have the effect of confirming that the German language is connected to two different political identities. The dividing line between self and other (Germany/Austria) will be maintained, often perhaps without readers being aware of it (that is, it will happen on the level of practical and not of discursive competence; see Giddens 1991). Other relevant identities, for example a German-speaking Swiss one, will not be implicated and so will not be confirmed.

THE PSYCHOLOGICAL PATH

The working of the boundary between an "us" and a "them" is the home turf of social psychology, which has belabored "ethnocentrism" and sundry related phenomena throughout the twentieth century:

> A differentiation arises between oneselves, the we-group, or in-group, and everybody else, or the other-groups, out-groups. The insiders in a we-group are in a relation of peace, order, law, government, and industry to each other. Their relation to all outsiders, or other-groups, is one of war and plunder, except so far as agreements have modified it. (Hogg and Abrams 1988: 17).

One should expect the social identification approach to be of immediate interest here. It sees self-categorization as an explanation of how individuals are turned into groups:

> Just as we categorize objects, experiences and other people, we also categorize ourselves. The outcome of this process of self-categorization is an accentuation of similarities between self and other in-groupers and differences between self and out-groupers, that is, self-stereotyping. To be more precise, self-categorization causes self-perception and self-definition to become more in terms of the individual's representation of the defining characteristics of the group, or the group *prototype*. (Hogg and Abrams 1988: 21)

I do not intend to discuss this literature further because it is akin to the literatures on attribution theory and cognitive consistency that made their imprint on the discipline of international relations in the 1960s and 1970s and that turned out to be a blind ally. The foreign policy analysis literature on perception, belief systems, operational codes, *Feindbilder* (enemy images), and so on failed because it tended to begin and end with a self that was not socially situated and so did not focus directly on the *nexus* between the self and the other (see Bloom 1990 for a recent example). What made these studies less persuasive than they might otherwise have been was probably their treatment of language as an unproblematic vessel for the transformation of meaning from one bounded individual to another, instead of focusing on transformations inherent in language itself to understand those social relations that should be the object of study.

However, there does exist a body of Lacanian psychoanalytical literature that redresses this by studying identity formation as an attempt to overcome a lack, as a process of desire for the power of the other, that produces an image of the self. That is, it treats language as referential rather than relational. Anne Norton has followed this line of inquiry and has foregrounded and illuminated the role played by the socially marginal. "The categories of self and other," she wrote,

> are shown to emerge with clarity as categories only where they are empirically dubious. . . . Individual and collective identities are created not simply in the difference between self and other but in those moments of ambiguity where one is other to oneself, and in the recognition of the other as like. (Norton 1988: 4, 7)

One notes the affinity of Norton's proposal to study identity formation where self and other ambiguously overlap (particularly what she calls "liminar" groups) and social anthropology's insistence on studying boundary markers. Norton suggests that the capacity to recognize the other as like is tied to a certain external *bodily* similarity. The political significance of this seems enormous. She draws attention to Jean-Jacques Rousseau's dictum that the citizen's body *is* the body politic, quoting him to the effect that "the words subject and Sovereign are identical correlatives, the idea of which reunites itself under the single word 'citizen'" (1988: 28). She then uses the parallel drawn between the body and the body politic as a launching pad for an intriguing suggestion:

> Accompanying this conviction is another: that likemindedness is coextensive with a likeness of physiological constitution; that all men, insofar as they have the same bodies, have the same capacity for reason, the same emotions, the same desires. This conviction, which has lent particular ferocity to debates over racial and sexual difference, denies the role of politics and language in the constitution of the mind. (Norton 1988: 42).

This is an interesting starting point not least for the study of how collective identity formations are "gendered." The semiotician Yuri Lotman (1990) discusses an example that may throw further light on Norton's discussion of the role of the liminar for identity formation. Seventeenth-century Russians defined themselves, among other ways, in relation to a group that was resident on their territorial borders and was known to them as *svoi pagany* (our pagans). Being of Orthodox religion was the main marker of Russianness at this point in time-space. Yet the existence of a group that was somewhat heterodox but nonetheless (and ostensibly impossibly) "our" embodied the inevitable ambiguity of identity formation and the inherent uncertainty of the categories us/them and self/other.

THE CONTINENTAL PHILOSOPHICAL PATH

The Continental philosophical path, that high road of modernity, is, as I have already intimated, paved with Marxian dialectics. One meets the self and the other as raw material for a possible dialectical *Aufhebung* (sublation, elevation) in the name of reason and progress in a number of different loci, for example, in Sartre:

It is strange that the problem of Others has never truly disturbed the realists. To the extent that the realist takes everything as given, doubtless it seems to him that the Other is given. In the midst of the real, what is more real than the Other? (Sartre 1957: 223)

In Habermasian "discourse ethics," the self and other are still ideally lodged in "ideal speech situations"—abstracted from power and indeed from the multiplicities of social bonds other than the bond of reasoned discourse. It is probably because of this lack of social placement that the most striking thing about the theorizing that has followed this path is its seemingly limited ability to offer new insights about collective identity formation.

One exception is Charles Taylor's book *Sources of the Self* (1989; see also Connolly 1985), which provides a magisterial overview of ideas of the self in the Western tradition. He proposes that these ideas can be found along three dimensions: There is, first, the idea of obligation to others. Second, there is the idea that there exists an ideal, a fully fledged goal, a pregiven narrative into which the fullness of a self's biography should fall. The two major and vying contemporary narratives, Taylor suggests, are that of the hero script and that of the affirmation of everyday life. According to the first, the self should assert itself and soar above its fellows; according to the other, the self should simply keep plodding. There opens up a vista for studying different human collectives in terms of the different scripts by which selves and others are constituted. The third dimension is the idea of presentation of self. Developments along the last two dimensions will obviously have an impact on dynamics along the first. To give but two examples: If what is found along the third dimension is a nonreflective mode of self and social order, of the type that is to be found in the Homeric poems, then ideas about the other will necessarily look rather different from what they would look like in a reflective order. And if what is found along the second dimension is basically a hero script, then this will also have immediate repercussions.

The dialectics at play along the Continental philosophical path has one major effect on studies of the self/other nexus, namely, that they bring to those studies an assimilatory thrust. Even for a thinker like Jürgen Habermas, who is trying to rid himself of this tendency, one may argue that the central insistence on consensus as the very goal of dialogue preserves this tendency toward assimilation. It is instructive in this regard to see how theorizing of the self/other nexus tends to play itself out in response to gauntlets thrown by the travelers along what I call here the Eastern excursion. In the preface to the English translation of his doctoral thesis, for example, Habermas (1992) attempts to overcome these problems by discussing Mikhail Bakhtin. Even Taylor's discussion of the ontological standing of the self may be read as an answer to problems formulated by Bakhtin. The clash that may be observed here between dialectical and dialogical sensibilities seems to be of far-reaching importance for the study of the self/other nexus. Instead of turning further down the Continental philosophical path, then, I turn now to what is this book's main fount of inspiration, namely, the dialogical thinking to be found along the path of the Eastern excursion.

THE "EASTERN EXCURSION"

The fourth and last path along which theorizing of collective identity may be found, the Eastern excursion, is not a well-trodden path like the high road of modernity; rather, it began as more or less isolated little forays into uncharted territory. I shall mention but four of the authors who have taken this path. Besides trying to theorize the self/other nexus, what they have in common is that they are marginal to the high road and, hardly unrelated, that there has been a surge of interest in their writings over the last couple of decades. There is first Georg Simmel, who discusses the importance of the margin of the collective self, what he refers to as "the stranger":

> The state of being a stranger is of course a completely positive relation. . . . The stranger is an element of the group itself, not unlike the poor and sundry "inner enemies"—an element whose membership within the group involves both being outside it and confronting it. (1970: 144)

Strangers—the sociologically marginal—play an important role in collective identity formation inasmuch as their very presence brings the question of who is self and who is other to the fore. The ambiguity of strangers may serve to highlight the possible ambiguity between these two categories themselves. Norton's liminars are exemplified and, as it were, embodied in groups of strangers.[3]

Then there is Carl Schmitt, who maintains that the state defines itself by being the unit that distinguishes public enemies (*Feind*) from friends (*Freund*). If a given state fails to do so, its authority will immediately be challenged by some other unit that will take on this burden. Schmitt sees the public enemy in our epoch exclusively as a concern of the political unit, which to him is the sovereign nation-state. This public enemy

> does not have to be morally evil, he does not have to be aesthetically ugly, he does not have to appear as an economic competitor, and it can . . . even be advantageous to have business dealings with him. He is nevertheless the Other (*Andere*). (Schmitt 1936: 14)

Whereas Simmel drew attention to the margin between self and other and Schmitt pared politics down to the act of distinguishing between them, Friedrich Nietzsche's great contribution was to begin to dissolve these categories (Dallmayr 1981: 27). Nietzsche stressed that the world does not simply present itself to human beings; rather, the activity of knowing is a formulation of the world. This knowing cannot take place from any solid foundation, and so the self will know the other and everything else only as a series of changing perspectives, not as a foundational fact. Indeed, it is the knowing that makes the self, not the other way around. Nietzsche's perspectivism concludes "that 'I' am a number of different ways of knowing and that there is no such entity as a permanent or privileged self" (Strong 1992b: 174). At the same time, he warned about the dangers of ressentiment, that is, of taking one's identity from the postulation of a negative other: "*Ressentiment,* born of weakness, to no one more harmful than to the weak man himself—in the opposite case, where a rich nature is the presupposition, a *superfluous* feeling to stay master of which is almost the proof of richness" (Nietzsche [1908] 1992: 46).[4]

If it is a defining trait of all these three that they more or less break with a dialectical understanding of the self/other nexus, it was left to the fourth to describe a fully fledged alternative to it. Mikhail Bakhtin's work was an attempt to redress exactly what he saw as the hollowness in philosophizing about the self. He believed that what he called "epistemological consciousness" or even "epistemologism" pervaded "all nineteenth-century and twentieth-century philosophy." By "epistemologism" he meant the reification of a knowing and sovereign self, cut off from the consciousness of the other:

Epistemological consciousness, the consciousness of science, is a unitary and unique consciousness, or, to be exact—a single consciousness. Everything this consciousness deals with must be determined by itself alone: any determinateness must be derived from itself and any determination of an object must be performed by itself. In this sense, epistemological consciousness cannot have another consciousness outside itself, cannot enter into relation with another consciousness, one that is autonomous and distinct from it. Any unity is its *own* unity; it cannot admit next to itself any other unity that would be different from it and independent of it (the unity of nature, the unity of another consciousness), that is, any sovereign unity that would stand over against it with its *own* fate, one *not* determined by epistemological consciousness. (Bakhtin 1990: 89)

What is wrong with this epistemologism is exactly the absence of the other. Without the other, Bakhtin insisted, the subject actually cannot know either itself or the world because meaning is created in discourse, where consciousnesses meet. In opposition to what had happened along the Continental philosophical path, Bakhtin thus in the early 1920s was already asserting that the other has the status of an epistemological as well as an ontological necessity. Whereas Bakhtin thus actively chose to distance himself from the broad path of Continental philosophy, this distance was further enhanced by the fact that he carried out his work inside the Soviet Union. He was removed from contact with the Continental tradition, even if he had wished to maintain a more active relationship with it.[5] The importance of all this to an archaeology of thinking on self/other perspectives has first and foremost to do with how Bakhtin's theorizing of the self/other nexus was reconfronted with the high road of modernity exactly at the time when a number of theoreticians veered off this road in Paris. One recalls that 1967 was the year when Jacques Derrida published no fewer than three seminal books, *Of Grammatology* being foremost among them. And it was in 1966 that Julia Kristeva introduced Bakhtin to a "Western" readership. As Kristeva's editor Toril Moi pointed out, this introduction occurred in a text that bore the marks both of the "high structuralism" that Kristeva and others were writing themselves away from and of what was to come after structuralism. It is worth quoting Kristeva at some length here:

> Bakhtin foreshadows what Emile Benveniste has in mind when he speaks about *discourse,* that is "language appropriated by the individual

as a practice." . . . Bakhtin, however, born of a revolutionary Russia that was preoccupied with social problems, does not see dialogue only as language assumed by a subject; he sees it, rather, as a *writing* where one reads the *other* (with no allusion to Freud). Bakhtinian dialogism identifies writing as both subjectivity and communication, or better, as intertextuality. Confronted with this dialogism, the notion of a "person-subject of writing" becomes blurred, yielding to that of "ambivalence of writing." . . . The notion of dialogism, which owed much to Hegel, must not be confused with Hegel's dialectics, based on a triad and thus on struggle and projection (a movement of transcendence), which does not transgress the Aristotelian tradition founded on substance and causality. Dialogism replaces these concepts by absorbing them within the concept of relation. It does not strive towards transcendence but rather towards harmony, all the while implying an idea of rupture (of opposition and analogy) as a modality of transformation. . . . More than binarism, dialogism may well become the basis of our time's intellectual structure. (Kristeva [1966] 1986: 39, 58–59)

Dialogism may at least be the best starting point for the study of collective identity formation. As Kristeva stressed, by doing away with the totalizing belief in progress inherent in dialectics, dialogism definitely offered itself as an alternative path along which to theorize identity (Holquist 1990). Indeed, it seems clear that the dialogical understanding of identity formation evolved out of a growing dissatisfaction with the dialectical interpretation and the political practices it inspired. In the case of Bakhtin, whose texts may yet await a broader reception in the social sciences, his writing self is directly implicated in this break: Writing as he did in a situation in which public discourse had been all but mopped up by Stalin and in which the possibility of public face-to-face discourse had all but vanished, he presented as an alternative the idea that texts could carry on a dialogue with one another across time and space. Kristeva came to read Bakhtin while growing up in Bulgaria, where she was also exposed to a crushing grounding in Marxian dialectics. The writing and reception of her piece were part of a general reorientation away from modern totalizing analyses. I have chosen to call this path "Eastern" because of the pivotal role played by Bakhtin and an "excursion" because of the force with which Bakhtinean and in an even greater degree Nietzschean insights grew into a path in their own right and curved back to offer an alternative to the Continental philosophical path. This is the story of the arrival of "poststructuralism." Indeed, in his aforementioned *tour d'horizon* of the intellectual landscape at the beginning of the 1990s, Richard Bernstein goes so far as to juxtapose what is left of the high road of modernity and poststructuralism as together making up the "new constellation" of social theorizing. Collective identity formation was a major concern of the new arrivals, as is evident, for example, from the way Michel Foucault explained why he had adopted Nietzsche's genealogical pose:

> The purpose of genealogy, guided by history, is not to discover the roots of our identity but to commit itself to its dissipation. It does not seek to define our unique threshold of emergence, the homeland to which metaphysicians promise a return; it seeks to make visible all of those discontinuities that cross us. . . . If genealogy in its own right gives rise to questions concerning our native land, native language, or the laws that govern us, its intention is to reveal the heterogeneous systems which, masked by the self, inhibit the formation of any form of identity. (Foucault 1977a: 156, 162)

There are many "Easts" in the world, and none of them is without signification. The focus of this book is European identities and the role played by its geographically immediate Eastern others. Since there is no inclusion without exclusion, this focus cannot but background the role played by other Easts. I mention this here not only because it has a bearing on what is being discussed in the succeeding chapters but particularly because one response to the thinking of Derrida, Foucault, and others explicitly fastened onto the East/West and self/other nexuses. I have in mind Edward Said's work on Orientalism, which was so successful in re-presenting these nexuses that the very word "Orientalist" has left its mark as a standard charge against those who oversee the role of "Easts" in the forging of "Wests." Said's work is also of interest because he raised a crucial methodological point (to which we will return in the conclusion):

> Unlike Michel Foucault, to whose work I am greatly indebted, I do believe in the determining imprint of individual writers upon the otherwise anonymous collective body of texts constituting a discursive formation like Orientalism. . . . Foucault believes that in general the individual text or author counts for very little; empirically, in the case of Orientalism (and perhaps nowhere else) I find this not to be so. (Said [1978] 1985: 23; for an elaboration, see Said 1983: 178–225)

There is one more reason why I have called this path the "Eastern excursion," however, and that has to do with the importance for it of the writings of Emmanuel Lévinas. Although Lévinas has only reached a broader readership in the 1990s, his importance as a source of inspiration for Derrida and other poststructuralists makes him part and parcel of the general development under discussion.[6] Lévinas himself grew up and received important impulses as a practicing Jew in prerevolutionary Vilna (now Vilnius), often called "the Jerusalem of the East" (Kemp 1992). Like Kristeva, then, he came to Paris not only from a geographical but also from a philosophical East.

Having just insisted on rooting the study of self/other relations in space and time, it may seem paradoxical to turn to a transcendental thinker like Emmanuel Lévinas for an example of how otherness is treated. Yet because besides Bakhtin he is the thinker on otherness par excellence and is perhaps even less known among IR scholars than is Bakhtin, I will nonetheless do so (but see Der Derian 1994 and the discussion between Campbell [1996] and Warner [1996] in *Millennium*). Lévinas condemns an ontological approach to the self as basically a violent one and therefore insists on the need to take a transcendental approach. In this way, the story of the self becomes sacred but also *social* history, derivative from the appearance of the other, mediated in language. The face of the other summons the self into existence:

> To be sure, the other (*l'Autre*) that is announced does not possess this existing as the subject possesses it; its hold over my existing is mysterious. It is not known but unknowable, refractory to all light. But this precisely indicates that the other is in no way another myself, participating with me in a common existence. The relationship with the other is not an idyllic and harmonious relationship of communion, or a sympathy through which we put ourselves in the other's place; we recognize the other as resembling us, but exterior to us; the relationship with the other is a relationship with a Mystery. The other's entire being is constituted by its exteriority, or rather its alterity, for exteriority is a property of space and leads the subject back to itself through light. (Lévinas 1989: 43)

This meeting has a timely, historical dimension, inasmuch as the other, because of its association with death—that ultimate other whose coming is certain—defines the future.[7] The other emerges more clearly as a social entity as Lévinas turns toward the sphere of everyday life:

If the relationship with the other involves more than relationships with Mystery, it is because one has accosted the other in everyday life where the solitude and fundamental alterity of the other are already veiled in decency. One is for the other what the other is for oneself; there is no exceptional place for the subject. The other is known through sympathy, as another (my)self, as the alter ego. (Lévinas 1989: 47)

Once we have fallen to earth, as it were, ontology seems to have reentered the story. There remains a tension between the fact that the other is an alter ego and the fact that "the Other is what I myself am not." Lévinas stresses the possible asymmetry of power here, where the I may be rich and powerful whereas the other may be poor and weak. And he stresses that the other cannot be conceived of as freedom because freedom invites either submission or enslavement and thus leads to its own extinction. Enter the problem of *collective* identity formation, that is, politics. The other upsets order, simply by being other, and what is one to do when there is a multiplicity of others?

Indeed, if there were only two of us in the world, I and one other, there would be no problem. The other would be completely my responsibility. But in the real world there are many others. When others enter, each of them external to myself, problems arise. Who is closest to me? Who is the Other? Perhaps something has already occurred between them. We must investigate carefully. Legal justice is required. There is need for a state. (Lévinas 1989: 247)

This is where Lévinas self-consciously begins to engage with the canon of theorizing on the modern state. The point he wants to make is about the contrast between his own concern and the general thrust of that canon:

But it is very important to know whether the state, society, law, and power are required because man is a beast to his neighbour (*homo homini lupus*) or because I am responsible for my fellow. It is very important to know whether the political order defines man's responsibility or merely restricts his bestiality. It is very important, even if the conclusion is that all of us exist for the sake of the state, the society, the law. (Lévinas 1989: 247–248)

There is a tension here. On the one hand, his transcendent thinking makes him skeptical toward the totalizing demands of the state; the state of Caesar is "the last refuge of idolatry":

Developing from the form it received from the Graeco-Roman world, the pagan State, jealous of its sovereignty, the State in pursuit of hegemony, the conquering imperialist, totalitarian, oppressive State, attached to a realist egoism. As such it separates humanity from its deliverance. Unable to exist without adoring itself, it is pure idolatry. This striking vision arises independently of any text: in a world of scruples and of respect for man derived from monotheism, the Chancellory, with its *Realpolitik,* comes from another universe, sealed off from sensibility, or protest by "beautiful souls," or tears shed by an "unhappy consciousness." (Lévinas 1989: 274)

Yet on the other hand, since he pries not into the case of the state in its generality but into the specific state of Israel, he does not leave the matter there. Initially, his is a seemingly universalizing move on behalf of the state form as such:

The sovereignty of the State incorporates the universe. In the sovereign State, the citizen may finally exercise a will. It acts absolutely. Leisure, security, democracy: these mark the return of a condition, the beginning of a free being. This is why man recognizes his spiritual nature in the dignity he achieves as a citizen or, even more so, when acting in the service of the State. The State represents the highest human achievement in the lives of western peoples. The coincidence of the political and the spiritual marks man's maturity, for spiritual life like political life purges itself of all the private, individual, sentimental chiaroscuro on which religions still nurture themselves. (Lévinas 1989: 259–260)

Yet it immediately becomes clear that Lévinas is not simply celebrating the state of Israel as one state among many. Israel also has a messianic side, which soars above the "political bookkeeping" of the "proud West"; it is *more* than "a State like any other" (1989: 283). Israel is a state harboring a great civilization, and

a great civilization . . . is universal, that is to say it is precisely capable of whatever can be found in any other civilization, of whatever is humanly legitimate. It is therefore fundamentally non-original, stripped of all local colour. Only those civilizations labelled exotic (or the exotic and perishable elements of civilizations) can be easily distinguished from one another. (Lévinas 1989: 265)

Levinas was born in 1906, when Vilna was still part of the Russian empire. One of the lasting influences on him from that time onward has been the work of Fyodor Dostoyevsky, and particularly *The Brothers Karamazov*, from which he quotes repeatedly. It is not hard to see how Alyosha Karamazov's idea that everybody is responsible for everybody else would appeal to the philosopher of alterity, or the similarities between Dostoyevsky's treatment of the relationship between state and spirit (the Grand Inquisitor and the starets) and Lévinas's way of approaching that problem. And yet, though Dostoyevsky the novelist is widely known and lauded, his political pamphleteer self, as a Great Russian nationalist, is not widely known. Not only did Dostoyevsky support imperial Russian rule throughout the territory that it possessed during his lifetime, but he also encouraged its further expansion into Constantinople, perhaps even to India. The way Dostoyevsky mustered support for these claims among his compatriots was exactly by appealing to a transcendental version of the commonplace nineteenth-century ideas of historical and ahistorical nations, namely that of the Russian civilization, which according to him encompassed all of humanity: "Yes, the Russian's destiny is incontestably all-European and universal. To become a genuine and all-round Russian means perhaps to become a brother of all men, a *universal man,* if you please" (Dostoyevsky [1876–1881] 1954: 979).

Whether Lévinas simply takes Dostoyevsky's outpourings on the historical mission of Russia and applies them to Israel must be further studied; my claim for now is simply that their textual moves are similar. (The importance of this for our undertaking will become clear in a moment.) Dostoyevsky constructed his claim by maintaining that Russia was more generous and more capable of universalism than "Europe." He thus invoked a comparison and established a hierarchy. What about Lévinas? To him, Israel is the Chosen People of the Book because it is better at taking responsibility for the other than are others: "It is a strange and uncomfortable privilege, a peculiar inequality that imposes obligations towards the Other which are not demanded of the Other in return. To be conscious of having been chosen no doubt comes down to this" (Lévinas 1989: 286).

Lévinas is aware of the enormity of this claim, guarding against criticism as he presents it by saying that others may see here nothing but a petitioning nationalism. As far as I am concerned, this is indeed so. But there is more. According to Lévinas, "the Third" must stand in relation to the self and the other as "a sovereign judge who decides between two equals" (quoted in Bauman 1992: 113). Lévinas is on record as having had a chance to try out this role. In an interview about Israel's responsibility for the massacres of Palestinians in Sabra and Chatila in 1982, Shlomo Malka and the philosopher of alterity exchanged words as follows:

> S.M.: Emmanuel Lévinas, you are the philosopher of the "other." Isn't history, isn't politics the very site of the encounter with the "other," and for the Israeli, isn't the "other" above all the Palestinian?
>
> E.L.: My definition of the other is completely different. The other is the neighbour, who is not necessarily kin, but who can be. And in that sense, if you're for the other, you're for the neighbour. But if your neighbour [ostensibly Lebanese Phalangists] attacks another neighbour [ostensibly Palestinians] or treats him unjustly, what can you do? Then alterity takes on another character, in alterity we can find an enemy. (Quoted from Lévinas 1989: 294)

It is hard to make heads or tails of this, to determine why this should imply a "completely different" understanding. In one context, Lévinas treats the Jewish people as an entity that can be meaningfully discussed as constituted by an other for which it takes more responsibility than that collective other takes for the Jewish people. And yet, when presented with a case where this clearly did not happen, the propensity to collectivize the other evaporates. Lévinas makes the political choice of first being a nationalist and only second a philosopher of alterity who ostensibly has a responsibility to bear witness. The question arises, then, of whether the uneasiness inspired by this shirking of responsibility on the part of Lévinas is simply the result of an idiosyncracy on his part—his failure to act as what he calls "a sovereign judge"—or whether it is intrinsically linked to his framing of the political. As Lévinas is among the authors on whom work on identity in international relations may be expected to draw, there will be a chance to return to this question as part of the discussion of how the issue of collective identity formation entered the discipline.

INTERNATIONAL RELATIONS AS SELF/OTHER RELATIONS

Though one may safely say that Lévinas does not engage fully with the political, one must also note that there is a *general* reluctance to address the concerns of the discipline of international relations in the vast literature on collective identity formation. In turning to a discussion of how these insights were led into the discipline, however, one notes immediately that the first full-length study to address world political concerns did not appear from inside the discipline. It was the work of a literary critic, Tzvetan Todorov ([1981] 1984), who, as a Bakhtinian of Bulgarian background and the mentor of Julia Kristeva, was also part of the "Eastern excursion." His book *The Conquest of America: The Question of the Other* treated the early-sixteenth-century Spanish legal-clerical debate about the status of "the Indians" of the New World. In addition to demonstrating the importance of the meeting of civilizations to the discipline of international relations (cf. Alker 1992), Todorov suggested that one may "locate the problematics of alterity" along at least three axes:

> First of all, there is a value judgment (an axiological level): the other is good or bad. . . . Secondly, there is the action of *rapprochement* of distancing in relation to the other (a praxeological level): I embrace the other's values, I identify myself with him; or else I identify the other with myself, I impose my own image upon him; between submission to the other and the other's submission, there is also a third term, which is neutrality, or indifference. Thirdly, I know or am ignorant of the other's identity (this would be the epistemic level). (Todorov [1982] 1992: 185)

Todorov demonstrated how the relation between self and other cannot be grasped on one level alone by comparing the relations of people like Hernán Cortés and Bartolomé de Las Casas to "the Indians." Where axiology is concerned, Las Casas loved the Indians more than Cortés (discussions of whether or not a given creature is "human" or not would also belong along this axis). On the epistemic level, however, Cortés's knowledge of the Indian was superior to that of Las Casas. On the praxeological level, both proposed a relationship of assimilation—the submission of the other. Todorov's distinction explodes the kind of easy thinking that is based on the premise that if only human collectives came to know one another better, they would also act less violently toward one another.[8] His typology seems useful. One may, for example, specify the critique made of Lévinas above by maintaining that his value judgment singles out Jews as a human collective possessing a unique mission. I would hold that such a view cannot but have consequences along the praxeological axis, for example, by inducing a proclivity to disregard Israeli culpability in Israeli-Palestinian relations. What a specific self/other nexus would look like in terms of these three axes must, however, remain an issue for empirical research; it is not a matter of conjecture.

Todorov's monograph was the first fully fledged application of the self/other problematique to a historical discursive sequence, but the monograph that extended this kind of analysis into the discipline of international relations was arguably James Der Derian's genealogy of diplomacy (1987). The human collectives that served as Der Derian's selves and others were states, and the focus of his analysis was their mediation of estrangement. The tension between a dialectical and a dialogical reading of the relations between selves and others was a main theme of the first section of this chapter, where it was discussed as a dividing line in social theory at large. Now I will argue that it is also a feature of Der Derian's work. I suggested that a dialectical and a dialogical reading could be seen to be perching uneasily in Kristeva's Bakhtin article from 1966, where she traced them both back to Hegel: "The notion of dialogism, which owed much to Hegel, must not be confused with Hegel's dialectics, based on a triad and thus on struggle and projection" (Kristeva [1966] 1986: 58). In Der Derian's work on diplomacy, the theoretical accent was firmly on the idea of alienation, with all the dialectical baggage that term entails. And yet Bakhtin made an uncited cameo appearance; a reference to "this year's Other" suggested a very much looser relationship between the self and the other than that postulated by a dialectical reading, and the book's conclusion was indeed dialogical: "Until we learn how to recognize ourselves as the Other, we shall be in danger and we shall be in need of diplomacy" (Der Derian 1987: 167, 297, 209). The point I am trying to make is simply that at the moment when the self/other problematique finally reached the discipline of international relations, there was a repetition of the shift away from a dialectical to a dialogical reading that had taken place in social theory at large some twenty years earlier.

Drawing particularly on Jean Baudrillard, Der Derian has since gone on to suggest that the entire business of identity formation has become hyperreal and thus no longer involves human collectives as others, only simulations thereof: "We [the US] have become so es-

tranged from the empty space left by the decline of American hegemony and the end of the Soviet threat that we eagerly found in cyber-
space what we could no longer find in the new global disorder—
comfort and security in our own superiority" (Der Derian 1991: 15).

Another theorist who introduced self/other theorizing to the discipline was Michael J. Shapiro. Having off-handedly remarked in
1988 that foreign policy generally is about making an other, he went
on to apply a number of the insights discussed earlier to questions of
war and peace. Carl von Clausewitz is usually read as having a
purely instrumental view of war, as treating it, as it were, epistemo-
logically: An actor reacts to an externally perceived threat in such
and such a way. However, Shapiro offered a reading that argues that
war for Clausewitz is actually an ontological phenomenon, that
"war is a major aspect of *being*, it emerges as a production, maintenance, and reproduction of the virtuous self, a way (for men) to
achieve an ideal form of subjectivity" (1992: 460). His main textual
evidence is a long quote from Clausewitz's *On War,* the gist of which
is that war is a "trinity—composed of primordial violence, hatred,
and enmity . . . within which the creative spirit is free to roam. . . .
the first of these aspects mainly concerns the people; the second the
commander and his army; the third the government." Now, if it is
the job of a government to nourish ontological enmity, this makes
for a rather different relation between governments than if its job is
an instrumental continuation of politics by other means.

Shapiro began to undertake the mapping of the hero scripts that
have been and are at work in studies in international relations.
Self/other relations have to be understood in their historicity; they
are aspects of historically contingent ideas of self, which again are
rooted in historically contingent ideas about time and space. Shapiro
gave as an example the way technological change automates and
speeds up the process of telling friend from foe during battle, with an
unintended consequence being that soldiers die from friendly fire.
Another example concerns the implications of real-time network news
from the battlefront for identity formation and questions of political
legitimacy.

In an analysis of the nature of the social bond that drew heavily
on Jacques Lacan and availed itself, of all things, of the Marquis de
Sade's writings, Shapiro remarked that

in the Sadean scenes, what may appear to be mere cruelty, when one causes pain in another, can be read as the desire by the perpetrator to identify with the pain of his/her victim. . . . Lacan saw Sade as one who helped to recognize that the problem of the self is not one bound up with a harmonious nature and the good life but rather one of a dynamic involving law and transgression. (Shapiro 1993: 117, 127–128)

This is certainly another view than the one presented by Lévinas, in which the other is seen as something on the order of an angel (cf. Lyotard 1988: 110–115, Lévinas note). In such situations, seen from the other's side of the self/other nexus, the others may, as suggested by Sartre, seem to be hell. Yet by being assigned the role of victim, the other is still not denied its humanity. Here is one notion, that there is one single humanity that has certainly informed world politics and that simply cries out to be analyzed. Shapiro has since briefly turned his attention to the social construction of humankind at large in terms of self/other relations and has pointed out that under present conditions, humankind must man two different frontiers (1993: 90–100). The need to man the frontier against the rest of animate nature—which partly, as Anne Norton would have us expect, happens as a meditation on the nature of those animals seen as marginal to man, that is, apes and monkeys—has been with the species since the time of man's first cave paintings. Furthermore, the growing technological refinement of cybernetic organisms (cyborgs, replicants, and so on) has added an anxiety in popular culture as well as among social theorists about how to delineate man and machine. It follows that there is no need to postulate an invasion from outer space in order to demonstrate how the largest human collectivity imaginable constructs itself socially in terms of a delineation from others.

Shapiro, having announced that foreign policy is about making others, does not proceed to demonstrate what an analysis along these lines would look like; this is exactly the task that David Campbell set himself in the monograph *Writing Security: United States Foreign Policy and the Politics of Identity*. Campbell programmatically quotes Judith Butler to the effect that "the construction of identity is not the deconstruction of politics; rather, it establishes as political the very terms through which identity is articulated" (Campbell 1992: 259). The book is a thick description of U.S. foreign policy as a seamless web of discourse and political practice that has played itself out through a series of engagements with others from the time of Cortés up to the Gulf War. The U.S. self is understood as a narrative structure, and it is argued that "for a state to end its practices of representation would be to expose its lack of prediscursive foundations; stasis would be death" (Campbell 1992: 11). Because of the role played by immigration in its genesis, the United States is presented as the imagined community par excellence, and this is seen as an additional factor that increases its need of having its representational practices recognized and confirmed.

Campbell's is an ethical concern: He follows William Connolly (1991) in arguing that the trick is for a human collective to be able to carry out its practices of representation while living in difference; that is, without "othering" other collectives. This, however, is exactly what the United States has failed and is still failing to do. One of the consequences is that it is perpetually on the lookout for new collectives to other:

> If we take the cold war to be a struggle related to the production and reproduction of identity, the popularly heralded belief that we are witnessing the end of the cold war embodies a misunderstanding: while the objects of established post-1945 strategies of otherness may no longer be plausible candidates for enmity, their transformation has not by itself altered the entailments of identity which they satisfied. (Campbell 1992: 195)

Campbell gives a detailed reading of how foreign policy, with its focus on border maintenance, is a particularly apposite practice for identity formation, but he also stresses the internal consequences of this. His reading of early U.S. Cold War diplomacy and the work of the Washington State Legislative Fact-Finding Committee on Un-American Activities, for example, stresses that

> concomitant with this external expansion was an internal magnification of the modes of existence which were to be interpreted as risks. Danger was being totalized in the external realm in conjunction with its increased individualization in the internal field, with the result being the performative reconstitution of the borders of the state's identity. In this sense, the cold war needs to be understood as a disciplinary strategy that was global in scope but national in design. (Campbell 1992: 172–173)

As landmark studies tend to do, Campbell's overstates the case by insisting on its uniqueness. Detailed work along the ethnographical path has shown that human collectives are not more or less "real" for being imagined and for sustaining themselves by means of narratives of selves that involve the whole gamut of metaphor; they all do. In the light of this, it makes little sense to insist that the United States should be "more imagined" than other collectives. Being the state of an immigrant society, the state could not latch onto territory and history—the chronological and spatial dimensions of collective identity—in the same way as could contemporary European states. The question, then, is what the diacritics are that are involved in delineating or "limning" the U.S. self from others, and not what the degree of imaginedness is. Campbell, furthermore, admirably demonstrates that after the fall of the Soviet Union, there was no break in the U.S. narrative of self as constituted in opposition to one major other; rather, there was a groping for a new "object" of enmity to take its place: drug traffickers and users, Japan, Iraq. An opportunity to restructure the narrative of self was missed. Yet in the era of nationalism, it is at least arguable that such a reification and demonification of "the other" is business as usual in international relations (but to downplay the specificity of U.S.S.R./U.S. mutual othering, a constitutive trait of the Cold War, hardly adds to our understanding of that particular constellation of collective identities). To give but one example: Consider the Soviet Union of the 1930s. In this case, there was indeed something close to a collapse of the internal and the external other, as an ever sharper line was drawn between the *Homo sovieticus* of the future and the tired inhabitants of old bourgeois and feudal worlds. By thus separating friend from foe, the security of the former would ostensibly be assured; a representative *Pravda* passage (from 10 March 1938) held that "by extermining without any mercy these spies, provocateurs, wreckers, and diversionists, the Soviet land will move even more rapidly along the Stalinist route, socialist culture will flourish even more richly, the life of the Soviet people will become even more joyous."

Yet contrary to stated expectations, what ensued was not an increased sense of security of self, but, on the contrary, a heightened sense of insecurity, brought on by the very insistence on excluding the foe. Since actions and views could "objectively," that is, unintentionally, benefit the enemy, any one Soviet citizen was in constant danger of running the enemy's errand. The word *dvurushnik*—"double-dealer"—was widely used to denominate people who were illegitimately trying to pass themselves off as friends but who were shown by some spurious means to be doing the dirty deeds of foreign spies and their domestic associate wreckers. There was pervasive fear of being exposed as being with "the other" camp. The point here is not that the United States of the 1950s was "better" than the Soviet Union of the 1930s in this respect, but that it certainly was not "worse."

A more general question could be asked of the empirical line of criticism. Do power discrepancies and hegemonical status *in themselves* make for fiercer othering, a point often made in discussions of U.S. and European identity (for example, Davies, Nandy, and Sardar 1993)? This is a theoretical non sequitur. There is also empirical discursive evidence that may be mustered against the idea, for example, in the construction of a Central European identity, which definitely evolved from a position of weakness but was no less othering for that (see Chapter 5 in this volume). Assumptions to the effect that the less powerful are necessarily less othering may be due to a lapse into a view of power as a negative and not also a productive force, and to a general proclivity to blame the powerful for everything, that is, to what Nietzsche called ressentiment.[9]

Finally, the impression of the United States as a special and somewhat frictionless case is reinforced by Campbell's choice not to deal with the U.S. practices that resisted the dominant narrative of the U.S. self. One of the similarities that warrant the use of the label "poststructuralism," is the insistence that since meaning resides in language and since language is context bound and therefore unable to preserve stable meaning over time, contradiction resides in identity formation itself: "It is because contradiction is always anterior to the discourse, and because it can never therefore entirely escape it, that discourse changes, undergoes transformation, and escapes from its own continuity. Contradiction, then, functions throughout discourse, as the principle of its historicity" (Foucault 1974: 151). By backgrounding heterodox narratives of the U.S. self, the discontinuities are shaved away and the impression of a closed-down monolithic script for the U.S. self becomes much more unequivocal than it would otherwise have been.

Mention should also be made of Campbell's later work, in which he has attempted to draw on Lévinas for his discussions of international ethics.[10] In his work on the Gulf War, Lévinas's insistence on ethics as first philosophy is invoked as a benchmark by which to pass judgment ex post facto on a U.S. "we":

> It is the idea of affirming life that is the important criterion—and perhaps, albeit ironically, the overriding principle—here; for in a situation of *an-arche,* of radical interdependence, one does not seek final justifications, or commands, or morals, or rationalizations, or answers to the "why" outside of life, beyond the nexus of being and acting. . . . precisely because of our collective failure to acknowledge our prior responsibility to the Other, we have—as the case dealing with Iraq forcefully demonstrated—backed ourselves into a corner such that military combat seems to be the only decisive (although undesirable) option. Had we . . . recognized earlier our intrinsic interdependence with the problem we seek to handle, the range of choices might not have been so limited. (Campbell 1993: 96–98)

One may characterize this as a healthy, self-reflecting antidote to an American "can do" attitude. One may also characterize it as a well-intentioned, sympathetic, and vague piece of advice. Perhaps sensing this, Campbell has recently followed the lead of Simon Critchley (1992) in carrying out a twin reading of Lévinas and Derrida. The result is an exhortation for the purpose of politics to be "the struggle *for*—or *on behalf of*—alterity, and not a struggle to efface, erase, or eradicate alterity" (Campbell 1994: 477). Appropriately, this new reading of Lévinas is offered as a "starting point for rethinking the question of responsibility *vis-à-vis* ethnic and national conflicts," and as such it seems to find a response within the subfield of international ethics (see Warner 1996 for a reaction).[11] It does not, however, seem to offer new insight into collective identity formation beyond the moral call always to reflect on how the other summons the self.

To return to Campbell's main contribution: His decision to study that representation of the American self that was at any one time dominant, and not also those representations that challenged it, is even more surprising because state-society relations, which make up one important site for clashes of this kind, have been impressively theorized by two international relations scholars to whom Campbell and also Der Derian acknowledge a debt, namely, Richard Ashley and R. B. J. Walker. "In modern discourse," wrote the former,

the sovereign figure of man, defined in terms of a necessary limita-
tion and set in opposition to historically contingent limitations, sup-
plies the constitutive principle of both (a) the modern state, as sovereign *subject* of rational collective violence and (b) domestic society,
as *object* domain subordinated to the state's sovereign gaze. (Ashley
1989: 268)

The representatives of states construct an international realm, yet
this community is set up *complete with smokescreen,* since it passes
itself off as a "state of nature" and thus not a community at all, yet
remains a bounded field in which only the exclusive competence of
statesmen has any business: "Together the two effects of the realist
double move set up an irony of no small proportions. They constitute a community whose members will know their place only as an
absence of community" (Ashley 1987: 420). Walker foregrounds the
repercussions in terms of identity/difference:

> The principle of identity embodied in Christian universalism was
> challenged by the principle of difference embodied in the emerging
> state. This was perhaps not much more than a change in emphasis.
> But this change in emphasis had enormous repercussions. From then
> on, the principle of identity, the claim to universalism, was pursued
> within states. International politics became the site not of universalis-
> tic claims but the realm of difference itself. Here lies the essential
> ground of the relationship between the political theory of state and
> civil society ever since. (Walker [1987] 1993: 117)

One should perhaps also stress how this development was further
elaborated by the coming of nationalism. If the setting up of the state
system institutionalized the realm of the international as the realm of
difference, the coming of nationalism raised the insistence on identity inside the state to new heights. A theme developed by German
romantic nationalists, the conviction that anthropomorphized nations would live peacefully together once they were established as
homogenized political "selves" through the merging of the state and
the nation found its perhaps most explicit form in the writings of
Giuseppe Mazzini:

> Natural divisions, the innate spontaneous tendency of the peoples
> will replace the arbitrary divisions sanctioned by bad governments.
> The map of Europe will be remade. The Countries of the Peoples will
> rise, defined by the voice of the free, upon the ruins of the Countries

of the kings and privileged castles. Between these Countries there will
be harmony and brotherhood. (1912: 52)

This was hardly an accurate prediction. It is, among other things,
the ongoing falling apart of states and nations that makes for the
renewed interest in the workings of collective identity. Though they
have been somewhat occluded by Campbell, these clashes of political
projects in order to define competing selves have been made the home
turf of another corner of the field, namely, the Copenhagen school.
The writers of the Copenhagen school acknowledge their debt to
the theorizing of Ashley and Walker (Wæver forthcoming; Hansen
1997b); the common denominator of their work on self/other relations is that it focuses on identity formation and self/other relations
in terms of the clash of *different* discursive practices. There is, first,
the case of how state selves clash with society selves, for which they
have traditionally claimed the role of power container and identity
arbitrator (Wæver et al. 1993). In Europe friction between leaders
and polities on issues of migration and EU integration may be seen
to reveal contending conceptions of security, in which the *states'*
insistence on the pooling of sovereignty clashes with the *societies'*
insistence on maintaining the borders between ethnically defined nations. Campbell's analysis of the United States as one discursive practice brings out the way that an evolving view of the self as covering
a multinational formation among state-bearing strata clashes with
a longer-held view of the self as covering only one nation. To para-
phrase Campbell's point of departure, it shows that the very terms
through which identity is articulated reproduce political institutions
such as the state and the EU, and *that this is always an internally
contested practice.* With the battles waged in the United States over
the adoption of the North American Free Trade Agreement fresh in
memory, it is unlikely that such a problematique should not apply to
North America as well.

The Copenhagen school has also produced studies of how self/
other relations impinge on the possibilities for international cooperation. The collective self is predicated on certain key political ideas—
such as what constitutes a "state" or a "nation,"—and the collective
self will try to make these ideas the basis for institutionalization
when it partakes in political cooperation. As more than one project
of what could be referred to as isomorphism—the attempted recon-

struction of social structures in new environments—will invariably be involved, the ensuing political clashes can be studied as the very stuff of world politics. Thus the key figure of the school, Ole Wæver, may insist that this way of studying foreign policy offers a fully fledged identity-based alternative to traditional foreign policy analysis (see Wæver 1995; also Wæver 1992; Hansen 1996; Holm 1993; Neumann 1996; Wæver, Holm, and Larsen forthcoming).

This insistence marks a shift in writing practice that is of key importance to the application of collective identity theorizing to international relations. The international relations theorists who have extended this theorizing into the discipline have insisted on "speaking the language of exile," working from "the margins," and "living on borderlines" (Ashley and Walker 1990; Der Derian and Shapiro 1989; Ashley 1989), exile from, margin of, borderlines to modern practice *tout court,* that is. The analyses of the "Copenhagen school," however, come from a position that is not explicitly marginal in relation to such an all-encompassing entity. They content themselves with attempting to write in the margin of the main text of the discipline itself (see Chapter 2 for an explicit example).

The text that firmly and unequivocally transposed the question of collective identity away from the margins and into the mainstream of the discipline was, however, Alexander Wendt's 1992 article "Anarchy Is What States Make of It: The Social Construction of Power Politics."[12] His technique was simple enough. The article starts by identifying the debate between neorealists, such as Kenneth Waltz, and neoliberals as the discipline's central "axis of contention." The former privilege structure as an explanational factor, whereas the latter plunge for process. Wendt then makes two claims: first, the structurationist claim that the dichotomy between these two is false because the two are mutually constitutive, and second, the claim that neoliberals have no systematic theory of process understood as complex learning processes.[13] He then sets out to formulate such a theory by drawing on "constructivist" work. The "constructivists" are, of course, none other than the international relations theorists who have just been shown to have extended theorizing about collective identity into the discipline. Wendt gives as his reason for calling them "constructivists" that he wants to "minimize their image problem," and he castigates them for having devoted "too much effort to questions of ontology and constitution and not enough effort to the causal and empirical questions of how identities and interests are produced by practice in anarchic conditions" (Wendt 1992: 393, 425). In this way he manages to acknowledge the importance of this theorizing for his own work, while at the same time distancing himself from it and so making the ensuing theory more presentable for the mainstream to which his theory is offered. Wendt then subsumes the identity formation approach under the neoliberal preoccupation with institutions and relates this to the discipline's core concern with anarchy and self-help:

> An institution is a relatively stable set or "structure" of identities and interests. . . . institutions come to confront individuals as more or less coercive social facts, but they are still a function of what actors collectively "know." Identities and such collective cognitions do not exist apart from each other; they are "mutually constitutive." . . . Self-help is an institution, one of various structures of identity and interest that may exist under anarchy. Processes of identity-formation under anarchy are concerned first and foremost with preservation or "security" of the self. (Wendt 1992: 399)

The meaning of the "structure" of anarchy to states is thus undergoing a constant reinscription as their identities change. The intersubjectively constituted structure of identities and interests in the system must be acknowledged by international theorists as a structural, endogenous, and constitutive factor. I would argue with Timothy Dunne (1995) that this has been the core concern of the English School of International Relations for years. Their concept of an ever growing "international society" of states is offered precisely as a way to capture how conceptualizations take on material quality as they are perpetually reconstructed and taken more and more for granted as factors playing a role in foreign policy decision making. The dynamic idea of an expanding international society, then, is an intersubjective structure of the type discussed by Wendt (see, for example, Bull 1977). The great merit of Wendt's analysis in this regard lies in the way he explicitly links this problematique with the question of collective identity formation. He then goes on to discuss how states constitute one another's identities by borrowing a key assumption from symbolic interactionists:

> Conceptions of self and interest tend to "mirror" the practices of significant others over time. The principle of identity-formation is

captured by the symbolic interactionist notion of the "looking-glass self," which asserts that the self is a reflection of an actor's socialization. (Wendt 1992: 404; cf. Bronfenbrenner 1961)

Thus, "alter" and "ego" mold one another by taking up different "roles" and playing them out in a "path-dependent" way: "The fact that roles are 'taken' means that, in principle, actors always have a capacity for 'character planning'—for engaging in critical self-reflection and choices designed to bring about changes in their lives" (Wendt 1992: 419). Wendt gives as an example a Soviet variation of what game theorists call "Trollope's ploy"—that is, to take someone up on an offer that has not been made: Soviet "new thinking" attempted to make "the West" act in a new way that would allow a new Soviet identity in international relations.

So by kitting out the issue of collective identity formation in the ritual "neorealist versus neoliberal" attire of an article in *International Organization,* Wendt managed to nudge this concern toward the center stage of the discipline. Everybody studying collective identity formation in IR will benefit from this widening of working space. There was, of course, a price to pay. Attention should be drawn, then, to this price, that is, to what now may be sacrificed on the altar of what Wendt refers to as "rationalism," "systematic theory," "Science." One such concern is acknowledged by Wendt himself when he justifies his unequivocal focus on states by insisting that "any transition to new structures of global authority and identity—to 'postinternational' politics—will be mediated by and path-dependent on the particular institutional resolution of the tension between unity and diversity, or particularism and universality, that is the sovereign state" (Wendt 1992: 424). Indeed, as already noticed, this is one of the themes that the Copenhagen school has made their own. However, Wendt's state-centrism is not in and of itself the major sacrifice. The main problem is not specifically that states are singled out as the collective actors to be studied but, rather, the more general insistence that human collectives are *unequivocally bounded actors.* A second problem is the regression to the psychologizing assumptions that were so popular within the discipline in the 1960s and that patently led nowhere, when these unequivocally bounded actors are rigged with the psychological makeup of a modern, unequivocally given, self. Wendt explicitly brackets how the struggle to delineate self from other in international relations must simultaneously be a struggle to pin down the identity of one among many possible and rival selves. The price is the reification of the very category of self. In the event, the possibility of studying the *multidimensionality* of identity formation is ceremoniously sacrified (ceremoniously rather than unceremoniuously, since Wendt [1992: 394, note 12] explicitly sides with "modernist" against "postmodernist" constructivists, thus implying that he treats the self as a foundation).

In a later article, Wendt goes on to make a number of additional suggestions, for example, that "identification is a continuum from negative to positive—from conceiving the other as anathema to the self to conceiving it as an extension of the self" (1994: 386). As demonstrated by Todorov, however, what is at stake here—the value judgment made of the other—is only one of three axes along which self/other relations may be studied. When Wendt postulates his continuum, he runs the risk of reducing the question of the other to a question of various degrees of assimilation or submission. In terms of ethics, furthermore, Lévinas's insistence that the other cannot be conceived of as freedom (because freedom invites either submission or enslavement) might be kept in mind. Wendt also postulates rising interdependence and the emergence of a "'common Other,' whether personified in an external aggressor or [a] more abstract threat like nuclear war or ecological collapse" (1994: 389) as factors that *may* facilitate collective identity formation. However, as demonstrated in Shapiro's work on collective identity formation, since the social construction of humankind necessarily involves delineation from other animate species as well as from cyborgs, the social construction of humankind in and of itself involves delineation from "common others." Thus Wendt's candidates for that role are simply extras.

There are problems also with the activation of rising interdependence here, and these problems may be treated together with Wendt's claim that the transnational convergence of domestic values may also facilitate collective identity formation: "As heterogeneity decreases, so does the rationale for identities that assume that *they* are fundamentally different from *us*" (Wendt 1994: 39). Does it? Normatively, it is an appealing thought that closer acquaintance makes for less othering, yet the claim is simply wrong. Empirically, it is refuted by the work of a thousand anthropologists. Two points should be made here: First, since what is at issue in delineation is not "objective" cultural differences but the way symbols are activated to become part of the capital of the identity of a given human collective, it is simply wrong that global homogenizing trends make it harder to uphold delineation. Any difference, no matter how minuscule, may be inscribed by political importance and serve to delineate identities, as shown by the example of the *Kartoffel/Erdapfel* given above. Second, increase in knowledge about the other (which may go together with "homogenization") has to do with what Todorov calls the epistemic axis, empathy with the axiological axis, and action with the praxeological, and they may not be positively correlated. Todorov's example, that although Cortés knew more about Indians than did Las Casas, he "loved" them less, and Bauman's insistence that those who helped refugees from the Holocaust did not necessarily know more or think in a particular way about them beforehand, come to mind. Wendt's work has the great merit of having propelled the study of collective identity forward in the sense that he placed it before a wider IR audience. And yet if his studied insensitivity to the multidimensional character of identity formation is taken up by the discipline as de rigueur, it may easily hamper the further theorization of collective identity formation in international relations.

CONCLUSION

The discipline of international relations may draw on a rich and multifaceted literature for its study of collective identity formation, and it may do so in a number of ways. Since it is a pervasive theme of this literature that the formation of the self is inextricably intertwined with the formation of its others and that a failure to regard the others in their own right must necessarily have repercussions for the formation of the self, it would be paradoxical to end this chapter by excluding certain approaches in the name of a chosen one. This notwithstanding, certain insights stand out as particularly important analytical how-tos. There is, first, the basic insight from the anthropological path, that delineation of a self from an other is an *active* and ongoing part of identity formation. The creation of social boundaries is not a consequence of integration but one of its necessary a priori ingredients. The focus for studies of identity formation should therefore be the socially placed one of how these boundaries come into existence and are maintained. Students of international relations have studied physical and economic borders for a long time. The concern with these types of boundaries needs to be complemented by a focus on how *social boundaries* between human collectives are maintained. Since strangers and other marginal elements of human collectives "embody" their borders, the role played by these elements in the identity formation of the collectives at large stands out as a particularly promising area for investigation.

Any social field will harbor more than one type of politically relevant collective identities. Particular care must be taken not to prejudice analyses by singling out only one type of human collective, say, nations, to the neglect of others. Similarly, when studying, for example, the self/other nexus of two states, attention must be paid to the fact that those states are at the very same time involved in maintaining their collective identities vis-à-vis other types of human collectives—societies, say, or an organization of which they both are members. Collective identities emerge as *multifaceted* and must be studied as such.

This argument may be extended to incorporate a perspectivist approach, which stresses that a certain collective identity cannot be unequivocally privileged, because self and other are not only mutually constitutive entities but also are necessarily unbounded. The self and the other merge into one another. It has been one theme of this chapter that this merging used to be understood dialectically—self and other were seen to merge into some kind of a new entity as part and parcel of the progressive flow of reason. Some thirty years ago there was a shift away from this understanding and toward a dialogical understanding, whereby no such goal or even development is posited for the exchanges between self and other. A similar shift in sensibilities may be observed in the discipline of international relation's study of collective identity formation since it somewhat belatedly got under way at the end of the 1980s.

In analyzing the self/other nexus, it is particularly hard not to ponder the ways in which the writer is implicated in what he or she writes about. Writing is also a normative concern, and the question of responsibility cannot be ducked. It is not enough to reflect on what we do (that is, on why we study this or that slice of world politics) and why we do it. We must also pay attention to what that which we do, does. If our analyses are used to facilitate the "othering" of this or that human collective, say the house of Islam or China, by another, say "the West," then this raises the question of how we are implicated in the unfolding of world political practice. Since consequences cannot be foreseen in their full range, perhaps such effects cannot be helped (that, of course, is no argument against reflecting on the possibility). And yet, certain analyses—Huntington's (1993) essay on the clash of civilizations comes to mind—seem to offer "othering" as a piece of practical policy advice for gluing a particular human collective together. Integration and exclusion are two sides of the same coin, so the issue here is not *that* exclusion takes place but *how* it takes place. If active othering is proposed as the price of achieving integration, that price seems to be too high to pay. Analyses of collective identity formation should contribute, however timidly, to our living in difference and not to some of us dying from otherness.

That normative concern is there, and it loses none of its force for not always being heeded. But the study of collective identity formation offers more than moral exhortations and a way of studying intersubjectively constituted structures of identities and interests that are endogamous and constitutive to the international system. To a discipline that has had notorious problems with pinning down its subjects and has often defined them in terms of their alleged and abstract "interests," it offers no less than the possibility finally to theorize the genesis and maintenance of the human collectives of world politics. Analyses of self/other nexuses hold out the promise of a better understanding of who "the actors" are, how they were constituted, how they maintain themselves, and under which preconditions they may thrive. If these are marginal concerns, they are marginal only in the sense that they may best be studied by an examination of the margins of world politics.

The empirical analyses that make up the next six chapters of the book draw on the theorizing along the Eastern excursion to offer specific readings of how human collectives are represented.

2

Making Europe: The Turkish Other

The presence of the Turk in Europe is incidental. They remain at the end of five hundred years as much strangers as they were at the beginning. European ideals and words, like "nation," "government," "law," "sovereign," "subject," do not apply to them.
— PAVEL MILYUKOV IN 1916, QUOTED IN RIHA 1969: 257

A variety of others have been and are instrumental in the process of forging European identity. From the confrontations with Islam and the Spanish conquest of the "New World" to the scramble for colonial possessions at the end of the nineteenth century and beyond, European historians and philosophers have grappled with the clash between "infidels" or "barbarians" and "civilized" peoples (Harbsmeier 1985). Ethnically and culturally peripheral minorities also serve as internal others. Outstanding historical examples include Jews and Freemasons. The most important contemporary candidates for otherness, arguably, are the postcolonial immigrants from Africa, the Middle East, and the Indian subcontinent. The ancient Greeks entertained the idea of an internal other in relation to which the Greek city-state defined itself, the *pharmakos* ("magician"; "poisoner"; "the one sacrificed in expiation for the sins of the city") (Derrida 1981: 132).

Nonetheless, the dominant other in the history of the European state system remains "the Turk," and because of the lingering importance of that system, we have here a particularly important other. In contrast to the communities of the New World, "the Saracen" and "the Ottoman" had the military might, the physical proximity, and a strong religious tradition that made it a particularly relevant other in the evolution of the fledgling international society that evolved from the ashes of Western Christendom and that took up a pivotal position in the forging of European identities. From the fourteenth century to the nineteenth century, the Ottoman Empire occupied and controlled a quarter of the European continent, comprising some of Europe's most coveted territory. Yet as Thomas Naff contends, its relationship with the emerging Euoprean state system was an ambiguous one: "The logical conclusion ought to be that the Ottoman Empire was, empirically, a European state. The paradox is that it was not. Even though a significant portion of the Empire was based in Europe, it could not be said to have been of Europe" (Naff 1985: 143). Although there was interaction between the Ottoman Empire and the European powers in war and commerce, "it was specifically denied on both sides that the European powers and Turkey possessed any common interests or values . . . and there were no common institutions, such as united the European powers, in whose working they co-operated" (Bull 1977: 14; Watson 1987).

It was only in 1856, with the Treaty of Paris, that the Ottoman Empire was officially recognized as a permanent part of the European balance of power; it was the first non-European power to gain that status. The Preamble to that treaty declared that the independence and integrity of the Ottoman Empire was vital to "the Peace of Europe," and Article 2 gave the Sublime Porte (that is, the capital of Istanbul and, by extension, the sultan) the right "à participer aux avantages du droit public et du concert europeen [to take part in the benefits of international law and the Concert of Europe]" (Gong 1984: 113; also Wight 1977: 116). This status was codified at the Hague Conference in 1899, in which Turkey was included as one of the participants, and was confirmed again by the 1923 Treaty of Lausanne.

The purpose of this chapter is twofold. First, charting the relations between European society and the Ottoman Empire may highlight the role of agreed cultural and social values in the maintenance of international order. Such an analysis may also show how these values often underlie agreement on the more procedural rules and institutions emphasized by rationalist writers concerned with the notion of an international society, as mentioned in Chapter 1.

Second, by underlining the importance of the other for the very formulation of international society, I intend to suggest some basic problems in Europe's present-day relations with non-European states. Inasmuch as European identity is tied to the existence of an other, this other will be constitutive of Europe, and so European representations of that other will necessarily be marked by that very fact. In that case, exposing the existence of an other may remove an unnecessary obstacle to working relations between European and non-European societies. Since the other is a human invention, and although the cultural differences between self and other may be real enough, it is after all historically arbitrary who at any given time fills the role of other.

THE MIDDLE AGES: THE SARACEN

As is well known, the term "Europe" had only a marginal existence before the fifteenth century. Pim den Boer describes the best-known uses of the term in the period between the time of ancient Greece and the fifteenth century:

> In 711, Tariq ibn Ziyard and his forces crossed into Spain at what then came to be known as Jebel-al-tariq (the mountain of Tariq), which is the source of the name Gibraltar. The Moors advanced across the Pyrinees, but in 732 were decisively defeated near Pointiers by a coalition army led by Charles Martel, the "mayor of the palace" (chief minister) of Austrasia, the eastern Frankish domains of Champagne and the Meuse and Moselle area with Rheims as capital. A contemporary chronicler, originating from Cordoba, referred to Charles Martel as the consul of Austrasia and used the term *europeenses* to describe the coalition army. . . . After a Saracen attack on Narbonne, Frankish forces founded the Spanish province south of the Pyrinees. In Rome, on Christmas Night in the year 800, the Pope's protector Charlemagne, was crowned Holy Roman Emperor. The Frankish king was seen as the successor to the Roman Emperors in the West and as having restored the *imperium romanum*. Poems refer to Charlemagne as *rex, pater Europae* and he is praised as *Europae veneranda apex*. (den Boer 1995: 26–27)

One notes that these are military settings and that the constitutive other in relation to which Europeans and Europe are referred to are "Moors" and "Saracens." One also notes that "Europe" and "Europeans" as terms that denote human collectives were not privileged in relation to terms such as "Franks," "the Holy Roman Empire," or "Christendom."[1] Christendom, as it stood in the eleventh century, combined a Stoic, universalist belief in the essential unity of humankind with a missionary dynamic to convert the infidel. According to the medieval canonists, the pope had rightful jurisdiction over all human beings, faithful and nonbeliever alike. As a corollary, he was given the right of direct interference in non-Christian countries to protect Christians living there, to correct perceived misgovernment, and, in some cases, to depose rulers. The tricky question, however, and one that would plague Europeans for the next five centuries, was whether the infidel had rightful domain over his land at all, or whether Christians had an explicit duty to conquer. In essence, there was a tension between universalism and exclusivity.

The early Augustinian solution to the dilemma leaned toward exclusivity, by giving papal sanction for holy wars of conquest against the nonbelievers; hence the medieval Crusades. In his book on what he refers to as "Western Views of Islam in the Middle Ages," R. W. Southern comments on the importance of the Crusades that "before 1100 I have found only one mention of the name Mahomet in medieval literature outside Spain and Southern Italy. But from about the year 1120 everyone in the West had some picture of what Islam meant, and who Mahomet was" (1962: 28). The Crusades, then, marked the Saracen positively and specifically as Islamic, and not only negatively as a nonbeliever. A more specified other called for a more specific relationship. Under Pope Innocent IV (1243–1254), a canonist compromise was reached that claimed that force could be used against the infidel only to redress an injury and that Christian conversion was to be brought about by peaceful missionary methods only.

As pointed out by Maxime Rodinson,

> [the] image of Islam was not drawn simply from the Crusades, as some have maintained, but rather from the Latin Christian world's gradually developing ideological unity. This produced a sharper image of the enemy's features and focused the energies of the West on the Crusades. (Rodinson 1987: 7)

These two processes fed off one another. The increasing solidarity of Christendom gave greater power to the Crusade against the other; the Crusade against the other helped to promote solidarity among the members of Christendom.

Of course, although they were marked by growing cultural solidarity constituted in opposition to the Saracen, political relations within Christendom were also marked by the frequent proclivity for military alliances with the very same Saracen. The fall of Acre in 1291 saw the hopes for the great Crusades diminish, as dispersed Christian power centers parted ways. As Rodinson remarks:

> It had been some time since the war against the Eastern infidels had been able to unite the West in a common struggle. The plan for the expansion of a united Christian Europe gave way, once and for all, to nationalistic political projects. (1987: 29)

One must, however, take issue with this as a summing up of relations between "the Saracen" and "Europe." First, "the Saracen" was not Europe's but Christendom's other: It is only with the next period that a European self becomes a political project strong enough first to vie with and then to overtake and succeed a Christian self. "The Saracen" was first and foremost a religious other. Second, it was not the case that the growing political differentiation of Christendom diminished the role of the Islamic other. On the contrary, the presence of an other that could be characterized as the embodiment of evil continued to unify and strengthen the disparate Christendom of the fourteenth and early fifteenth centuries. Following the foundation of the Ottoman Empire in the early fourteenth century and the gradual increase of military pressure on Christendom, however, "the Saracen" gave way to "the Ottoman Turk." And just as "the Saracen" was present at the creation of Carolingian Europe, "the Ottoman Turk" was present at the creation of the Europe of the modern state system.

THE RENAISSANCE TO WESTPHALIA: THE OTTOMAN TURK

Although attempts were made to create a common Christian front at the council of churches at Ferrara-Florence, it collapsed because of a lack of unity among the European states. The Orthodox delegates accepted unity with Rome in order to obtain help against "the Turks," who were then at the gates of Constantinople. However, when the Russian delegates came back to Moscow, Grand Duke Vasily II refused to acquiesce in the church union and declared their actions null and void. When Constantinople fell in 1453, Metropolitan Jonas declared from Moscow that it was God's punishment of the Greeks for having united with Rome (Strémooukhoff 1953). It is apparent, then, that in this case the dualism between Christendom and "the Turk," so formidable on a rhetorical level, was not strong enough to marginalize the differences within Christendom itself.

It is in these years, when Christendom was being politically fractured under the strain of the Ottoman onslaught, that the term "Europe" began to be used frequently and took on political importance. It was, for example, a favorite term of Pius II in his papal years from 1458 to 1464, and he had actually, before he became pope, been the first to use it in a book title. Pius's priority as pope was to rekindle the crusading zeal of Christendom, and in this connection he bolstered his appeals to Christendom—the referent for which had so obviously been partitioned by the Great Schism—with appeals to "our Europe, our Christian Europe." Europe, by dint of being vaguer in its outlines, was an easier term under which to preach unity. And this unity was unequivocally directed against that Islamic military opponent who was the Ottoman Turk.

Early Renaissance images of "the Turk" served to underline the degree of medieval Christian hostility that survived even among those Europeans inspired by the new ethic of humanism. Therefore, during the Renaissance period of European-Ottoman relations, one finds not only a struggle between competing military powers but also a conflict of ideologies and of competing social, economic, and political systems. The Turkish peril was viewed as the latest phase in the centuries-old assault of Islam on Christianity. Consequently, for their understanding of this challenge, Europeans drew heavily upon the crusading literature of the Middle Ages.

In addition, Renaissance writers invoked writers such as Hesiod, Xenophon, Herodotus, and other ancient Greeks, who saw their own system of city-states as the realm of dynamic change and who saw the barbarians in the East as living in a world that was condemned to be forever static (Hay [1957] 1966: 2–6). This tradition, which of course concerned the forging of different selves in terms of different others, was pressed into service, combined with medieval representations, and re-presented as Renaissance perceptions of the Ottoman menace.

When news of the fall of Constantinople (1453) spread through the Italian city-states to northern and central Europe, few chroniclers engaged in the cool, power-political assessment of the defeat that would have been typical of the discourse on *raison d'état* that was becoming an important part of overall political discourse. Instead, they concentrated on the agonies and atrocities suffered at the hands of the infidels. Hence, for example, when informed of the event, King Christian I of Denmark declared that "the grand Turk was the beast rising out of the sea described in the Apocalypse" (quoted in Schwoebel 1967: 4). Rather than attributing Turkish victory to the well-organized, highly disciplined army of Sultan Mehmed II, European observers railed against the divisions and dissensions among Christians, who preferred undercutting one another to defending the faith. In Robert Schwoebel's words: "If the Turks were barbarians, it followed that they must be inferior to civilised Europe on all accounts; and, in the face of overwhelming evidence to the contrary, even the military abilities of the Turks were disparaged" (1967: 19).

More significantly, representations of the other were used to reinforce and strengthen the collective of Europe. The Turk was seen as a pernicious force sent by God to scourge Christendom for its sins. To fend off this evil, all that was required was for Christians to repent, unite, and take up the defense of the faith. Consequently, in the period after the fall of Constantinople, one finds proponents of the chivalric tradition of courage, honor, and piety as well as conservative calls for the restoration of the papacy. The Turkish threat worked toward reviving a waning loyalty to the Republica Christiana and gave new life to the old cry for peace and unity in a Christendom subject to the pope. As a result, after 1453, the papacy (first under Nicholas V and later under Pius II) took bold steps to reinvigorate the medieval Crusade. First, it offered material and financial assistance to military campaigns, primarily through the use of indulgences. And second, it intervened to pacify and unify Europe through an appeal to Christian conscience. Despite the increasing dedication of Renaissance princes to national aggrandisement, support could still be summoned for the medieval ideals of a united Christendom. As Pius II proclaimed in one of his exhortations to his flock: "An unavoidable war with the Turks threatens us. Unless we take arms and go to war to meet the enemy, we think all is over with religion" (quoted in Schwoebel 1967: 71).

There was, to be sure, some recognition of the growing force of temporal considerations. In his appeal to the princes of Europe to keep up the fight, Pius acknowledged the need to combine religious with practical arguments. He therefore sought to demonstrate that an unopposed Ottoman advance was an imminent threat to the temporal interest of the rulers—that is, the *raison d'état* fear of one power striving for mastery over Europe. In fact, Rodinson alleges that by the end of the fourteenth century "the Turk" was seen more as a secular or cultural menace than as an ideological threat:

> At this stage (around 1500) European rulers did not consider Christian expansionism worth the sacrifice of their own political (and eventually national) interests; nor did the general public see this as justification for a call to arms throughout Europe, as earlier had been the case with the Crusaders. . . . From then on, to the realists, the Ottoman Empire became a power like any other and even a European power. (1987: 32–33)

Rodinson puts his finger on how this other is transformed from a primarily religious to a primarily military-political other, and this is indeed central. However, one must challenge his view of the consequences of this transformation. It was *not* the case that "the Ottoman Empire became a power like any other and even a European power." The representations of the other's specificity as such changed, and consequently what this particular other meant to the European self also changed, but the existence of the other as an other, and *not* as part of the European self, definitely did not change. Furthermore, even in the early sixteenth century, after the bulwark of Christendom had begun to crumble, representations of Islam and "the Turk" continued to draw heavily on medieval representations of the Saracen. The representations that dominated the previous period continued to echo in European discourse. Evidence for the resonance of medieval images can be found in the anti-Turk tirades that remained fashionable in Renaissance political oratory. At diplomatic congresses, the marriages of princes, or the inaugurations of popes, an orator could be expected to deliver an *exhortatio ad bellum contra barbaros,* which was part of his standard repertoire (Schwoebel 1967: 150). Whether such orations were motivated by serious religious concerns or by political expedience, the result was the same. Through them, the representation of "the Turk" as the enemy of faith and culture was perpetuated.

One such Renaissance orator was Giovanni Botero. Although in many respects a classic proponent of *raison d'état* (see, for example, Meinecke [1924] 1957), Botero believed that additional factors needed to be considered when waging a campaign against "the other." In the following excerpt, one sees the uneasy tension between the logic of *raison d'état* and the logic of culture in his attitude toward "the Turk":

> There are only two ways of uniting against the Turk with any hope of success. Either the rulers of all the countries that border upon his dominions should attack him at the same moment on all sides, not with limited strengths but using all available resources—and in this way all the parties would have an equal interest in ultimate victory. Or another and more noble way would be for many princes to unite together with no other interest than the honour of God and the exaltation of the Church, and to attack the Turk at one or several points. . . . I do not know by what justice the reason of state (if something so irrational, not to say bestial, merits the name of reason) has shown itself more hostile to Christians than to Turks and other infidels. Machiavelli cries out impetuously against the Church, and yet utters not a word against the infidels; and the Christian rulers are intent upon each other's downfall as though they had no other enemy in the world. . . . And what came of this? The barbarians first drove us out of Asia and then subjugated the Greeks. This is the fruit of modern policy. (Botero [1589] 1956: 164–165, 222–223)[2]

To Botero, then, a logic of culture exists and must take precedence over a logic of *raison d'état*. The demands of *raison d'état* nevertheless brought the two hostile rivals, Christian Europe and the Ottoman Empire, into increased contact. Until the death of Mehmed II, alliances and pacts against the Ottoman Empire had been the most prominent feature of European international relations. At this time, however, significant Ottoman involvement in European conflicts began to appear, as the warring city-states of Italy sought Ottoman aid against their enemies. Consequently, between 1495 and 1502 Sultan Bayezid II sided with Milan and Naples against a Franco-Venetian alliance. Moreover, European powers quickly learned to do business with "the Turk," including him in their diplomatic machinations. The first alliance between Ottomans and Europeans occurred in 1536 during the struggle for the Holy Roman Empire between Charles of Spain (who was the Holy Roman Emperor Charles V) and Francis I of France, when the latter signed a treaty with the Ottomans for an attack against the Italian states. Although the military articles became superfluous once Francis made peace with Charles, friendship and cooperation continued to characterize Ottoman-French relations. In fact, some have argued that with this alliance "Christendom" disappeared as a relevant political term (for example, Baumer 1944). Rodinson supports this view of the predominance of *raison d'état*:

> [By] the late sixteenth century, religious arguments completely gave way to political realities. In 1588, Elizabeth I even went so far as to inform Sultan Murad II that, as far as she was concerned, Spain was nothing but a nation of idolators with Philip II as their leader. An alliance based solely on ideology was now proposed: strict monotheists against untrustworthy Catholics. (1987: 34–35)

However, this interpretation has been challenged by, among others, Franklin Baumer, who demonstrates that Elizabeth I took great pains to dispel the impression that she was conspiring with "the Turk" against other Christian powers. Furthermore, he contends that in spite of diplomatic overtures toward "the Turk" in the sixteenth century, this new diplomacy was not considered respectable by either contemporary political or legal standards. "In short, despite the growing secularization of European politics and the religious schism, the idea of 'the common corps of Christendom' continued to hold its ground to an astonishing degree in official as in other circles" (Baumer 1944: 27–28).

Indeed, even the Ottoman-French treaty of 1536 illustrates some of the lingering cultural gaps between the Ottomans and the Europeans. Whereas France regarded the agreement as a formal treaty, the Ottomans saw it as no more than an *ahdname*—a contract granted unilaterally by the sultan. The unilateral character of this agreement therefore "reflected the Muslim-Ottoman view of the inferiority of Christian Europe" (Naff 1985: 148). And on the other side, whereas today we might interpret these diplomatic relations as constituting de facto European recognition of the Ottoman Empire, such was not the case in the eyes of contemporaries. Negotiations and alliances were not accompanied by any official redefinition of the status of "the Turk" or by acceptance of the Ottoman Empire as a legitimate member of that community of states that was about to congeal (Schwoebel 1967: 204).

In order to capture the specificity of the Ottoman other at this stage, it may be instructive briefly to contrast these representations with those made of the "Indians" of the New World. I mentioned in Chapter 1 that at the time of the Spanish conquest of the New World a hefty debate ensued about how to categorize the Indian other. The Spanish theologian and jurist Francisco de Vitoria (1483–1546) saw the problem in terms of Christian universalism and social particularism and wrote in *De Indes* that

> the barbarians in question . . . cannot be barred from being true owners, alike in public or in private law, by reason of the sin of unbelief or any other mortal sin, nor does such sin entitle Christians to seize their goods and lands. (Quoted in Gong 1984: 36; see also Hurrell 1996)

In positing the existence of a *jus inter gentes*—a natural law applicable to all men, Christian or non-Christian—Vitoria, although not averse to the idea of holy war in principle, sought to legitimate peaceful conquest while respecting the rights of the Indians in the New World. This tension between universalism and exclusivity was most immediate, however, in the peculiar relationship between Europe and the barbarian in question here, namely, the Ottoman Turk. The Ottoman Empire was regarded with greater antipathy than the non-Christian territories of the New World, given its geographical relationship to Europe and its military prowess. Religion remained a factor in the representation of the Ottoman Turk as Europe's other, but the military-political aspect dominated. The hostility that characterized the relationship was no longer a question of Christian versus nonbeliever but, rather, sprang from the profound similarity between the two religions of Christianity and Islam. Both believed they were the unique possessors of the whole of God's truth, and both combined a universalist faith with proselytizing zeal.[3] Whereas "the Saracen" was a religious other to Christendom, "the Ottoman Turk" may perhaps be seen as the generalized challenger, on a par with the European self as to codification of a monotheistic religion, efficiency of political organization, and military prowess.

THE OTTOMAN TURK IN THE MODERN STATE SYSTEM

At Westphalia in 1648, European princes continued their break away from the overarching control of the Holy Roman Empire and from the claims of the papacy to pronounce on the validity of treaties concluded among Christian powers. In addition, the sovereignty of states was advanced through a reaffirmation of the principle of *cujus regio, ejus religio,* which had been introduced at Augsburg in 1555 (Bull 1990: 76–77). This principle of "whose region, his religion" specified that it was up to the king to decide which religion should be followed throughout his realm. Through the dictates of sovereign absolutism, a legal system of autonomous states was established, formally superseding the medieval notion of Christendom as one political unity. The process of state building, which intensified after Westphalia, often served to sharpen cultural differences among the newly sovereign European states. As princes turned inward to summon the military, economic, and bureaucratic strength required by the logic of *raison d'état,* bonds that they had shared as members of the Holy Roman Empire were to some extent severed (George and Craig [1983] 1990: 3–16). Immanuel Kant, a later thinker on international relations, believed that these cultural differences and the lively competition that such differences would produce would work in the interest of progress (Hinsley 1963: 62–80; Gallie 1978: 8–36). Although weakened, certain cultural bonds nevertheless continued to tie Europe together.

Despite the doctrinal secularist formal representation that emanated from Westphalia, a representation of relations between sovereigns as being also a religious affair remained to be activated. Europe as a whole was decidedly Christian in character, and its Christianity was frequently contrasted with the Islam of the Ottoman and Mogul Empires, the Hinduism of India, and the Confucian tradition of imperial China (Purnell 1973: 14). Furthermore, although Hugo Grotius, the prominent Dutch jurist of the period, recognized the legality of treaty relations with infidels, he did admit the existence of a particular bond uniting Christian states and acknowledged the special rules regulating relations among their sovereigns: "Grotius may thus be understood as embracing a minimum content of universally applicable rules of the *jus gentium* . . . with a pluralist overlay of additional norms based on custom or consent or the values of the peoples concerned" (Kingsbury and Roberts 1990: 47–48). Grotius, however, continued to privilege individuals over states as the ultimate political agents, and this made it possible for him to maintain a dual conception of international society: an outer circle of all humankind, bound by natural law, and an inner circle of Christians, bound by the laws of Christ. States dominated by Christians were, further-more, different from states dominated by non-Christians, and so Grotius went so far as to call for a general league of Christian states and a crusade against "the Turk" (Grotius [1625] 1979: 146).

As represented by Europeans, the Ottoman Empire was pro-foundly unsuited to the new Westphalian system. The postmedieval European idea of the state—a territorially defined entity apart from dynasty and organized in accordance with man-made rules—was alien to Muslim political theory. Muslim theories of the state derived from the concepts that God is the source of all authority and law and that government exists to enable the community of true believers (*ummah*) to fulfil its obligations to God. Consequently it was the community rather than the state that constituted the basic Muslim polity. And further, as Naff writes, orthodox viewers held this Mus-lim community to be morally superior to all other societies:

> Until God's intention of a universal true-believing community under a single law and ruler was achieved, the world would be divided into two spheres: Dar ul-Islam—the abode of Islam where Islamic law obtained; and Dar ul-Harb—the abode of war where infidels lived outside the law of God and against whom holy war, jihad, must be waged until the universal idea became reality. (1985: 144)

Such competing universalistic religious representations, be they Christian or Muslim, did not mesh with notions of equality, sover-eignty or nonintervention—the key planks of the new, *raison d'état* European diplomacy. Thus in 1693 when William Penn put forth his scheme for an organized European society of states, dedicated to the maintenance of peace and stability, he recommended that the Ottoman Empire be included only if it renounced Islam. As we shall see later, this notion of an "entry requirement" for European society has persisted, even to the present day.

In 1683 a league of Christian forces halted the Ottoman thrust into Europe outside the gates of Vienna, bringing about a decisive change in the historic competition between the two adversaries. The Treaty of Carlowitz (1699) marked the turning point for Europe and "the Turk," confirming Europe's military superiority and signaling the Ottoman Empire's retreat from Central Europe. The Treaty of Carlowitz was also the first instance in which "the Turk" was invited to participate in a European congress. In addition, by signing the treaty, the Ottoman Empire acknowledged the formal existence of non-Muslim states for the first time (McKay and Scott 1983: 76). Indeed, 1699 initiated what Bernard Lewis (1995) refers to as Europe's period of "reconquest and empire" with regard to the Sublime Porte. But despite the decline in military threat, the cultural threat of "the Turk" remained. Hence, as Lewis argues, the European expansion into the Ottoman Empire was of a different kind from the colonialism that characterized Europe's relation to North America, China, or India, inasmuch as it was predicated on the prolonged and multifaceted contacts of two "intimate enemies." As a result, Europe pursued its former conqueror with a particular intensity.

In addition, the time of reconquest and empire was seen by many as a reincarnation of the old religious war—a continuation of the Crusades. What is interesting to note, however, is the increased use of the Greek term "barbarian" to describe "the Turk," as opposed to the strictly religious notion of "infidel" or "nonbeliever." This change in terms would seem to fit with the growing secularization of the state system that had begun at Westphalia and is yet another reminder that the phenomenon of the Easterner as Europe's other predates the coming of Christendom and Islam. In other words, civilization, defined by criteria such as "humanity," "law," and "social mores," seemed to supplant religion in Europe's external differentiation from non-European communities. What took hold was a set of "intercultural relations" between Europe and "the Turk," relations that drew a sharp distinction between civilization and barbarism (Gong 1984: vii).

The European sense of identity and superiority deepened in the following century and helped to reinforce the unity of European society. Moreover, in describing those components that were uniquely European, eighteenth- and early-nineteenth-century publicists subordinated the logic of *raison d'état* to the "common ground of culture" that existed among European states. The international lawyer G. F. Martens, writing in 1795, spoke of Europe as "a society of nations and states, each of which has its laws, its customs, and its maxims, but which it cannot put in execution without observing a great deal of delicacy towards the rest of the society." Both Emmerich de Vattel and L'abbé Dominique-Georges-Frédéric de Pradt went a step further to describe Europe as a kind of "republic" (all quoted in Gulick [1955] 1967: 10–11). But perhaps the most eloquent exponent of the collective idea of Europe as opposed to the Turkish other was Edmund Burke, who elaborated the notion of a "Commonwealth of Europe." Burke accentuated the cultural "similitude" throughout Europe of the monarchical principle of government, the Christian religion, the Roman law heritage, and old Germanic customs and feudal institutions. In fact, he went so far as to portray Europe as "virtually one great state," claiming that "no citizen of Europe could be altogether an exile in any part of it" (Burke 1907: 155–157; Welsh 1995).

An integral part of this definition of the Commonwealth of Europe was the attempt to distinguish it from the Ottoman Empire. As a result, during the Ochakov Affair of 1791, Burke was a vocal opponent of William Pitt's realpolitik scheme to aid "the Turk" in his fight against Russian advances:

> He had never before heard it held forth, that the Turkish empire was ever considered as any part of the balance of power in Europe. They had nothing to do with European power; they considered themselves wholly Asiatic. . . . They despised and condemned all Christian princes, as infidels, and only wished to subdue and exterminate them and their people. What had these worse than savages to do with the powers of Europe, but to spread war, destruction, and pestilence among them? (Burke, recorded in Hansard 1816: vol. 28, cols. 76–77)

In Burke's conception of the kind of cultural homogeneity needed to sustain order in European international society, there was no room for "the Turk."

Despite these impassioned pleas from European patriots, however, "the Turk" was definitely a player (Gulick [1955] 1967: 15). Throughout the eighteenth century, Britain and France maintained diplomats in Constantinople as part of their campaign of military and commercial expansion. Furthermore, after the defeats in the wars of 1768–74 and 1787–92, the Ottomans themselves began to recognize that their empire could no longer be defended without European allies. As a result, the sultans adopted certain aspects of European diplomacy, most notably Selim III's establishment of permanent embassies in Europe in 1793. Before 1793 the sultans had sent individual missions for specific purposes, after which they returned to Constantinople; "the absence of permanent resident Ottoman embassies reflected a basic assumption of superiority: diplomacy was unnecessary during the centuries of Ottoman power"

(McKay and Scott 1983: 204). In the economic realm, the Ottoman decline in power resulted in the infamous capitulation treaties in which European powers obtained huge concessions and rights of immunity in exchange for their alliances. One instance of such capitulation was the Treaty of Kücük Kaynarca (1774), which codified Russia's decisive territorial gains on the Crimea and gave it extensive commercial rights on the Black Sea as well as the right to establish its own consuls, an independent church in Constantinople, and a special relationship with the Porte's Christian minorities (Anderson 1966: xi). The granting of such rights of extraterritoriality to Europeans became a "badge of inferiority" for the Sublime Porte (Gong 1984: 8).

The culmination of the Ottoman Empire's increasing reliance on Europe came in 1799 with its Tri-Partite Alliance with Britain and Russia against Napoleonic France. For the European powers, the pact was motivated by military and power political concerns—that is, the need to check French hegemonic aims—and the need to postpone the crumbling of the Ottoman Empire, lest it should reveal a dangerous power vacuum in Europe. Beyond such considerations of *raison d'état,* the alliance had little substance and was therefore destined to crumble once the French threat subsided. What followed was a century of shifting diplomatic arrangements between European states and the Ottoman Empire, directed at ensuring the empire's survival and at preserving the European balance of power.

Thus in the early stages of the Greek War of Independence, European statesmen such as Prince Metternich and Viscount Castlereagh allowed the interests of *raison d'état* to override their religious sympathies with the struggle of Christian rebels against Muslim rule. Revolution would destroy the fragile conservative order that had been established at the Congress of Vienna and would only open the way for hegemonic aims toward the disintegrating Ottoman Empire, especially where Russia was concerned. This status quo policy was echoed by Russia itself in a memo of 1829, which stated that "the advantages of the preservation of the Ottoman Empire outweigh its disadvantages" (quoted in Gong 1984: 71; the quotation is from a memorandum delivered by a special task force set up within the foreign ministry to review Russia's policy towards the Porte in its entirety). There was a shift from seeing the Ottoman Turk primarily as the barbarian other to civilized Europe toward seeing him as an "odd man out." Instructively, European discourse on how to order relations with this odd man out went by the term "the Eastern question" (Anderson 1966).

THE SICK MAN OF EUROPE AND THE YOUNG TURK

During the second Mohammed Ali Crisis, which began in 1838, Lord Palmerston organized a collective effort on the part of the European great powers to prevent Ottoman collapse. Subsequent Palmerstonian diplomacy would be directed toward propping up the empire in order to avoid strengthening Russian power on the Continent. In a conversation with the British naval commander Sir Hamilton Seymour in 1853, Tsar Nicholas I could afford to allude to the Porte as a "sick man" that Europe had "on its hands" (Rodinson 1987: 59). Significantly, although the metaphor of the "sick man" was of Russian coinage, for reasons that will become eminently clear in the next chapter Russian representations of Turkey emphazised its non-Europeanness. The "of Europe" that was added to the term "sick man," adding ambiguity to the Turk by offering him a principled place among the European hale if he could only heal himself, was a later elaboration.

The representation of Turkey as the "sick man of Europe," although dominant, did not crowd out echoes of other representations. A clear example is the Christian legitimist campaign that was waged by Tsar Alexander I at the Congress of Vienna. Alexander's scheme for the post-Napoleonic peace called for a fraternal association of sovereigns guided by the precepts of Christianity. His "Holy Alliance" was to be dedicated to "the Holy and Indivisible Trinity," and underwritten by all the European nations "united in Christ." Although the tsar's proposal was largely treated as an anachronism by the other powers, an altered form of the text was nevertheless signed by all parties save Great Britain, the Vatican, and, not surprisingly, the Ottomans themselves (Palmer 1974: ch. 18). In fact, the whole affair demonstrates to what extent Alexander differed from the Western powers and bears witness to Russia's perceived need to underline its European identity by means of an even more Eastern other.

Furthermore, in 1836 the British politician Richard Cobden was still doubting the "acceptability" of "the Turk" as a member of the European concert framework. In particular, Cobden protested against the inclusion of Turkey in Europe's calculation of the balance of power, as well as to the exclusion of the United States. The latter, he contended, enjoyed the economic standing and tradition that made it fit for partnership with Britain. But with regard to the former, he asked: "Upon what principle is Turkey a member of this European system? The Turks, at least, will be admitted by everybody to form no party to this 'union'" (quoted in Gulick [1955] 1967: 16).

And finally, although most historians cite the 1856 Treaty of Paris as the date by which the Sublime Porte was officially accepted as a member of the European state system, this acceptance was not accompanied by an admission of equality with "the Turk." In fact, as Hedley Bull argues, during the nineteenth century "the idea that international society was world-wide and all-inclusive lost ground, both in theory and in practice, to the idea that it was a privileged association of Christian, European, or civilized states" (1990: 82).

International lawyers of the nineteenth century perpetuated this cultural dualism with their positivist assertion that advanced international law did not apply to the territories outside of Europe. As W. E. Hall wrote:

> It is scarcely necessary to point out that as international law is a product of the special civilisation of modern Europe, and forms a highly artificial system of which the principle could not be supposed to be understood or recognised by countries differently civilised, such states only can be presumed to be subject to it as are inheritors of that civilisation.

Legal theorists also seem to suggest that a symbolic act of admittance had to occur before such territories could be considered part of the European "club"; states "outside European civilisation," Hall continued,

> must formally enter into the circle of law-governed countries. They must do something with the acquiescence of the latter, or of some of them, which amounts to an acceptance of the law in its entirety beyond all possibility of misconstruction. (Quoted in Wight 1977: 115)

According to Gerrit Gong, nineteenth-century lawyers gradually developed a formal European "standard of civilization" to demarcate those states "which were full members of the 'civilized' international society from those which were merely part of the European international system" (1984: 10–42). Gong suggests that the very codification of such a standard—necessitated by increased contact with the non-European world—helped to define more clearly the customs of European international society, customs that had heretofore been implicit and assumed by its members: "What the 'civilized' world had in common became apparent only when juxtaposed with the 'barbarous' and 'savage' worlds." Thus the standard included requirements based on long-standing European practices such as the protection of basic individual rights (life, dignity, and freedom of travel, commerce, and religion); an organized and efficient state bureaucracy; a fairly nondiscriminatory domestic system of courts, codes, and public laws; adherence to international law and the maintenance of avenues for diplomatic interchange; and conformity with accepted norms and practices of civilized international society and the outlawing of practices such as slavery and polygamy.

This spirit of exclusivity is perhaps best exemplified by natural law theorist James Lorimer. Drawing on Joseph Gobineau's racialist ideas, he made a clear distinction between civilized and barbarous humanity and accorded each a different stage of legal recognition. Plenary political recognition was to extend to all existing states of Europe, colonial dependencies with European settlers, and former European colonies. But only partial political recognition—and therefore only limited membership in the "family of nations"—was to be granted to Turkey (as well as to Persia, China, Siam, and Japan). "In the case of the Turks," stated Lorimer, "we have had bitter experience of the consequences of extending the rights of civilisation to barbarians who have proved to be incapable of performing its duties, and who possibly do not even belong to the progressive races of mankind" (quoted in Wight 1977: 122). For Lorimer, then, even the partial acceptance of the Ottoman Empire in 1856 had been premature. In his mind, "the Turk" had not yet attained the "standard of civilisation" that would allow him to sustain orderly international relations. To Lorimer, the Ottoman Turk was first and foremost a sick man, whose Europeanness remained in doubt.

The evolution of Ottoman diplomacy was accompanied by internal changes within the Ottoman Empire. The defeat of "the Turk" at the hands of superior European military and economic might had necessitated a grudging self-examination on the part of Muslim leaders and intellectuals. The humiliation of military defeat was aggravated by an accompanying awareness of their own arrested cultural development. Europe was no longer considered an inferior entity to be converted; rather, it was seen as a military, economic, and political giant to be emulated. With European assistance, reforms were initiated in the realms of education, technology, communication, transportation, and political and judicial institutions, to give the Porte some semblance of a secular, European-style state.

More important, the European powers themselves continuously demanded a widening and deepening of these domestic changes toward conformity with European standards. In other words, in order to play in the Concert of Europe, "the Turk" was expected to learn new tunes. Thus Ottoman reforms were introduced at critical junctures in European concert diplomacy. For example, in 1839, at the height of the Mohammed Ali Crisis over Egypt and Syria, the Ottomans introduced new measures guaranteeing the security of life and property and drew up a new penal code for the empire. In addition, the reform edict of 1856, which not only reaffirmed privileges and immunities for non-Muslim communities but also enshrined a new principle of religious equality throughout the empire, appeared a month before the Treaty of Paris. Turkish hesitations about Russian demands for an agreement guaranteeing the position of Orthodox Christians within the Ottoman Empire were a vital part of Russo-Turkish relations from the time of the Treaty of Kücük Kaynarca onward. And finally, the first Ottoman constitution was promulgated in December 1876, at the time of another Balkan crisis that threatened to involve the Ottomans in a war with Russia. It is evident, then, that the molding of alliances depended as much on the logic of culture as on the dictates of power political realities. If the Porte was to be granted European support, it had to tailor its domestic realities to the standards of European civilization. One must acknowledge that the reform demands of the European states were also oriented toward their own economic interests or the interests of non-Muslim communities. These interests often conflicted with the goals of the Ottoman elite (Berkes 1964: 147-154). As we shall see, the attitude of furious surprise by which Constantinople met European cultural demands is still very much with us.

By the time the Ottoman Empire had completed its entry into Europe's state system, most Islamic societies outside the empire had already been made subject to European colonial expansion. But it would be wrong to suggest that the synthesis of European and Muslim societies was total: "What occurred was an integration of systems and the material and technological accoutrements of modern societies. Values, outlooks on life, behaviour patterns, and beliefs remained culturally disparate" (Naff 1985: 169). Thus, for example, at the Second Hague Conference of 1907, the continuing presence of capitulations was used to accord the Ottoman Empire second-class status and to prohibit it from nominating a permanent member to the Court of Arbitration. Although "the Turk" was a part of the system of interstate relations, the logic of culture denied it equal status within the community of Europe.

Indeed, where Russia was concerned, the theme of Christian unity versus Ottoman domination of Christian peoples remained a staple in the Russian historiographical and political treatment of the Eastern Question. For example, in 1877 the leading historian Sergey Mikhaylovich Solovyov wrote that "the Eastern Question surfaced in history from the moment when European man saw the difference between Europe and Asia, between the European and Asian spirit" (quoted in Kinyapina 1963: 17). As late as 1916 the leading Russian liberal Pavel Milyukov used the idea of the other as proof that Russia was better equipped than the Porte to take care of the Straits and Constantinople. Quoting a contemporary British writer, he argued that "the presence of the Turk in Europe is incidental. They remain at the end of five hundred years as much strangers as they were at the beginning. European ideals and words, like 'nation,' 'government,' 'law,' 'sovereign,' 'subject,' do not apply to them" (quoted in Riha 1969: 257; compare Weisensel 1990). In the case of Russia, we have an outstanding example of how the idea of "the Turk" as the other is used to bolster the case for Russia's own Europeanness, which, it will be demonstrated at length in Chapter 3, was in doubt in quarters at home as well as in Western Europe.

With the shift in representations of the Ottoman Turk from being a barbarian to being the sick man of Europe went a toning down of the centrality of this other for the European self. Generalized colonialism was one reason; the growing preoccupation with Russia that will be discussed in Chapter 3 was another. References to "the Eastern Question" suggested that Turkey was *the* East, but there were also other Easts. There was a certain homogenization of the Ottoman Turk as other, and this trend definitely became even stronger as the Ottoman Empire gave way to a Turkish nation-state. This, however, should in no way be taken to mean that Turkey was represented as just another country. Once again, echoes of former representations may be heard.

CONCLUSION: TURKEY

With the demise of the Ottoman Empire in the wake of the 1908 revolution of the Young Turks and the defeat in World War I, a representation of Turkey began to take shape as a normalizing and modernizing nation and, with its entry into NATO, even as a trusted ally. More important, in being represented as a case of normalization, the transformation from a sick man to a reborn and young body politic also made "the Turk" less central as a constitutive other.

Among the arguments made in Chapter 3, perhaps one of the least controversial ones is that after an indecisive interwar period and after World War II the Soviet Union definitely came to occupy the position of constitutive other. A question about which to speculate, then, is how possible it would be for the political entities that have emerged to take over from "the Saracen" and "the Turk" in his various guises to once again become Europe's most important other. I should like to leave that question for the conclusion of the book, however, and round off this chapter by a discussion of the more immediately tangible question of how relations between the major successor state to the realm of the Saracen and Ottoman Empire on the one hand, and Europe on the other, still can be said to carry the marks of that constitutive exclusion of "the Turk" that was so central to the becoming of "the European." I should like to examine three examples: a newspaper tiff between a leading British columnist, Edward Mortimer, and the Turkish ambassador; an interview given by then Turkish prime minister Tansu Çiller to *Time* magazine; and a speech by the Dutch minister of foreign affairs and head of the EU Council of Ministers Hans van Mierlo to the European Parliament.

On 3 April 1990, when Edward Mortimer reviewed contemporary European perceptions of Islam and Turkey in a newspaper article in *Financial Times,* he found that they echoed the views of Penn, Lorimer, and other Europeans discussed above, thereby bearing witness to the continued operation of the logic of culture. His findings are worth citing at some length:

> Educated Turks especially, heirs to the militant secularism of Kemal Ataturk, are shocked to find their European identity judged by reli-

gious criteria. Yet the success of Ataturk's revolution looks far less certain today than it did a generation ago: almost every day brings new evidence of the strength of Islam in Turkey, not as a set of private religious beliefs but as a public phenomenon, moulding people's behaviour in the political and social arena. Nor in fact has it ever ceased to be the state religion in Turkey, in the sense that its institutions, unlike those of other religions, are financed and directly controlled by the state. Few Christians nowadays would wish to see Christianity reinstated as the established religion of Europe in that sense. But for good or ill the Christian legacy remains a key component of European identity. That is bound to affect the argument over where Europe's border should be drawn, and its relations with Moslem communities both inside that border and beyond. (*Financial Times*, 3 April 1990)

Mortimer's analysis must have hit a raw nerve. Turkey's ambassador to London quickly published a response, maintaining that "Turkey has been an integral part of Europe for six centuries and surely has a role to play and is a voice to be heard. The logic of an argument that Europe could renege on its commitment to Turkey's eventual full membership of the European Community now that the iron curtain is up is insupportable" *(Financial Times*, 20 April 1990).

The interview by Tansu Çiller was made during the run-up to the negotiation of a free trade treaty between Turkey and the EU that was viewed as an important step on Turkey's way to EU membership. Çiller's argument was that a failure by the EU to deliver would certainly propel the Islamicist Welfare Party to power and thus tip Turkey further toward the Middle East and away from Europe:

Now the European Parliament has to make its decision. It can say either yes or no—there is no third alternative. Delay means no to me and to all the people of Turkey; if nothing else, the fundamentalists will make sure that it is understood as a no. And it is not just Turkey that is concerned here: there are also the millions of Turkic-speaking people of Central Asia who are looking at two models: ours or the Iranians'. . . . I see my task as changing the history because Turkey can become a bridge for peace between the two areas. If it does not, the two regions will be divided and in confrontation with each other. We can be the link. We are democratic; we are secular; and our economy is the first open, sophisticated economy in the area. . . . The radicals, the fundamentalists and the extreme rightists will capitalize on any delay in the decision as a no vote and as an objection to Turkey by Europe. They will make sure that is understood by the people. So it is going to strengthen the radicals and may even move them into power—move the anti-Europe, antidemocratization, anti-Westernization, antisecular forces into power. . . . Now it's me versus them. I represent Westernization, secular government, liberalization, the link with Europe. (*Time* magazine, European edition, 20 November 1995)

Turkey applied for membership in the European Community (EC) in 1987 (Özdalga 1989). The opinion on membership (number 1589) duly published by the Commission of the EC on that occasion discussed economic and political matters, but the reasons it suggested for not accepting the Turkish application were not explicitly those mentioned above. The application stalled, officially for economic reasons. On 15 January 1997, however, van Mierlo delivered a speech to the European Parliament on behalf of the Dutch presidency of the EU in which he said that he understood Turkey's frustration over the issue. And then he went on to argue that it was "time to be honest" and admit that the problem was also one of admitting a large Muslim country into the European Union. Do we wish this to happen? van Mierlo asked, adding that no one had posed this problem officially before.

Present-day representations of Turkey thus carry with them the memory of earlier representations. These memories are among the factors operative in today's Turkish-European discourse, and this discourse remains part of the discourse on European identities. It is instructive to note that the Turkish ambassador to London tried to re-present these memories by offering a representation of Turkey as "an integral part of Europe for six centuries" pitted against representations that cast Turkey as an external or at best marginal presence in Europe. And just as Russians have pointed to Turkey to bolster their own claim to Europeanness, Çiller pointed to Iran in order to boost the European standing of the country that she headed. Of course, Çiller's worry that a failure of negotiations with the EU might "strengthen the radicals and may even move them into power— move the anti-Europe, antidemocratization, anti-Westernization, antisecular forces into power," was not exactly her greatest worry, which can be seen from the fact that she herself turned around and made a deal that brought these very forces to power in Turkey. The point, however, is that Çiller deemed it effective to pursue this line of argument when taking part in English-speaking discourse. She expected European politicians to have a horizon of expectation that would be accommodating to this kind of argument. As van Mierlo pointed out to one of the key audiences also addressed by Çiller, one would be hard put to argue that she was wrong in this regard.

The main reason given for presenting a reading of "the Turk" as Europe's other was the very clear-cut way in which Turkey has been represented. Admittedly, this discussion has perhaps presented a picture that is a bit too stark in that it has largely failed to highlight the ongoing struggles over representations of "the Turk." Since Cardinal Nicholas of Cusa suggested that the two parties should simply sit down together and see what would come out of that, voices arguing in favour of dialogue with the Turk have repeatedly been heard in European discourse. These voices have nonetheless routinely been drowned out. In the case of Russia, which I will discuss next, however, both the variation of representations and the scope of the representations offered have been much broader. If "the Turk" really became what we may call a marginal or liminal other in the guise of "the sick man of Europe," we have in the case of Russia a European other that, I will argue, has been marginal all along.

3

Making Europe: The Russian Other

In Silesia we saw many reinforcements on their way to join the Russian army; large bodies of Cossacks; but what astonished us more than anything was a body of several hundred Asiatical Tatars armed with bows and arrows, and carrying a light spear. Their equipment altogether was most strange. They have the Chinese face, and are exactly like the fellows one sees painted on tea-boxes.

— LORD ABERDEEN IN 1813, QUOTED IN BALFOUR 1922: 80

Whereas one of the main reasons for devoting the previous chapter to European representations of "the Turk" had to do with the historical centrality of such representations for European identity formation, one of the main reasons why this chapter discusses representations of "Russia" has to do with its sweeping contemporary salience. In addition to its centrality for overall discourse on European identity formation, the question of where Russia fits in is a central component of ongoing discourse on the European security order, and is frequently its focus. It is the central part of most day-to-day deliberations over institutional particulars, such as the way to handle the expansion of organizations like the EU and NATO. It also permeates discussions of economic developments, not only discussions concerning the markets for such raw materials as petroleum and aluminum but also the overall question of what is most often referred to as the transition of former Communist economies.

When these developments come under the scholarly gaze, as they frequently do, the result is usually work on the practical problems involved in handling Russia in a particular policy area or discussions of the systemic forces that were at the heart of the breakdown of the Soviet Union and how these forces now work in favor of or against the inclusion of Russia in what is regularly named Western or European institutions. Russianists also find a regular market for writings about the political struggles over what is named reform (or, again, transition) as these struggles unfold in Moscow, St. Petersburg, and the amorphous Russian provinces. One favorite Russianist argument, known to every policy maker and academic, draws on the long history of struggle between Westernizers and Slavophiles, modernists and traditionalists, democrats and patriots, in order to demonstrate that metaphors of the past are very much part of the Russian political present (see Neumann 1996 for an example). During the Cold War, this argument would usually include parallels between the operating modes of Ivan the Terrible and Stalin. At the beginning of the 1990s, parallels between Peter the Great and somebody often named Tsar Boris were very much in vogue.[1]

Where Russia is concerned, then, the legitimacy and relevance of discussing how the handling of day-to-day questions of policy are influenced by references to the past are seldom questioned. Neither does one need an excuse for drawing parallels between sixteenth-century and twentieth-century rulers. By extension, one should also expect there to be a scholarly debate about how European and Western metaphors of the past color the handling of the question of where Russia fits in. Very few politicians and diplomats, and only the most ardent positivist scholars, would probably object to the genealogical presupposition that the way a political question has been variously discussed in the past will impinge on the political business at hand. And yet when it comes to the question of where Russia fits in, there is very little by way of scholarly reflection on how this complex of issues has been handled previously. Whereas the chapter on Turkey could proceed by way of criticizing the generalizations made by other scholars, the relative dearth of studies concerning European representations of Russia means that this chapter will first have to demonstrate what the major representations were. Since other scholars have offered few generalizations, furthermore, mine will in a larger degree have to grow out of that material itself. In other respects, this chapter will proceed along the same lines as the previous one.

THE SIXTEENTH AND SEVENTEENTH CENTURIES: MUSCOVY

Whereas contacts between, on the one hand, Novgorod and Kievan Rus' and, on the other hand, political entities to the west of them had been lively enough for there to have developed a number of representations during the High Middle Ages, the earliest period to be examined here is the one stretching from the early contacts involving representatives of what may only now and still tenuously be referred to as European political entities—1493 where Denmark is concerned, as late as 1553 for Britain—to Peter the Great's accession to the throne. European representations of Russians during this period focused on the political entity of Muscovy. Sigismund von Herberstein's *Notes upon Russia*, clearly the most widely read work of the period, still referred to Novgorod as the "most extensive principality in all Russia" ([1551] 1851, 1852: 24), although he makes it clear that it had come thoroughly under the sway of Muscovy.

The institutionalization of relations coincided with the spread of the Renaissance to the rest of the alleged entity of Muscovy, as well as with the so-called Age of Discovery. Significantly, however, the "discovery" of Russians neither was nor is treated on a par with the "discovery" of the Indies, for example. This is a first indication of a theme that will be developed throughout this chapter, namely, that European representations of Russia show a marked proclivity for treating Russians as what can be called the liminar case of European identity.

Indeed, a case can be made that in the discursive shift discussed in the previous chapter, whereby representations of "Christianity" were first imbricated in and then occluded by representations of "Europe," the difficulties of categorizing Russia conferred on it not only a liminar, but also a pivotal status. Enea Silvio Piccolomini, who went on to become Pope Pius II and who, as already mentioned, wrote the first book with the word "Europe" in its title, counted Russians as Europeans because of their Christianity (Groh 1961: 20). And yet this was a contested point throughout the period. At the beginning of the 1500s Rabelais held them to be unbelievers (*mécréants*), and in his usual carnivalesque fashion he referred sweepingly to "Moscovites, Indiens, Perses et Troglodytes" (quoted in Lortholary 1951: 11, 16). There were two issues involved here. The first concerned firsthand knowledge of the Holy Scriptures, which was held to be impeded for the Russians by their lack of scholarship. The Danish diplomat Jakob Ulfeldt, who went to Russia in the 1570s, reported that "their clergymen are not learned, and understand no other speech than the Russian; of learned men there are none" (quoted in Møller 1993: 112). The other concerned the heretical teachings and practices emanating, among other things, from this sorry state of affairs. In 1620 A. J. Prytz treated both in a doctoral thesis at the University of Uppsala with the title *Theses de quaestione: Utrum Muschovitae sint christiani* (Lortholary 1951: 281 n. 41). He concluded in the affirmative, but the point in this connection is that his dissertation was very much part of an ongoing debate in which the question was widely held to be in serious need of discussion (the Swedish king was in attendance at the thesis defense).

The question of the status of the Russians as Christians was further complicated by the close ties they were seen to maintain with non-Christian people. Indeed, representations of Russia were often directly mixed up with representations of Muslim political entities. In 1603 John Smith was taken prisoner by Crimean Tatars (a dry run for the captivity from which Pocahontas would release him four years later). When he reported back on his whereabouts, he held that "Tatary and Scythia are all one; but so large and spacious, few or none could ever perfectly describe it; nor all the several kinds of barbarous people who inhabit it" (quoted in Wolff 1994: 11). Sir Jerome Horsey was quite explicit about these political ties, writing at the end of the sixteenth century that Tsar Ivan III "cast off the yoke of homage his predecessors always did unto the great Scythian emperor of the Kryms." Then, clearly scandalized, he went on to tell the story of Ivan's second marriage:

> And when his good queen died, Empress Anastasiia, who was canonized a saint and so worshiped in their churches to this day, having by her two sons, Ivan and Fedor, then he married one of the Circassian princesses, by whom he had no issue that he would be known of. The manner and solemnity was so strange and heathenly as credit will hardly be given to the truth thereof. (Horsey 1968: 264–265)

Circassians were Muslim, and this political association of the most intimate kind with Islam could be nothing but "heathenly." Perhaps it was practices such as these that made Horsey refer to Russians as "Scythians." Referring to Russians as "Scythians,"

"Tatars," "Kalmucks," and so on does, at any rate, make its debut as part of European representations of "Asiatic" and "barbarous" Russia in this early period. Hartog sees the Scythians of Herodotus as "a people midway between two different spaces, on the frontiers of Asia and Europe" (1988: 30). It may be because it captures this ambiguity that the practice of referring to Russians as "Scythians" remained part of European representations into the twentieth century.

The dominant version of this period included two other themes in addition to the master theme of Christianity. These were the questions of the civility of the Russians and of regime type. In all three respects Russians were found wanting, and it was for all these reasons that the period stressed their barbarity, their characteristic lack of civility. Ulfeldt found that his host, who happened to be Ivan IV (known as "the Terrible," in itself an interesting translation of *grozny*, "threatening" or "forbidding"), did not meet his expectations of royalty: "Never did I see a man, be he of whatever low estate, sit and eat less properly than this mighty Tsar [*Kejser*]" (quoted in Møller 1993: 119).[2] And the bodily practices of the tsar mirrored the practices of the body politic: Ulfeldt did not find the equals that he expected to find in what was after all, or after a fashion, a Christian country. Another traveler who was scandalized by Russian bodily practices was Jerome Horsey, who commented on Ivan IV's style of government in the following manner:

> Knyaz Boris Tupulev, a great favorett of that tyme, discovered to be a treason worcker against the emperor, and confederatt with the discontented nobillitie, was drawen upon a longe sharpe made stake, soped [sharpened] to enter his fundament thorrow his bodye, which came owt at his naeck; upon which he languished in horable paine for fifteen howres alive, and spake unto his mother, the Duches, brought to behold that wofull sight. And she, a goodly matronlye weoman, upon like displeasure, geaven to 100 gunners, whoe defile her to deathe one after the other; her bodye, swollen and lieinge naked in the place, comanded his huntsmen to bring their hongrie dogs to eat and devouer her flesh and bones, dragged everiewher; [and Ivan said] "such as I favour I have honored, and such as be treytors will I have thus done unto." . . . I could innumerat many more that have felt the like severitie and crueltie of this emperors heavy hand of displeasur, but I forbade to trouble the modest eyrs and Christian pacience of such as shall read it. (1968: 279; see also Cross 1971: 73–74).

In an age where one of the Elizabethan capital punishments involved being boiled alive, what was shocking was perhaps not first and foremost the practice as such but that it was meted out on good Christians of rank.[3] But the sexual practices of the populace were also constructed as being heavily wanting. As George Turberville put it in an "Epistle to his especiall friend Master Edward Dancie" from 1587:

> Perhaps the muzhik hath a gay and gallant wife
> To serve his beastly lust, yet he will lead a bowgard's life.
> The monster more desires a boy within his bed
> Than any wench, such filthy sinne ensues a drunken head.
> The woman to repay her drowsie husband's dettes
> From stinking stove unto her mate to bawdy banquets gets.
> (Reproduced in Cross 1971: 70–72)

And in 1646 Adam Olearius deplored the fact that references to bodily practices permeated Russian speech:

> The Russians are in general a very quarrelsome people who assail each other like dogs, with fierce, harsh words. . . . They have nothing on their tongue more often than "son of a whore," "son of a bitch," "cur," "I fuck your mother," to which they add "into the grave," and similar scandalous speech. Not only adults and old people behave thus, but also little children who do not yet know the name of God, or father, or mother, already have on their lips "fuck you," and say it as well to their parents as their parents to them. (Quoted in Cross 1971: 94)

So given the dominant representation of Russia, John Milton's comment about Muscovy in the mid-1600s, that it was "the most northern region of Europe reputed civil" (quoted in Roberts 1964a: 386), must be called charitable. The weight ascribed to bodily practices in the representations of Russia in this period is indeed striking. In their different ways, Michel Foucault and Anthony Giddens both stress the importance of disciplining the bodies of subjects for the disciplining of the body politic at large, with Giddens arguing that "routine control of the body is integral to the very nature both of agency and of being accepted (trusted) by others as competent" (1991: 57). If this is acknowledged as a salient issue on the level of subjectivity, it is a small step to seeing its relevance in the representation of one human collective by another also. Russia was represented as other, among other things, by dint of the bodily practices of its population.

If this is so, it would make bodily practices the negative flip side of the preoccupation with regime type, which was the third ingredient of the dominant representation of this period. Horsey's outrage at the treatment by Ivan IV of his aristocracy was one instance of the general condemnation of the despotism of Russian rulers. As M. S. Anderson puts it in his magisterial study of the period's English writings on Russia:

> Francis Bacon expressed the feelings of all educated Englishmen when he wrote of Ivan IV that "he is advised by no Council, but governeth altogether like a tyrant." The same point is made, usually at considerable length, in every systematic account of Russia, first- or second-hand, original or translated, published in English in the sixteenth or seventeenth centuries. Eden declared that "In authoritie and dominion over his subiectes, the prince of Moscovie passeth all the monarchies of the worlde; For he depriveth all his noble men and gentelmen of all theyr holdes and inventions at his pleasure. He trusteth not his owne brethren, but oppresseth all with lyke servitude." Fletcher, much better informed, found that "The state and forme of their government is plaine tyranicall, as applying all to the behoofe of the prince, and that after a most open and barbarous manner." (1958: 19–20)[4]

Russians were represented as barbarians. And yet the very same closeness to savage and infidel peoples that was seen as jeopardizing their status as civil Christians may in other cases furnish a context that adds to a representation of Russians as being themselves civil. This may be seen, for example, in what was, after its publication in 1549 (English translation, 1551), ubiquitously held to be the standard text of the period, namely Sigismund von Herberstein's *Notes upon Russia: Being a Translation of the Earliest Account of That Country Entitled "Rerum moscoviticarum commentarii"* ([1551] 1851, 1852). To Herberstein the Don "divides Europe from Asia" (1852: 11), and so he referred to Moscow as a town situated in Asia. Crucially, however, to be civil was in this period a universalist trait, in the sense that it was not tied to geographical place and was not divisible. There did not yet exist different "civilizations"; there was only the civil world and the noncivil, that is, the barbarian or savage world. There is, however, a marked tension in Herberstein's text where this issue is concerned. For example, he wrote that "beyond the rivers Petchora and Stzuchogora are various innumerable races, who are called by the one common name of Samoged, which implies, 'men who eat one another.' . . . These races do not come to Moscow, for they are savage, and avoid communion with other people, and civilized society" (Herberstein [1549] 1852: 39). The implication is, then, that such a thing as civilized society may be found in Moscow. Nonetheless, elsewhere Herberstein goes on to avail himself of the epithet "barbarian," for example, to describe one "Dimitry Danielovich, a man who, considering that he was a barbarian, was of remarkable dignity and truthfulness" ([1549] 1852: 74). Of course, an easy reconciliation would have it that the good Dimitry Danielovich simply did not belong to the civilized Moscow set. This reading would, however, probably overlook the crucial issue.

Michael Harbsmeier (1987) concludes from an extensive reading of sixteenth-century German travelogues, of which Herberstein's is the major specimen where Russia is concerned, that the case of Russia stands out as an unwieldy challenge to the rapidly changing European cosmology of the first half of the period under consideration here. During the Renaissance, he maintains, there was a shift away from a religious cosmology based on the two axes of us-them (Christianity versus Islam) and ancient Christians–contemporary Christians. Whereas the former of these axes remained, the latter was supplanted by one that was based not on religion but on whether one was educated or not. Harbsmeier explains the shift partly as a response to the schisms of the Reformation, which brought about efforts by elites in different parts of a religiously and politically fracturing Christendom to establish new common ground as *cultured*. He maintains that no attempts were made to include Russians within Europe on the ground that they were cultured. On the strength of the present discussion, this may be an overstatement. The point still stands, however, that the representation of Russia as a European country should have been easier inside the fading European cosmology than in the emerging one. Harbsmeier then highlights the main taxonomic problem that arose inside this old cosmology by pointing out that both the numerous wartime broadsheets and a number of travel accounts tended to describe the conditions of life in Russia in much the same terms as other travelers used to describe conditions under Ottoman rule. At the same time, however, these travelogues would describe Russian religious life as "a series of deviations from truly Christian rules of conduct and behaviour" (Harbsmeier 1987: 348).

In this period, when Christianity remained the outstanding marker of identity and when "Christendom" was still vying with "Europe" as a marker while retaining the meaning of the former term, such a differentiation of spheres political and religious was truly remarkable. It struck to the core of the anxieties surrounding the refashioning of European selves, from multilayered entities whose cohesion was furnished exactly by Christendom to, for the elite, selves that were tied to rising states. "Despotic Christian ruler" was an oxymoron, and one that the period preferred to leave in peace instead of resolving.[5]

This representation of Russia was so pervasive that a challenge to it appeared only at the very end of the period. A follower of Jakob Böhme, Quirinius Kuhlmann, went to Russia and attempted to make the tsar abdicate in order to speed the coming of the fifth Jesuitical world kingdom and world salvation. Before this idea of Russia as the land of the future had time to establish itself in European discourse, however, Peter the Great had its proponent burned at the stake, in 1682, the very first year of his reign (Naarden 1992: 20; Gollwitzer 1964: 68).

One also has to look to the margins of European discourse in order to find representations involving strategic issues. This theme was almost drowned out by the dominant theme of Christianity and the two other themes of bodily practices and regime type, and yet it was not completely absent. Dieter Groh holds Hubertus Langeutus to have been the first to worry about Russian expansion. In a letter to John Calvin written in September 1558, Langeutus commented on the Livonian War, which commenced that year, that "si ullus principatus in Europa crescere debet, ille erit [if there is a principality in Europe that will grow, it is this one]" (quoted in Groh 1961: 25). The same war, which lasted until 1583, occasioned the use of a parallel that we have already seen at work in subsequent periods, as the Vatican worried that a Livonian victory would propel Muscovy to dominance in the Baltic Sea area and beyond.[6] It was pointed out that, like the Goths, who had not been stopped even by the power of

the Roman Empire, the Russians were also coming from the north
(Groh 1961: 26). And some twenty years later, during the Polish-
Lithuanian king's war against Muscovy, the Vatican expected him to
be Europe's *antemurale,* or rampart, which should "omnes Moscos
et Tataros sub pedibus contereret [force all Muscovites and Tatars
underfoot]" (Groh 1961: 27).

Once again, however, particular care must be taken so that representations such as these are not foregrounded anachronistically. Alliance against Russia was *not* a regular European practice in this period (or, for that matter, in the twentieth century). Suffice it to note
that in 1490, that is, almost a full century before the Polish-Lithuanian
Kingdom was called upon to be Europe's *antemurale* against Russia,
Holy Roman Emperor Maximilian I's ambassador N. V. Poppel had
already asked Ivan III for an alliance against the Jagiellonians. The
forging of military alliances with "the Turk" was a possibility, and
so it was with Russia. This point only jeopardizes the relevance of
the present undertaking for an understanding of present European
representations of Russia if the narrow social interaction that is alliance formation is dehistoricized and foregrounded to the detriment
of all other social practices. An enquiry into European representations of Russia must, like all studies of the role of cultural factors in
world politics, face essentialization on the one hand, and the accusation of irrelevance on the other.

THE EIGHTEENTH CENTURY: TSARIST EUROPE IN THE NORTH

Peter the Great's accession to the throne set in train hefty re-presenting
activity throughout Europe and established new representations that,
although challenged first and foremost by romantics, nonetheless
dominated European discourse on Russia until the Napoleonic Wars.
As it happened, Peter's coming to power was immediately framed in
two parallel ways: (1) Because of how he behaved, he was seen as
a bit of a barbarian, but a barbarian who redeemed himself by
showing what was constructed as a willingness to shed his ways and
learn from Europe. By the lights of general political reasoning, this
view was then transposed from the king's body to his body politic.
(2) Concurrently, the hope was expressed that Peter's Russia, which
quickly established itself as the dominant Baltic power and by extension as part of the European states system, could be a valuable ally
against "the Turk." Indeed, Peter's establishment of himself as *im-*

perator coincided with the appearance of the name "Russia" in the titles of European books about the country (Groh 1961: 47), and so the name "Russia" and the power Russia actually appeared in the European system of states at the same time.

Gottfried Wilhelm Leibniz's representation of Peter's arrival seems exemplary both where the double framing and the emphases are concerned and has the added interest of highlighting the interplay of the two others, Russia and Turkey, in European identity formation. His "Egyptian plan" of 1672 had outlined how the Sun King's France should forge Europe together behind its leadership in a military campaign to wrest Egypt from the Ottoman Empire (Yapp 1992). In this connection he had already written that Russia could become a good ally against the Turk. In a 1696 letter to H. W. Ludolf, he went on to state that

> I wish it could be done in the same way as with the Ethiopians! If such a vast Empire were to be ruled in order to bring about a more cultured Europe, and therefore to harvest larger fruits in ways Christian but there is hope, if we are vigilant. Tsar Peter knows the vices of his people and he wants to abolish barbarity. (Quoted in Groh 1961: 33)[7]

At the same time, Leibniz also famously wrote that "if the tsar is going to debarbarise his country, he will find a Tabula Rasa." At this point, Leibniz held that Russia might be destined to become a bridge between Europe and China (Groh 1961: quote on 33; 34). There were two sides to this: Russia, under the firm hand of an enlightened despot, might on the one hand become a conduit for Europe's enlightened heritage; on the other hand it thereby also risked contamination by Europe's decadence, and this might dull its ability to reinvigorate that heritage.

Groh concludes from this that "Leibniz was the first to include [or accept; *Aufnahme* is the noun used] Russia into the political constellation of Europe" (1961: 37). It must be stressed, however, that this happened as part of a universalizing thrust. Leibniz was interested in charting and abetting the universal march of progress, and so his writings about Russia were consistently directed to this general goal. Therefore, the point of his interest in Russia was not to treat that country in its specific otherness, but to subsume it under the European same. Since this same was the same of an abstract universalism centered on a Europe in becoming, the critical thrust of his writings on Russia were directed toward the goal of demonstrating not only to Russians but to a Europewide audience that their continent as well as the world at large had to march in the direction of this same.

The dominant metaphor for the arrival of Russia as an actor as well as a learner in the European state system was coined in this period and is still very much present in European representations of Russia. This is the metaphor of Peter's founding St. Petersburg as a "window on the West." One notes, however, an extremely instructive displacement here. The metaphor goes back to a letter written by Voltaire's friend Count Francesco Algarotti to Lord Hervey in 1739, in which he wrote that "I am at length going to give you some account of this new city, of this great window lately opened in the north, thro' which Russia looks into Europe" (Algarotti [1769] 1971: 183).

Aleksandr Pushkin popularized this in his *Bronze Horseman*, explicitly giving Algarotti as his source, in the succeeding period, when one could speak of a "window on the West," which, by implication, was opened from the east. However, Algarotti saw a window opening *in the north,* as well he had to, since this period did not know the idea of an east and a west in Europe (Confino 1994). After all, the long war against Sweden and its allies by which Peter was seen to establish himself as the dominant power around the Baltic Sea is still known as the Great *Northern* War. It is hard to overestimate the implications of this change of compass directions for European representations of Russia (and it is because the idea of an East/West divide in Europe now seems self-evident that it is so easy to overlook the fact that this divide did not exist for those writing during the eighteenth century). As a result of the Thirty Years War, what had previously been seen as two distinct state systems, one focused on the Baltic and the other on the Continent, came into contact with one another; the northern power Sweden was among the powers present at Westphalia (Watson 1984). And yet at the time of the Great Northern War, the idea that there existed a separate configuration around the Baltic was still pervasive. This, after all, is one of the reasons why Groh can say that Leibniz was the first to include Russia in the political constellation of Europe.

The Great Northern War foregrounded the balance of power that centered on the Baltic Sea in European discussions and attached it firmly to the idea of the overall European balance.[8] In this way, the perceived importance of Russia as a serious player in European politics was much enhanced, and so was the possibility of further Russian expansion toward the south (not yet toward the west). Indeed, it may be argued that "this outcome of the Northern War, the withdrawal of Sweden to Scandinavia and Finland, helped to dissolve the whole idea of 'the North' by neatly separating for the first time Sweden from Russia and Poland" (Wolff 1994: 156).[9] To put it another way, as Russia became dominant in "the North," this immediately set in train a re-presentation of the coordinates of Europe that was to result in the forging of the East/West divide during the next period, a divide that is still pivotal.

The advent of Russian dominance around the Baltic Sea was not immediately represented as a direct military threat to Europe, but it was clearly seen as making one possible. Peter, as Daniel Defoe wrote in the wake of Peter's rout of Charles XII of Sweden at Poltava, had "a Country of Slaves behind him, of near 2,000 Mile square, all the Inhabitants are subject to him, as a Gentleman's Hounds in England are to his Huntsman," and he engaged them not in "conquering but ravaging and tearing to pieces." Four years later, a newspaper article speculated that the Great Northern War might be "the occasion of bringing down a Foe upon Europe, more formidable than the Goths and Vandals, their Ancestors" (both quoted in Anderson 1958: 58–59). Here is an embryonic representation of "the barbarian at the gate" (indeed, in the latter text, Russians are concurrently constructed as "a race of Savages" and a "Barbarous Race"). And in 1724 a daily by the apt name of *Plain Dealer* had already proposed a policy for dealing with the barbarian:

> If early Measures are not taken, by Way of Prevention, against the threaten'd Evil, the UNIVERSAL EMPIRE, which Spain and France have successively alarm'd Europe with a fruitless dread of, seems, in Reality, to be coming upon us, with all the Terrors of a Fifth General Monarchy. (Quoted in Anderson 1958: 72)

It must be stressed that these representations were not inscribed with the same urgency as they were to be during the following period, when a Left Hegelian, Arnold Ruge, could call for a preventive strike by Europe against the barbarian at the gate. For example, in elaborating the territorial relative gains point that "one must take care that in seeking to increase real size, one does not diminish relative size," Montesquieu remarked that during the reign of France's King Louis XIV, "Muscovy was as yet no better known in Europe than was the Crimea" (1989: book 9, ch. 9, 137). The Crimea was at this time a khanate and arguably the least well known of the areas around what the dominant version saw as Europe's geographical borders, that is, the territories west of the Don and the Sea of Azov. (This construction was taken over from antiquity; in the second century before our era, Ptolemy singled out the river Don as a border between Sarmatia Europea and Sarmatia Asiatica; see Halecki 1950: 85.) For Montesquieu, the fact that Russia was little known did not mean that it was not part of Europe. Indeed, he was critical of Peter's heavy-handed policy of Europeanizing Russia as being unnecessarily brutal. After all, climate was for him the most important social factor, and by virtue of its climate Russia belonged to Europe. The implication was that what may in this case quite literally be called the climate for learning was so good that the pupil could not help but succeed.

Such doubt was unusual at the beginning of the period and clearly ran counter to the dominant representation, which lauded Peter's Russia for its efforts to civilize itself. Due to the image of Peter as a learner, during his extensive travels in Western Europe he was approached by a number of people who tried to interest him in sundry plans and proposals concerning his intended reforms. Matthew Anderson points to the scholar Francis Lee as

> perhaps the first example of a type of interest in Russia which was to become increasingly widespread amongst the intellectuals of western Europe. The idea of the country as a vast field for governmental experiment, a gigantic specimen to which the most advanced legal and administrative ideas could be applied with a completeness impossible in western Europe, was to develop rapidly under the stimulus of Peter's reforms, and the attitude to Russia implicit in Lee's proposals was later to inspire Voltaire, Mercier de la Rivière, Jeremy Bentham, and a large number of less important figures. (Anderson 1958: 50)

What should also be noted is that these ideas presuppose Leibniz's idea that Russia was something of a tabula rasa. Leibniz's hopes that Russia could somehow reinfuse universal reason into Europe also seemed to animate a number of these proposals. When Catherine the

Great invited the renowned scholar John Brown to come and assist in the running of the affairs of state, he wrote to a friend that

> if you indulge me in carrying my imagination into futurity, I can fancy that I see civilisation and a rational system of Christianity extending themselves quite across the immense continent, from Petersburg to Kamschatka. I fancy that I see them striking further into the more southern regions of Tartary and China, and spreading their influence even over the nations of Europe; which, though now polished, are far from being truly Christian or truly happy. Nay, I am fantastic enough to say with Pitt, that as America was conquered in Germany, so Great Britain may be reformed in Russia. (Quoted in Anderson 1958: 104–105)

A representation of Russia as the land of the future seems to be at work. Brown stressed that he was operating in the realm of potentialities. Yet Peter's reforms were seen as having immediate effects, inasmuch as Russians' grossness of manners receded and their knowledge of French increased, and the period was rife with nods in the direction of the increased Europeanness of Russians. For example, in 1753 Gotthilff Werner wrote that "the inhabitants of these parts were until recently quite untamed, barbarian and of *slavisk* [the Danish word, still in use, may mean "Slav" or "slavish"] temper, yet they have now become more civilized and have adopted the mores of the other Europeans" (Quoted in Møller 1993: 120).

Doubts about the ability of Russians and Russia to internalize these values were, however, frequently voiced. The idea that Russia was coming into European civilization had its flip side in the idea that it was emerging from an Asiatic one. Parallels, political and otherwise, were frequently drawn between Russia and the Ottoman Empire. Sir George Macartney maintained in a book published in 1768 that "the history of favourites and ministers in Russia is the history of bashaws and grand viziers in Turkey" (quoted in Anderson 1958: 98). When, at the end of the period, Edmund Burke on a number of occasions juxtaposed the two and maintained that Europe should follow a policy of support for one against the other, he voiced what was to become a main theme of the nineteenth century (see Welsh 1995).

Doubts about the Russian potential for breaking away from its barbarized state were often voiced in terms of manners. Just Juel, who visited St. Petersburg in its early days as King Frederick IV of Denmark's *envoyé extraordinaire,* was particularly uneasy about the easy flow of all kinds of liquids: The *imperator*'s fools blew their noses in one another's faces in the immediate vicinity of their master, and he and his men drank continuously. One night, in May 1710, during a large party that the tsar gave aboard a ship, Juel had had enough and tried to retreat to the top of one of the masts. Yet once the tsar saw that his guest was abandoning them, he took a glass full of vodka between his teeth and climbed up after him. "And there," Juel wrote, "there where I had thought myself to be most safe, not only did I have to drench that glass which he brought, but also four more, and I became so drunk that I was not able to descend without finding myself in the greatest peril" (quoted in Møller 1993: 120). One wonders what Norbert Elias would have made of all this.

In his reading of Danish representations of Russia, Peter Ulf Møller sees a master dichotomy at work in the insistences on Russian lack of etiquette, capacity to brave the elements and to down alcohol, and sturdy if noninventive behavior on the battlefield and elsewhere. Quoting from Johan Hübner's geographical handbook of 1741 to the effect that "the Russians have oftentimes shown themselves to be good soldiers, as they have been trained well by foreign officers in the art of war," he argues that Russians were constructed as body and nature, whereas Europeans were constructed as mind and civilization (Møller 1993: 108). Enlightenment discourse at large clearly drew on such a dichotomy, and this seems to be the locus from which arose the metaphor of the Russian *ursa major,* a metaphor that is still very much present in European discourse in its delatinized forms (Great Bear and so on; see also Anderson 1958: 97). Yet exactly because the idea that humans may be pure nature was a set piece of the Enlightenment, it did not come with an inbuilt prejudice where value judgment was concerned; savages could be noble or otherwise. More often than not, however, the Russian was seen as lazy and fatalistic, as, for example, Laurent Bérenger, French chargé d'affaires to Catherine, saw them:

> Perhaps the prime cause of his laziness is that he has no interest whatever in the fruits of his industry; it is inconceivable how little attachment to life a Russian seems to have. When the rivers freeze and thaw, one sees people crossing them regardless of the evident danger; and if

one tries to hold them back, warning them that they are risking death, they answer coolly, "Bog znaet" ("The Lord knows") and continue on their way. (In Vernadsky et al. 1972: 397)

In Møller's reading, Russia is to Europe as nature is to culture, and this is a stimulating reading. What this dichotomy fails to demonstrate, however, is how European representations of Russia as hovering between Asia and Europe inscribes the country with a crucial ambiguity. Nowhere is this more apparent than in the exchanges between Catherine and the philosophes, who agree in seeing Russia not only in a civilizing role vis-à-vis Muslim peoples in the south and even Turkey but also as the bulwark of Europe against Asia. ("If you really want to make me happy, inform me immediately of the massacre of fifty or sixty thousand Turks," Denis Diderot wrote to the sculptor Etienne-Maurice Falconet, who was at that time at work in St. Petersburg; quoted in Lortholary 1951: 131). In the latter half of the period, this ambiguity became a crucial matter in the overall clash between Voltaire and Rousseau, the discussion of which will take up the rest of the treatment of this period.

In his extremely entertaining book *Inventing Eastern Europe: The Map of Civilization on the Mind of the Enlightenment,"* Larry Wolff has recently described Voltaire as "the philosophical Cortés of Eastern Europe," and his history of Sweden's Charles XII as "the philosophical foundation for the representation of Eastern Europe" (Wolff 1994: 91, 362). The gratuitous parallel and the downplaying of Leibniz as precursor aside, it seems clear that Voltaire's consistent and universalist optimism on behalf of Russia added significantly to the dominant version of the period. For example, writing in 1760 under the obviously Russian nom de plume of Ivan Aletof, Voltaire published a poem in which he had his Russian alter ego introduce himself in the following manner:

> I come to form myself on the shores of the Seine;
> It is a coarse Scythian voyaging to Athens
> Who conjures you here, timid and curious,
> To dissipate the night that covers still his eyes.
> (Translated in Wolff 1994: 97)

This is enlightenment at work in the most literal sense. The parallel drawn between Russians and French on the one hand and Scythians and Athenians on the other could hardly be more explicit. The Russian is forced to play the role of the barbarian who steps into the light of civilization as if by his own accord, in order to become part of a European-based universal humanity. In the first half of the period, there was simply no interest in the specificity of Russia. Claude-Carloman de Rulhière, in a famous book written in the 1760s but not published before 1797, held that "scarcely has one spent eight days in Russia than one can already speak reasonably of the Russians; everything leaps to the eye" (quoted in Wolff 1994: 274). Of course it did, when Europeans already knew what they would see: Uninteresting matter about to form itself into more of the European same. This is the other extreme of Winston Churchill's much-quoted dismissal to the exotic from a later period, that Russia is an enigma wrapped in a riddle inside a mystery. If power is the knowledge necessary to tell the other his name, then Voltaire's and Rulhière's practices are the epitome of power at play.

As a correlate to this point about universalization, there is Wolff's persuasive argument, crucial to any treatment of Russia as one of Europe's others. His book is about the representation of *Eastern Europe,* and not of Poland, Rumania, or Russia, exactly because these representations were all of a kind.[10] The period freely bestowed epithets from antiquity onto modern human collectives: Russians became Scythians, Poles became Sarmatians, Romanians became Dacians, and so on. Russia was *not* seen to stand out from these other peoples in terms of being even more barbarous, but specifically because of Peter the Great's efforts and the military might that it bestowed on the Russian state. Given present-day efforts, not least by "central Europeans," to construct clear boundaries between themselves and a Russian other, which will be the topic of Chapter 5, Wolff's demonstration of how these peoples were lumped together in eighteenth-century European discourse takes on immediate political importance.

If Peter's efforts were what made Russia stand out, however, it is exactly against this trait of the dominant version that Rousseau pitted his own representation of Russia. In *The Social Contract* he was very clear:

> Russia will never be civilized, because it was civilized too soon. Peter had a genius for imitation; but he lacked true genius, which is creative

and makes all from nothing. He did some good things, but most of what he did was out of place. He saw that his people was barbarous, but did not see that it was not ripe for civilization: he wanted to civilize it when it needed only hardening. His first wish was to make Germans or Englishmen, when he ought to have been making Russians; and he prevented his subjects from ever becoming what they might have been by persuading them that they were what they are not. In this fashion too a French teacher turns out his pupil to be an infant prodigy, and for the rest of his life to be nothing whatsoever. The empire of Russia will aspire to conquer Europe, and will itself be conquered. The Tatars, its subjects or neighbours, will become its masters and ours, by a revolution which I regard as inevitable. Indeed, all the kings of Europe are working in concert to hasten its coming. (Rousseau [1762] 1973: book 2, ch. 8, 198–199)

As has already been demonstrated, the effortless transition from the theme of political regime to that of military confrontation is characteristic of the period. Furthermore, as Montesquieu's intervention reproduced earlier shows, the skepticism about Peter's means was not in itself new. The theme of the "noble savage," which may be found elsewhere in Rousseau's writings and also in those of L'abbé Raynal (see Duroselle 1965: 111), was not foregrounded here. Rather, the importance of the challenge to his contemporaries had to do with the idea that Europe set itself up as the propelling force of universal history. This at least seems to be the thrust of the reading made in a 1768 travelogue by Sir George Macartney, in which he wrote that

nothing was ever more just than Rousseau's censure of Peter the first's conduct; that monarch, instead of improving his subjects as Russians, endeavoured totally to change and convert them into Germans and Frenchmen; but his attempts were unsuccessful; he could not make them what he wished to make them, he spoiled them in the experiment, and left them worse than they were before. . . . Many ingenious men have amused themselves devising hypotheses, and forming conjectures, why the Russians should have so long continued in barbarism; why tho' emerging from it for a century past, they still continue the least virtuous, and least ingenious nation in Europe. Some have ascribed it to the climate, whilst many think it owing to the manner of education, and others attribute it to the form of government. The first of these causes seems to be of less force than the others; for the Swede who lives under the same parallel, certainly bears no resemblance to the Russian. (From Cross 1971: 204–207)

The definite break with the universalist assumptions that Voltaire and the dominant version brought to the representation of Russia came not with Rousseau, however, but with Johann Gottfried von Herder. Herder's 1769 travel journal, written as he sailed the northwestern coast of Europe, has a striking passage in which he presents what he called his "political seadreams":

> What a view from the West-North of these regions, when one day the spirit of [culture] (*Kultur*) will visit them! The Ukraine will become a new Greece: the beautiful heaven of this people, their merry existence, their musical nature, their fruitful land, and so on, will one day awaken: out of so many little wild peoples, as the Greeks were also once, a mannered (*gesittete*) nation will come to be. Their borders will stretch out to the Black Sea and from there through the world. Hungary, these nations, and an area of Poland and Russia will be participants in this new [culture] (*Kultur*); from the northwest this spirit will go over Europe, which lies in sleep, and make it serviceable according to the spirit. This all lies ahead, and must one day happen; but how? when? through whom? (Quoted in Wolff 1994: 307)

Herder stressed the graded unevenness between the cultural levels that were present in Russia: "The wild peoples are on the borders: the half-mannered is the country: then, the mannered seacoast" (quoted in Wolff 1994: 308). He held that Russia's heart lay between Europe and Asia and blamed Peter for not having built his capital at the Sea of Azov, close to the Black Sea. Herder also stressed that Russia was a land of the future that may benefit all mankind, but in his insistence that the world consisted of a number of distinct cultural nations, each having its own task to look after, he furthermore stressed that Russia was also a world unto itself. Thus, Herder's was an attempt to grasp Russia in its particularity, as a culture ambiguously poised between Europe and Asia and reproducing those ambiguities inside itself. ("The wild peoples are on the borders: the half-mannered is the country: then, the mannered seacoast.") It was not a clear-cut particularism, however, since the Russians' ambiguous position as a European nation allowed them to be represented in terms of what was seen as European history: "Out of so many little wild peoples, as the Greeks were also once, a mannered (*gesittete*) nation will come to be." It would, furthermore, be a mistake to overdo the particularism of Herder, since his fashioning together of the peoples to the east of Germany as Slavs and his description of them as living in a happy pastorale may also be read as a way of holding them up as a mirror for his Germans to emulate.

There can be no doubt that for those of Herder's German contemporaries who focused on the political implications of his culturalist ideas, political Pan-Slavism was less about Russia than it was about the necessity of all *Germans* living in the same state. One may see this, for example, when August Ludwig von Schlözer begins his *Allegemeine nordische Geschichte* (1771) by describing the Slavs as "that great, renowned, ancient mighty race which spreads so vastly in the North and about which we know so little" and then proceeds to tell the story of how the forging of a collective identity has paid a political dividend (quoted in Petrovich 1956: 19). Here again is a way of representing Russia in order to teach another collective self a lesson.

The theme of particularism also cropped up in the application to Russia of the new racialist representations of the latter half of the period, as when Georges-Louis Buffon in his book *Natural History* held that "there are as many varieties in the race of blacks as in that of whites; the blacks have, like the whites, their Tatars and their Circassians." Similarly, in annotating his own essay "National Characters," David Hume wrote that he was apt to suspect that blacks were naturally inferior to whites, among other things since "the most rude and barbarous of the whites, such as the ancient GERMANS, the present TATARS, have still something eminent about them" (both quoted in Wolff 1994: 348; also Hannaford 1996: 187–233). At this early stage of racialist thinking, however, the place of Russians in the biological hierarchy was not fixed. In 1776 Ferdinando Galiani took on the climate theory in no uncertain terms, and proposed instead that

> everything is about race. The first and most noble races originate of course from Northern Asia. The Russians stand out in this regard, and this is why they have advanced more in the course of 50 years than have the Portuguese in the course of 500. (Quoted in Lortholary 1951: 271)

One notes that in this case, Russia was held to be at the upper end of the racial hierarchy, the reason given being their geographical and therefore, by inference, biological proximity to what were to become known as Aryans. This runs directly counter to the idea that the Tatars and, again by inference of geographical and biological proximity, therefore the Russians were somehow at the fringe of the white race. Thus the racial theme became pervasive in European discourse only after this internal tension in the racialist argument had been stabilized.

During the eighteenth century, the dominant representation of Russia was of a power whose prominence in "the North," increasing with the partitions of Poland, entitled it to play a role in European politics. In 1778 Burke said about Russia that this "newcomer among the great nations stood supreme between Europe and Asia, and looks as if she intended to dictate to both. We see in her a great but still growing empire" (quoted in Groh 1961: 62; also Welsh 1995). Russia, however, was also a learner that of its own accord tried to cultivate itself to become part of mannered Europe. Granted that it was able to tackle this task and leave its barbarity behind, it even had some potential to reinfuse into Europe some of those animal spirits that the Continent was seen to have lost.

THE NINETEENTH CENTURY: TSARIST EUROPE IN THE EAST

During what has been called the long nineteenth century—from the French Revolution to the First World War—the representations were again different. The Napoleonic Wars brought Russian soldiers to Paris. Russia was recognized as a great power, and with the defeat of Napoleon, Russia, Great Britain, Austria, and Prussia made the Quadruple Alliance against France. Russia remained a fully fledged player in European politics throughout the period. Otto von Bismarck summed up a century of geopolitical thinking and practice with his adage that one must always try to be *à trois* in a world of five great powers. There was a debate about Russian intentions, with Russian fortunes in its wars with Turkey and Persia (and in 1904–1905 with Japan) being the main factor to influence assessments of its strengths and intentions. Let us not forget that the question of a possible Russian hegemony in Europe was not allowed fully to dominate the discourses of other great powers; Russia was not alone in being suspected of such intentions. Similar things were being said about France, particularly at the beginning of the period; about Germany as the period drew to a close; and about Great Britain throughout. When in 1817 the Whig daily *Morning Chronicle* wrote about Russia, then, Russian soldiers had left Paris not long before:

> Those who suppose that either the Russian people or the Russian Government are deficient in confidence in their own power, are but

little acquainted with them. A very general persuasion has long been entertained by the Russians, that they are destined to be the rulers of the world, and this idea has been more than once stated in publication in the Russian language. To do the Russians justice, their aggrandizement has never for a moment been lost sight of under the various Sovereigns, who, for a century, have filled the throne. The most arbitrary Sovereigns must yield to the prevailing inclinations of their people, and the prevailing inclination of the Russians is territorial aggrandizement. With such a feeling, and with the confidence which recent events have given them, to suppose that a colossal Power like Russia will be contented to remain without any other maritime communication than the Northern Ocean and the Baltic, both accessible only at certain seasons of the year, and that she will not endeavour to obtain for by far the most valuable part of her Empire the command to the situations which secure an entrance to the Mediterranean, argues not a great deal of political foresight. (Quoted in Gleason 1950: 42–43)

This view of Russia as a rival to the other great powers did, however, come side by side with the dominant idea that the great powers could work out spheres of influence arrangements and formalize their responsibility for the working of the international system. As the Tory daily, *Post,* wrote at the same time:

Let not the two nations whose languages (it is no vain boast) are one day to divide the world, interfere without necessity in each other's harvest—but let the rivalry between them be which shall govern best, and be the instrument of most improvement to the goodly fields which Providence has entrusted to their care. (Quoted in Gleason 1950: 56)

The strategic discourse focused on the Eastern Queston. The way Russia's wars influenced the European representations of it may be gauged from an example concerning the Russo-Turkish War of 1828–1829. Two quotations from *The Times,* of 22 April 1828 and 16 October 1829 respectively, show the vacillations involved:

England has nothing whatever to apprehend from the power of Russia. We have seen enough of the issue of the most vigorous attempts at universal empire ever to dread them from any quarter. The more Russia adds to the superficial extent of her territory, the more she increases her weakness, and brings upon herself the certainty of falling asunder, or breaking in pieces. (Quoted in Gleason 1950: 85)

But again we ask, when during the last 1000 years have such enormous acquisitions been made in so brief a period by any European conqueror, as those of Poland and Turkey by the Czar of Muscovy during the space of 15 years? When, in a single generation, were such masses of dominion superadded to any pre-existing empire. When were the relative positions of one power with each and all of the surrounding states so fearfully changed to their detriment as in this instance? . . . may it not be affirmed that twenty years ago the empire of Russia was not half European, and that while we write, Europe is almost half Russian? (Quoted in Gleason 1950: 86)

Russian rivalry with Turkey was considered a question of pivotal interest for the balance of Europe, with the British cabinet already deciding on one occasion in 1829 that, should Russia attempt the occupation of Constantinople, it must be opposed by force of arms (Gleason 1950: 96). Once Britain and France *did* decide to go to war, in 1854–1856, the emphasis on this intention was of course particularly strong. That war did not, however, bring about an end to calls for a preventive war. Arguing from the idea that history resides in a world *Geist* that must necessarily roll over minor local spirits, Arnold Ruge served up a particularly pithy variant of a standard Left Hegelian argument when he advocated a war between the European, or "Latin-Germanic," historically productive spirit and the Russian reactionary one (Groh 1961: 248–252).

The tension inside the strategic discourse of the nineteenth century between representations of Russia as being on the way to world hegemony versus having a legitimate right to play the role of a great power in and out of Europe may at first glance bring to mind the configuration of the strategic discourse of the Cold War. This will be a particular temptation for someone who is used to regarding strategic discourse in isolation from, as well as privileged in relation to, overall discourse. As the focus of inquiry here is overall discourse, however, the main point about the way Russia was treated in nineteenth-century strategic discourse may not be the weighing of its intentions but the very *acceptance* of Russia as a legitimate player in the Concert of Europe. Pim den Boer (1995) has highlighted how at this time considerations of the balance of power were a vital part of discourse about European identity at large. So in this central regard Russia would seem to have been included in Europe. And yet, although the inclusion in Europe that emanated from the inclusion in the balance of power is the main point, two other strands of nineteenth-century strategic debate tend to relativize this inclusion. There was, first, the tendency to view Russia not only as a power grasping for hegemony but also as doing this in the manner of a barbarian at the gate (as opposed to being seen as launching the attempt from inside). And, second, there was the tendency to try to refashion the idea of the European balance of power itself, so that the Europeanness that inclusion conferred on Russia could be relativized. It is hardly surprising that both these themes were particularly pronounced among Napoleonic French writers.

Napoleon at one point held that Europe and the rest of the world would soon be enmeshed either in the American republic or the Russian universal monarchy. After his fall, he is reported to have held that Europe would become either cossack or republican (cf. Rougemont 1966: 294; Cadot 1967: 516).[11] As part of the preparations for his Russian campaign, Napoleon had issued orders that the Ministry of Foreign Affairs should orchestrate the publication of articles to show that "Europe is inevitably in the process of becoming booty for Russia" (if it did not become republican, that is, dominated by Napoleonic France). One of the results of this was the publication, in October 1812, of a meticulously researched and annotated book by Charles Louis Lesur called *Des progrès de la puissance russe* (M.L. 1812). The book contained a modified version of a document that had been written for the French Directory by the Polish general Michael Sokolniki fifteen years earlier and that was now passed off as the testament of Peter the Great. The alleged testament was nothing short of a recipe for attaining European hegemony:

> Hold the state in a system of continual warfare, in order to maintain strict discipline among the soldiers and in order to keep the nation on the move and ready to march at the first signal. . . . utilizing any means, expand northward along the Baltic and southward along the Black Sea. . . . interest the house of Austria into chasing the Turk from Europe and, under this pretext, maintain a permanent army and establish docks on the shores of the Black Sea and, always advancing, extend to Constantinople. Support anarchy in Poland . . . and finish by subjugating her. . . . At any costs involve yourself in the quarrels of Europe either by force or by ruse. . . . All these divisions will then provide total latitude for the soldiers of the front lines, so that they may

with vigor and all possible certitude conquer and subjugate the rest of Europe. (Translation from McNally 1958: 174).[12]

Significantly, the rest of Lesur's book laid out the testament as befitting the stagnant country that Christianity had not been able to civilize, but it claimed that the testament had been garbled. As he put it in a follow-up volume published two years later on the Cossacks: "It is doubtful whether or not one can ever make them civilized. . . . their land, which they seem to occupy always in passing, appears in our eyes as a vast camp seated upon the frontier of Europe" (quoted in McNally 1958: 174). The metaphor of the "vast camp" suggests what another Frenchman, Vicomte de Bonald, explicitly referred to as the "nomadic character" of the Russians.

Throughout the period, the theme of the barbarian at the gate was reinforced by focusing on the existence of Muslim and therefore presumably Asiatic national minorities inside Russia, and using these as a *pars pro toto* to underline the Asiatic nature of Russia as a whole, as did Lord Aberdeen in 1813:

> In Silesia we saw many reinforcements on their way to join the Russian army; large bodies of Cossacks; but what astonished us more than any-thing was a body of several hundred Asiatical Tatars armed with bows and arrows, and carrying a light spear. Their equipment altogether was most strange. They have the Chinese face, and are exactly like the fellows one sees painted on tea-boxes. (Quoted in Balfour 1922: 80)[13]

There is only a small step from this to the idea that if one scrapes a Russian, the Tatar will emerge. Take away the borrowed feathers of European civilization and Russia's military might, and the barbarian (or even a savage, if one scrapes hard enough!) would emerge in the raw. As the founder of the *Manchester Guardian* Richard Potter put it to his fellow British MPs in 1832:

> Let a fleet be sent to the Baltic to close up the Russian ports, and what would the Emperor of Russia be then? A Calmuc surrounded by a few barbarian tribes, (Cheers) a savage, with no more power upon the sea, when opposed by England and France, than the Emperor of China had. (Cheers) (Quoted in Gleason 1950: 126)

Bruno Naarden has recently highlighted the fact that during the first half of the nineteenth century many intellectuals had been spellbound by Edward Gibbon's *History of the Decline and Fall of the*

Roman Empire, above all because in reading it they had at the same time to think of the Russia that had defeated Napoleon. Gibbon blamed Rome's downfall primarily on internal weakness. Many of his readers believed likewise that Europe had lost its vitality and was thus ripe for barbarian conquest. "The comparison between the fate of the ancient civilization and the possible future Russification of Europe became such a cliché that people spoke of 'the great parallel,'" Naarden concludes (1992: 13). And indeed, if one turns to Dieter Groh's standard work on European discussions of Russia in this period, the index has no fewer than twenty-nine references to this "great parallel" (Groh 1961: 15 et passim). These metaphors of the Russians as nomadic barbarians, always on the move, pegging their tents on the outskirts of Europe, looming like an incubus, belong to a fixed imagery that may also crop up occasionally in, say, contemporary French representations of the British (or, to take a similar example from a later period, British twentieth-century representations of Germans). The crucial difference is that in the case of Russia, this is a regularly invoked feature of discourse throughout the nineteenth century and beyond.

Going hand in hand with the representation of the barbarian at the gate, however, was an auxiliary attempt to disrupt the idea that Russia might have a place inside the European balance of power by changing that representation itself. The crucial author here is L'abbé Dominique-Georges-Frédéric de Pradt, who in a series of books exhorted Europeans to close ranks and gates against the Russsians:

> Russia is built up despotically and asiatically. . . . Europe must draw closer together and as she shuts herself up, Europe should cooperate in outlawing all participation in her affairs by any power which does not have a direct interest in them and which has the force to weigh down the balance to suit her own interests. (Quoted in McNally 1958: 182; also Cadot 1967: 174–175; Groh 1961: 128–131)

In a number of works published in the aftermath of the Napoleonic Wars, de Pradt, who was an archbishop and Napoleon's former confessor, went on to develop the thesis that "l'Angleterre règne sur la mer, la Russie sur la terre: tel est le partage actuel du monde [England rules at sea, Russia on land; Such is the real division of the world]." Russia must be kept from Europe, and the way to do it was to expand the idea of the balance of power to include America. Here is the genesis of the idea that Europe is situated between America and Russia and that European power politics must be conducted on the basis of this fact. Crucially, by changing the balance of power from an intra-European to a European-focused phenomenon, this idea annulled the idea that inclusion within the balance of power in and of itself should confer Europeanness on a particular power. Since it came at the exact time when there could no longer be any doubt about Russia's pivotal role in the European balance of power, this was indeed a crucial move. It is instructive, furthermore, that representations of the balance of power made at this particular time, which is often treated as paradigmatic of a mechanistic, "concert-style" way of conceptualizing European security, should be so permeated not by decontextualized balancing but by cultural politics. For those who believe in the possibility of decontextualized representations, it must be a source of dismay that even at its historical apex, representations of the balance of power can be shown to be not mechanical but very much culturally contextualized. The widening to include America and thus relativize the importance of including Russia was also a move that proved productive in the long run, since after the nineteenth century the relevance of inclusion into the balance of power for inclusion into Europe clearly faded.

The idea of the barbarian at the gate, then, lent a particular flavor to European strategic discourse on Russia. Russia was depicted as an ambiguous presence on Europe's border, a presence that could be associated with Europe but also with China. Thus it is not surprising to find as the central metaphor in what was perhaps the most widely read book of the period, Marquis de Custine's ([1843] 1975) travelogue on Russia in the year 1839, the idea that Russia was cordoned off from Western Europe by a "Chinese Wall" (Cadot 1967: 540, 173). What should be particularly noted, however, is where the marquis located this wall, namely, on the Vistula. For Custine, it was the military reach of Russia that determined where this wall was to be found, and not the cultural traits of the particular peoples who happened to live in the relevant territories. Bearing in mind the very recent debate about the delineation of "Eastern" from "Central" Europe to which I return in Chapter 5, this problematique is not without contemporary relevance.

It must be said that Custine's book drew some of its popularity from its ability to reach beyond the strategic discourse and latch the image of the barbarian at the gate onto the wider issue of a *Kulturkampf* between Russia and Europe. He was certainly not alone in this. One of the main reasons why the clashes over representations of Russia were so lively was that all the three main political orientations to be found within Europe actively drew on these representations to reproduce themselves. To liberals, radicals, and conservatives, Russia offered a political regime that was used to highlight the advantages of their preferred representations of European identity as a political program. Representations of Russia were bound up with various domestic political struggles.

For conservatives like Joseph de Maistre, who was the king of Sardinia's representative in St. Petersburg from 1803 to 1817, Russia was the one power that could help Europe to find its way back to its own proper self—that is, to the self of the ancien régime. There was a crucial prerequisite, however, since this could only take place if Russia were first Catholicized (Groh 1961: 101–113). But even without Catholicism, de Maistre held that the Russian people somehow possessed an inherent wisdom, in the sense of a lack of the rationality that the Enlightenment had set up as a European and global ideal. Russia should stay clear of the "poison" of individualism and religious reformations: "It would be unfortunate for us," he warned in a famous passage written in 1822 but published only in 1859,

> if she should be seized by one of those intellectual deliriums which have attacked nations not more reasonable, but more logical! . . . If this nation, after coming to understand our perfidious novelties and to like them, should conceive the idea of resisting any revocation or alteration of that which she calls "her constitutional privileges"; if some Pugachev from the university should put himself at the head of any party; if at one time the people should be troubled and, instead of her Asiatic expeditions, should start a revolution *a l'européenne,* I cannot express all that one could fear as a result. (Quoted in Reynold 1950: 389; see also Cadot 1967: 173)

This amounted to a representation of Russia as a bulwark not only of contemporary legitimism but of the ideas of the European ancien régime. Indeed, throughout the period, ultraconservatives throughout Europe employed representations of Russia in their interventions in general political debates (and, by the same token, it is hardly coincidental that texts in conservative journals and newspapers were generally much more relaxed about Russia's strategic intentions than were texts in liberal publications). For example, the British Tory Thomas Raikes wrote about a trip through Russia in a book published in 1838 that

> if a comparison were drawn between the respective situations of these classes in the two countries, I mean as to physical wants and gratifications, how much would the scale lean towards this population of illiterate slaves? The Englishman may boast his liberty, but will it procure him a dinner?—will it clothe his family?—will it give him employment when in health?—or when sick, will it keep him from the poorhouse or the parish? The Russian hugs his slavery; he rejects the airy boon of liberty and clings to more substantial blessings. He lives indeed without care for the present, or anxiety for the future. The whole responsibility for his existence rests with the lord. . . . the result is, that, while beggars abound in other countries, none are seen here; each mougik has a master and consequently a home. (Quoted in Gleason 1950: 225)

Most famously, Baron von Haxthausen, a conservative whose study of Russian peasant life established him as a central Russianist, was convinced that their communal life made Russians inherently peaceful (see Cadot 1967: 100–103).

In counterpoint to these different conservative representations, liberals of the period were not only quick to criticize Russia as a reactionary country, they also drew on what they saw as the fortunate experiences of their own countries to explain *why* Russia lagged behind Europe. As the French chargé d'affaires in St. Petersburg, Comte de la Moussaye, reported back to his Foreign Ministry:

> Domestically she is without law, without administration, and almost without industry. Some men, chosen bizarrely from all the classes and throughout the whole country, united under the name "legal commissars," are engaged in the task of compiling all the ancient and modern legal catalogues, in order to extract that which would be applicable to Russia. . . . Before them rises an insurmountable barrier; no code can exist without civil liberty, and, in one word, everyone trembles in the councils of the sovereign and at the head of the army. . . . It is a colossus that will survive perhaps only a day, but its fall can crush a part of Europe, which by a lack of foresight has raised Russia to this level. (From Polovtsoff 1902: vol. 1, 434).

In 1822 there appeared a book in Paris by a certain M. P. D. that pared all this down to one idea: Russia was held back by its lack of a substantial middle class (see McNally 1958: 181–182). The idea that Russia needed a middle class was also an interesting intervention inasmuch as it was a concrete proposal for a place that others saw either as an undifferentiated mass of powerless subjects before the tsar or as divided by class distinctions that were held to be particularly wide: "In the Russian empire Man may somewhere be found to live in the rawest and most untamed state, in other places he lives in barbarous half-culture, while there are also those who may be counted amongst the most well cultured (*dannede*) in the world," one reads in a Danish geographical handbook of 1809 (quoted in Møller 1993: 112). Russia, then, was ambiguous not only by being chronologically in a state of transition from barbarism to civilization but also by spatially harboring this process in all its unevenness. And in a book published in London in 1821, Madame de Staël combined these two ideas:

> In this mode of life there is a little resemblance to savages; but it strikes me that at present there are no European nations who have much vigor but those who are what is called barbarous, in other words, unenlightened, or those who are free. . . . They meet, as we go to a fête to see a great deal of company, to have fruits and rare productions from Asia and Europe; to hear music, to play; in short to receive vivid emotions from external objects, rather than from the heart or understanding, both of which they reserve for actions and not for company. Besides, as they are in general very ignorant, they find very little pleasure in serious conversation, and do not at all pique themselves on shining by the wit they can exhibit in it. Poetry, eloquence and literature are not yet found in Russia. . . . There is no Middle Class in Russia, which is a great drawback on the progress of literature and the arts; for it is generally in that class that knowledge is developed: but the want of any intermedium between the nobility and the people creates a greater affection between them both. (From Cross 1971: 304, 305, 306)

These ideas of the lack of a middle class and the gulf between elite and people, which to fast-forward out of turn for a moment are at the core of the present dominant version of Russia as learner, were thus already very popular with the liberal set at the beginning of the nineteenth century.[14]

Conservative representations of Russia stressed that, as a shard of a broken Europe, Russia could be held up as a mirror in which Europe could find its way back to itself. Liberal representations stressed that Russia was on its way to becoming more of the European same. Radicals, however, were perhaps even more insistent on using Russia as a foil to further their own identity politics.

In his study of how European socialists saw Russia, Naarden notes that in 1864 Marx referred to Russia in the first declaration of principles for the First International as "that barbarous power, whose head is at St Petersburg and whose hands are in every cabinet in Europe" (Naarden 1992: 49). He then goes on to demonstrate the working of what he in no uncertain terms refers to as "Marx's scheme of giving greater unity to the extremely heterogeneous and varied company of the First International by making use of the anti-Russian feelings which dominated public opinion in England" (Naarden 1992: 50).

This attempt, which was part of the central clash between Marxian and Proudhonian groups, failed, not least because Pierre-Joseph Proudhon and his followers were much more positive toward Russia than was Marx. And yet Proudhon's representations of Russia were not very different from the liberal version. It is instructive that he reacted to Russia's intervention to suppress the Hungarian revolution in 1849 by congratulating the Hungarians for their attempt to "save the Slavs and all of Europe from the conquest of the Cossacks" (quoted in Cadot 1967: 511). A lengthy quote from Friedrich Engels from 1890 that assesses Russia's strategic role for the labor movement and then the impact of the Crimean War of 1854–1856 further demonstrates that Russia was seen by radicals as passing through the phases on the way to their end goal of the European same:

> We, the West-European labor parties, have a twofold interest in the victory of the Russian revolutionary party. First, because the Russian Czarist empire forms the greatest fortress, reserve position and at the same time reserve army of European reaction, because its mere passive existence already constitutes a threat and a danger to us. Second, however—and this point has still not been sufficiently emphasized on our part—because it blocks and disturbs our normal development through its ceaseless intervention in Western affairs, intervention aimed moreover at conquering geographical positions which will secure it the mastery of Europe, and thus make impossible the liberation of the European proletariat. It has been the contribution of Karl Marx, first in 1848 and repeatedly since, to have emphasized that, for

this last reason, the Western European labor parties must of necessity wage an implacable war against Russian Czarism. . . . The Russian people were too much aroused by the colossal sacrifices of the war, the Czar had had to rely too much on their devotion, to be brought back without further ado to the passivity of unthinking obedience. For gradually even Russia had developed further both economically and intellectually; beside the nobility there now stood the beginnings of a second educated class, the bourgeoisie. In short the new Czar had to play the liberal, but this time *at home*. However, this gave a start to the internal history of Russia, to a movement of minds within the nation itself and its reflex, public opinion, which henceforth could be less lightly discarded, which, although still feeble, was making itself felt more and more, and thus arose an enemy against which Czarist diplomacy was to founder. For this sort of diplomacy is possible only as long as the people remain unconditionally passive, have no will except that imposed by the government, no function except to provide soldiers and taxes to achieve the objectives of the diplomats. Once Russian internal development, with its internal party struggles, had begun, the winning of a constitutional framework within which this party struggle could be fought without forcible convulsions, was only a question of time. But in such a situation the former Russian policy of conquest is a thing of the past; the changeless constancy of diplomatic objectives is lost in the struggles of the parties for control; the ability unconditionally to dispose of the forces of the nation is lost— Russia remains difficult to attack and relatively weak on the offensive, but in other respects it became a European country like any other, and the peculiar strength of its former diplomacy is forever broken. (Engels [1890] 1952: 25, 46–47)[15]

Engels was unique in his emphasis on social power (but not in his view that the lack of organized social life outside the state's control in the early part of the period was an asset for Russia rather than a handicap). In two other regards, however, this representation is typical of the period. First, Russia was represented as a socially and economically backward power. This view was part of the dominant version not only in constitutionalist-inclined countries such as Great Britain but also, if to a minor extent, among its partners in what started out as a Holy Alliance of 1815. Lest it be forgotten, the Austrian prince to whom Tsar Alexander I presented the original draft for what became the Holy Alliance later testified that he thought at the time that Alexander had gone out of his mind. Second

Engels's text makes a point of discussing and indeed fixing down to a year (namely, 1856) when Russia became "a European country like any other." Elsewhere, it stresses the economic process of "westernisation" (Engels 1952: 51). As already demonstrated, this particular question of to what extent, in which respects, and from what point in time Russia belonged to Europe was an obsession with almost every European who wrote down his or her views on Russia at any length during the period.

For the first time, during this period from the French Revolution to World War I, in European representations of Russia the discourses on strategy and the relative merits of regime types were inextricably intertwined. It would perhaps be an overinterpretation to see the representation of Russia as part of the representation of Europe's own prerevolutionary history. Nonetheless, just as the European discourse of the interwar period, which will be discussed shortly, seemed to be tied up with European anxieties about the future, so the discourse of the nineteenth century tied in with Europe's laying out of the chronological dimension of its own identity. Toward the end of the period, de Maistre's worry that "some Pugachev from the university" should try to act out European revolutionary ideas was, of course, taken up by others, in counterdistinction to the hopes of Engels and others for a similar development, and there was a shift in this regard. A marginal and often eschatological strand, which saw Russia as the land of the future, may also be noted as a counterpoint: After 1848 Ernest Coeurderoy invited Russia to come in and shatter Europe's bourgeois order, and for Bruno Bauer, Russia was Europe's "sphinx of the future" (see Cadot 1967: 520). In most other regards, however, the representations of the early part of the period dominated the field throughout. There is a reason why the useful works of McNally and Gleason, on which I have drawn extensively above, refer to the first few decades after the end of the Napoleonic Wars as the period of the "origins" and "genesis" of Russophobia in France and Britain respectively. The combination of a period of particularly thorough social changes in Europe and what was seen as a conspicuous change in the military record of Russia reworked the representations of Russia. There were people, then as now, who made it their task to warn against what one could now call the antagonistic othering of Russia that emanated from the insecurity of the alleged European self. Thus in 1838 the *Morning Chronicle* expressed a concern that Britain was worrying too much about Russia: "Let Russia be watched, and when detected in hostility towards us, let us retaliate, but do not let a great nation . . . make itself ridiculous by an insane Russo-Phobia" (quoted in Gleason 1950: 212). And yet in a period when ideas such as that Russia was about to march on British India were discussed at length, exhortations like the *Chronicle*'s could do little to change the dominant version of the day.

THE INTERWAR PERIOD: SOVIET RUSSIA

Initially, reactions to what is now known as the February Revolution were on the whole rather positive. For example, one of the first analyses to be published, on 21 March 1917 by the *Financial Times* of London, was headed "The Dawn of a New Era: How British Traders May Profit." The emphasis was on how Russia could now overcome "the 'dark forces' of ignorance and reaction which [had] held Russia in thrall these many years"; that is, the dawn would dispel the dark as integration into the world market brought progress (quoted in Mortimer 1988). This core liberal idea informed views in subsequent years as well. With reference to the introduction of the New Economic Policy, *The Times* wrote in December 1921 that communism was at an end and that it was "only a matter of hitting on a suitable formula for reintroducing capitalism." Two months before, David Lloyd George had told the British Parliament that Lenin "admits they have been wrong, he admits they have been beaten" and that the partial "re-establishment of capitalism" involved to some extent a condemnation of the doctrines of Karl Marx (both quoted in White 1985: 30). Such triumphalism was soon seen to be misplaced, and the dominant version became, rather, one of how the Revolution devoured its own children. The pervasive idea of Soviet Russia as a revolutionary political threat did have an adjunct inasmuch as there was much talk about a potential military threat. Nonetheless, even in Poland, which fought a war with Soviet Russia in 1920, Soviet Russia was seen by many as one of many threats, that is, as an integral part of a hostile international environment, rather than as the threat par excellence. Its character of being a revolutionary power and thus a political threat, with an extraterritorial presence through the organized Communist movement, made it a special case, here as elsewhere in Europe. Yet in Poland as well as in, say, France or Germany, it was seen as a legitimate player on the

European political scene (Neumann 1992). There is a need to stress this, since the situation during the Cold War is too often and too easily generalized to cover the entire Soviet period.

In 1921 the Third International (the Comintern) was issuing its theses demanding absolute loyalty of its sundry detachments, and all over Europe, there were labor movement splits over the representation of Soviet Russia. These remained vibrant at least until the time of the Second World War. In March 1940 the leadership of the British Labour Party issued a public statement apropos the Finnish situation in which it was argued that "the Red Czar is now the executor of the traditional imperialism of Czarist Russia. Stalin's men in Great Britain use the freedom which they enjoy to defend War and Tyranny, a war of conquest by an alien and powerful despot against a small outpost of republican democracy" (quoted in Bell 1990: 32). An "outpost" presupposes a hostile wilderness. With the advent of massive military threat, which was to be reinforced by the successes of the Red Army from the battle of Stalingrad onward, the ingredients of the Cold War representations were in evidence.

It would be a mistake, however, to extrapolate the Cold War situation of two relatively neatly separated and, between themselves, all-pervasive representations of the Soviet Union onto the interwar period, when the clashes over the representation were marked by considerably more flux. Three examples will follow. The first concerns that branch of racialist discourse—most conspicuously Nazi—that saw Slavs (not Russians specifically) as *Untermenschen*. Racialist discourse was widespread at the time, as was the idea of ranking different races against one another. Yet although there had often been a biological tinge to the argument of excluding the "Asiatic" Russians from the European self, the Nazi idea of excluding Slavs from humankind *tout court* was radically new.

A second example concerns the idea of Russia as the land of the future. In 1923 the League of Nations' high commissioner for refugees, Fridtjof Nansen, himself a nationalist and a royalist, wrote that for him, "it seems likely that Russia will one day not only deliver Europe materially, but also furnish its spiritual renewal" (Nansen 1923: 146; also Dahl 1994).

This idea of Russia as a nation whose "primitive health" and unfathomable patience made for a particularly advanced spirituality was widespread at the time, inside and outside of Christian milieus.

Nikolay Berdyayev wrote a number of books on the issue. These were first published from his exile in Paris and were then more often than not translated into English, German, and other European languages. In the interwar years, celebrating Soviet Russia was also part of radical chic. Sydney and Beatrice Webb's book *Soviet Communism: A New Civilisation?* appeared in 1925 and went into its second printing without the question mark. George Bernard Shaw argued that "the success of the Five Year Plan is the only hope of the World" (quoted in Bell 1990: 29; see also Caute 1973: 66). These well-known quotations reproduced a representation that was well established. The British Left Book Review was set up as late as 1936. For the next three years, a period that coincided, among other things, with the great Soviet purges, it "published 15 books dealing with the Soviet Union, all of them sympathetic and in some cases hagiographical" (Bell 1990: 29). These are other examples of the representation of which only the anthroposophist trickle remained after the Cold War was in place, namely, of Soviet Russia as the land of the future.

A third example concerns the view of socialist economic organization. In the interwar period, a theorist like Joseph Schumpeter could still advocate capitalist economic organization on normative grounds but predict that socialism would carry the day in what amounted to a struggle between two different economic organizational principles. In the Cold War period, when specialized argument of this type was subsumed by the catch-all representations of the Soviet Union and those were again in a very high degree subsumed along a left-right axis, one did not find this kind of pairing of arguments.

The interwar period, then, saw a number of tentative representations of Soviet Russia. With the radical exception of Nazi discourse, Russia was seen as part of Europe, but a somewhat errant part. Perhaps Carl Schmitt, who spent a life theorizing about the delineation of friend from foe, encapsulated this best: He held that "we in *Mitteleuropa* live *sous l'oeil des Russes* [under the eye of the Russians]," and that Russia was "a state which is more, and more intensely, statist [*staatlich*] than any state ruled by an absolute monarch." This, he maintained, was because Russia could be seen as Europe's radical brother, "who took the European nineteenth century at its word" (Schmitt 1963: 79–80; McCormick 1993). Schmitt's representation of Russia was shot through with fear not only of that particular state as a factor external to Europe but also of the possibility that Russia's present would be Europe's future. Thus when Soviet Russia emerged, the political threat that it posed was held to be serious enough to warrant an intervention by the European Allies, yet it was only toward the very end of the period and into the next that the representation of a unique, clear, and present threat took hold of European discourse. Whereas during the Cold War representations of Russia often underlined continuity with the previous period, it is imperative to insist on the importance of the break that is the Second World War.

THE COLD WAR: THE SOVIET UNION

During the Cold War the representation of the Soviet Union as an actual military and to some extent also a political threat was so pervasive that it was and is ubiquitously used in the delineation of a period of European history: the Cold War. The other inscribed itself in the temporal dimension of the European self's identity by giving a name to a period of its history. Indeed, the Soviet initiative to end the Cold War was made among other things by means of issuing an application to join Europe: the slogan of the "Common European Home." European reactions to these applications varied from bafflement that such an application should be necessary to assertions that the Soviet Union was (mostly) "in Europe but not of Europe," to wariness that the intention was to decouple Western Europe from the United States (see, for example, Nonnenmacher 1987).

These reactions mirrored the two pervasive representations of the Soviet Union of the Cold War period. The dominant version was of an Asiatic/barbarian political power that had availed itself of the opportunity offered by the Second World War to intrude into Europe by military means. In 1945 Churchill is said to have maintained, with reference to the Soviet Union, that the barbarians stood in the heart of Europe, and the following year Konrad Adenauer wrote to William Sollmann that "Asia stands on the Elbe" (Adenauer 1983: 191).[16]

This representation was also widespread in academic literature. In a book series on the formation of Europe published in France in 1950, the first paragraph of the first chapter of the volume on Russia is headed "La Russie est asiatique." The author, Gonzague de Reynold states that Russia cannot be judged by European measures, that there exists a primordial geographical antithesis between Europe and Russia, and that whereas the former is sedentary and thus civilized, the latter is nomadic and thus barbarian (1950: 25–28). One notes the ambiguity of these statements, given their inclusion in a book series on *European* history.

We have here the theme of the barbarian at Europe's gate, which may be traced throughout the period and which in the 1980s was kept alive in the discourse on "Central Europe," to which I return in Chapter 5. Central Europe was, in Milan Kundera's phrase, seen as *"un occidente kidnappé,"* that is, a part of the West occupied by the Russians. There is a dual emphasis here, with the military ingredient being mixed with *Kulturkampf.* European civilization was under seige by the Soviet barbarians, and the main trait (but, as we will see later, by no means the only one) identifying them as barbarians was their politico-economic system. Raymond Aron (1965) held that by not differentiating between politics and economics, the Soviet system betrayed its "pre-modern" character. Others held that the Soviet model was a model for modernization, in fact *the* alternative model to the "Western" one. Such ideas came through with most clarity in the idea of *tiersmondisme*—the idea that the industrialized West constituted the first, the Communist world the second, and everybody else the third world. One notes a similarity between the classifying schemes of civilized-barbarian-savage (where the barbarian stands out by being politically and economically organized on a grand scale, whereas the savage is not) on the one hand and *tiersmondisme* on the other.

The Communist politico-economic model was sometimes lumped together with that of the vanquished Nazi enemy and labeled "totalitarian," to be distinguished from the model of the West; hence book titles such as *Démocratie et totalitarisme* (Aron 1965; Arendt [1951] 1973). The epithet "totalitarian" is one example of how U.S. discourse on the Soviet Union permeated European discourse (on U.S. discourse, see Dalby 1988, 1990; Nathanson 1988). It was in widespread use in Britain in the 1950s and early 1960s and reemerged in France in the 1970s and 1980s (see Desjardins 1988: 64ff.). When "totalitarian" was not used, Russia was referred to as "authoritarian." This dichotomy between democratic and totalitarian or authoritarian replaced the master dichotomies civilized/barbarian and European/Asian and had affinities to a number of others such as free/unfree, market/plan, West/East, defensive/offensive.

Although the military threat emanating from the Soviet Union was deemed to be massive, the morale of their soldiers was often held to mirror an alleged Russian *Volksgeist* ("national character") of sloth, drunkenness, and laziness. These two representations coexisted, often within the same sentence. As the American geopolitical thinker Edward Luttwak formulated it in a television interview, "Drunk they defeated Napoleon. Drunk they beat Hitler. Drunk they could win against NATO." The rickety social and economic foundations on which Soviet power, including its nuclear capability, was seen to rest nevertheless made it the undimensional superpower; whereas the United States was a superpower because of its overwhelming capabilities in a number of different fields, the Soviet Union was a superpower first and foremost by dint of its nuclear capability. This representation came complete with a discussion of whether the superpower was a "status quo" (satiated) power or whether it was "revisionist" (expansionist). In the beginning of the period, when there was a stress on the political threat, the tendency was to see it as expansionist, in Europe and elsewhere, even as grasping for worldwide hegemony. At the end of the period, the tendency was to see it as status quo–oriented in Europe but to some extent expansionist elsewhere. Again, this was a conceptually constipated debate, which took place within a tightly restricted register.

An alternative representation of the Soviet Union saw this state not only as the deliverer of Europe from the scourge of Nazism (the "halo of Stalingrad") but also as a model for Europe to emulate.[17] "I have looked, but I just cannot find any evidence of an aggressive impulse on the part of the Russians in the last three decades. . . . [The Soviet citizen] criticizes [the régime] more frequently and more effectively than us," Jean-Paul Sartre proclaimed in the early 1950s, in defiance of the representation of the Soviet Union as the military and nondemocratic aggressor (quoted in Judt 1992: 154, 156). Tied first and foremost to the organized Communist movement, whose strength in Europe was very uneven, this alternative representation was also perpetuated by others (but by no means all) who invoked a socialist identity. Within a totalizing, evolutionist, and teleological historiosophy, the Soviet Union was seen as more advanced than capitalist Europe, not first and foremost in empirical terms but by virtue of its very politico-economic model. Thus a celebration of domestic economic or political performance was not at the core of the representation, which was first and foremost a celebration of the model *in abstracto*. This model was seen as having an evolutionary, invigorating potential on Europe, and Europe (or parts thereof) were in turn seen as a possible sophisticating influence. As Martin Brionne wrote in 1946: "This old civilization that it is assaulting will absorb and enrich it. This, indeed, could be France's essential contribution. Russia saw the Communist breakthrough; France could lead it into maturity" (quoted in Judt 1992: 160).

This is a representation of Russia as the land of the future. In the years immediately after the Second World War, the clash of the two representations of the Soviet Union took place at the core of European politics. In some countries, notably in northern Europe, developments in Czechoslovakia in 1948 were seen as a Communist coup with Soviet backing. Consequently, most Social Democrats saw it as confirmation of the dominant representation of the Soviet Union. The Soviet intervention in Hungary in 1956 had the same kind of effect in countries such as France. As Gilles Martinet commented:

> The left intelligentsia dreams of a revolution that cannot occur in France. Therefore, it projects this dream elsewhere and wants to discover in a far away land . . . that [which] does not exist in France. Such political exoticism causes it to lend its own aspirations and phantasms to societies which are in fact extraordinarily remote from this image. . . . The Soviet intervention in Hungary deals a decisive blow to these illusions. (Quoted in Desjardins 1988: 12)

"Phantasms" or not, three features stand out where European representations of the Soviet Union during the Cold War are concerned. One is the very high fit between the several representations and the general right/left divide within which political life was generally seen as being organized. The social representation of the Soviet Union was integral to Europeans' social representation of political identity as such and so was a part of everyday politics. This lent a particular urgency to the question of representing the Soviet Union and meant that a lot of political energy was expended on the matter. Another is the way in which the dominant and alternative versions were able to define the entire discourse on the Soviet Union. Particularly immediately after the Second World War, few attempts were made to come up with alternative representations of the Soviet Union. A number of ideas about particulars were floated, but the main outlines were hardly questioned. A conversion thesis, seeing a coming together of modern systems simply because of some studiously unspecified contingencies of modern systems, was sometimes advanced. It hardly said more than that "we" would assimilate "them" in some unspecified long term and would be somewhat transformed in the process. Perhaps the only notable exception was to be found in the marginal anthroposophist discourse, which included the idea that just below the surface of the Soviet state there remained alive a spiritual Russia with the potential to enrich and perhaps even renew spiritual life in Europe. The anthroposophist discourse thus reformulated a representation with a checkered but long pedigree (I return to this below).[18]

Yet another feature of the discourse at large was how the shift in backing of the two versions did invariably go in the direction of the dominant version and invariably seemed to be tied to developments in what was at the time called Eastern Europe, that is, the lands between the Soviet Union and Germany that were under Soviet political sway. The examples of Czechoslovakia in 1948 and Hungary in 1956 have been mentioned, and so should reactions to the 1968 intervention in Czechoslovakia and perhaps also the 1979 intervention in the central Asian neighboring state of Afghanistan. The obvious reason why defections from the alternative version come about in this manner was that it did not depend on what was seen as developments internal to the Soviet Union itself (economic output, span of published opinions, or the like), so it could not in its own terms be judged on this ground. It could only be judged on relations that were seen as being in some degree external, such as those between socialist countries. One may, however, speculate about the degree to which the tangible geographical aspect of these events played a role. The events of 1948, 1956, and 1968 were all widely seen as a question of how to delineate Soviet power relative to European countries; this is one of the main reasons why the idea of "*un occidente kidnappé*" could be so effective. Each intervention was in some degree seen as an onslaught not only on the particular country in question but also on Europe as such. And as each intervention had the effect of confirming and adding to the military threat, so, inversely, by detracting from the attractiveness of the Soviet Union as a political model, with each one the political threat was dulled. Thus at the end of the Cold War, very little was left of the idea of Soviet Russia as a political threat, though that had been the main dimension of threat in the interwar years.

CONCLUSION: EUROPE'S PANGOLIN

At present, representations of Russia concern its future more than its present. Russia is often seen as a learner of European economic and political practices. Economically, it has emerged from under the ruins of a failed modernization strategy and is now in the process of getting in place the prerequisites of a capitalist economy: a market with supporting institutions and a middle class to run it. Politically, it is beginning to develop a differentiated elite structure with supporting institutions and a legal system based on the idea that written laws bind all actors. Thus it is seen as substituting the successful modernization strategy for the unsuccessful one that it had followed before. However, to a degree unheard of in contemporary Europe, political power is bound to the bodies of persons and not to the bodies of institutions. Hence the importance of a European policy of supporting the leader (Mikhail Gorbachev, Boris Yeltsin) rather than the emerging system *in abstracto*. To the extent that this construction is challenged, and that is not a very large extent, the question is not whether this is what is happening but what and how important the role of Europe and the West was in bringing about this change.[19]

Other representations do exist. The Estonian politician Tiit Maade, for example, went on the record in 1989 with the view that because Russian women had for centuries been raped by Mongol and Tatar men, the Russian people were untamed and wild and tended to spread like a blob over all the territory they could find (quoted in *Svenska Dagbladet,* Stockholm, 24 July). During and immediately after the breakdown of the Soviet Union, other Baltic politicians frequently spoke in the same terms. At present, however, this representation has to some extent been suppressed by the dominant version just given, but it remains what one Lithuanian ambassador calls "common folk wisdom" in the Baltic states. Tiit Maade's contemporary invocation of a racialist language as a way of establishing the superiority of the civilized Balts over the barbarian Russians is a strong echo of once more-prevalent representations of Russia.

The idea of Russia as a learner does of course imply that Russia is becoming more like "us," less "different." In accordance with what was said earlier about the impossibility of fixing any one identity, I will not dwell on the fact that this "us" to which Russia is presumably growing more similar is forever changing by context and may be "the West," "Germany," or "the Baltics" as well as Europe. The main point is that as Russia is "learning" successfully, it is expected to become less of a threat. What is heavily disputed is whether the idea that it is a learner will remain a dominant identity in Russian political discourse itself. The idea of learning, after all, presupposes a disequilibrium, and so for Russians there is an obvious tension between accepting the role of "learner" from Europe and maintaining the notion that Russia is a European great power, a notion that presupposes some kind of equilibrium with (other) European great powers.

Whereas it is sometimes stressed that the market is already in place and the rest will therefore quickly follow, even that Russia is a place for a possible capitalist *Wirtschaftswunder* (economic miracle), an alternative version has it that the learning process may quickly be discontinued. Aggressive nationalists may take over, and a military threat to Europe may follow. It is sometimes stressed that Russia's being a bad learner in one particular but crucial area, namely, that of human rights in general and minority policy in particular, shows that the possibility of an aggressive nationalist policy vis-à-vis Europe may be imminent. Russia's seeming inability to treat its ethnic minorities, such as Chechens, and also the "near abroad," perhaps even the Baltics, as nations on a par with the Russian nation itself suggests an insecurity of self that may also result in an aggressive nationalist policy vis-à-vis Europe. Learners should pass tests, and in Europe, Chechnya was made a test of Russia's prospective European policy. Less conspicuously, Russian reactions to expansions of the EU and NATO are seen as tests of the extent to which Russians have learned that these particular institutionalizations of European and Western selves are not and cannot be potential threats to Russia.

A dominant representation of Russia that stresses a learning aspect and, to a lesser extent, a potential military threat dominates the contemporary European discourse. By authorizing itself as a teacher who has the right to sanction bad learning behavior, Europe creates one dominant problem for its Russian policy. As every teacher knows, there is a clear limit to the amount of sanctions that can be meted out before the pupil will respond by challenging the teacher's authority, and the teaching will simply have the effect of underlining the difference between the two parties. In order effectively to shape the pupil not as different but as similar, a teacher needs at least some degree of recognition from the pupil. The representation that dominates in Europe by being reiterated over and over, by people holding positions that add weight to their statements, attempts to solve this problem by recognizing Russia not as a fully fledged great power but as a great power by courtesy. There is a focus on human rights, particularly minority rights. These are areas that also figure prominently in other European discourses, for example, in the one on the institutionalization of European integration. Russia is seen as part of Europe in the sense that Russia is Europe's apprentice and a potential apostate. The discourse on Russia is prominent among political discourses, but hardly dominant. It is, for example, a disputed point whether the actualization of a Russian threat is the most immediate challenge to the configuration of the international system, or whether that role is played by the possibility of a change in Chinese or even Indian foreign policy, by Islam, by the possibility of a worldwide ecological crisis, and so on.

How to sum up Russia's specificity as Europe's other? Perhaps one may take a cue from a minor anthropological classic. Mary Douglas discussed the taxonomic practice of the Lele and fastened onto their problems in categorizing the pangolin (a scaly anteater to some):

> The pangolin is described by the Lele in terms in which there is no mistaking its anomalous character. They say: "In our forest there is an animal with the body and tail of a fish, covered in scales. It has four legs and it climbs in trees." (Douglas [1957] 1975: 33)

The pangolin is seen to have properties that do not go together, and so it threatens the very principles of Lele taxonomization and, by extension, taxonomization as such. Since taxonomy is at the core of the worldview and thus the identity of the Lele themselves, this is an extremely serious matter:

> They would never say, "We avoid anomalous animals because in defying the categories of our universe they arouse deep feelings of disquiet." But on each avoided animal they would launch into disquisitions on its natural history. (Douglas [1966] 1984: 173)

For this reason, the pangolin is constructed as a monster but also by some as the totem animal of a fertility cult. One could argue that for the last five hundred years Russia has been Europe's pangolin.

Being a pangolin that does not fit in is, however, still very much being part of the taxonomy, and a very important part at that. It is not the case that Russians "have traditionally been perceived as non-European," as one recent generalization has it (Delanty 1995: 11). The representations of Europe have been sundry and various, as have the representations of Russia, but what one has here is not a case of simple leaving out. No matter which social practices a period has foregrounded, be they religious, bodily, intellectual, social, military, political, economic, or otherwise, Russia has consistently been seen as an irregularity.

The point may be taken too far. Identity is a fluid, many-stranded, and perpetually negotiated phenomenon, and so all identities are ipso facto ambiguous. Russia has, furthermore, not been alone in being constructed as an ambiguous presence on Europe's border; it was demonstrated above how, before the advent of the Napoleonic Wars, this was the lot of all human collectives inhabiting territories stretching from the Baltic to the Black Seas. To this could be added the ambiguity concerning the Europeanness of all the others in relation to which Europe is constructed: "the Turk" of the previous chapter and the United States, for example.

And yet Russia stands out for its five hundred–year history of always *just* having been tamed, civil, civilized; just having begun to participate in European politics; *just* having become part of Europe. Since the Enlightenment it has, furthermore, been seen as a pupil and a learner, whether a successful one (the dominant version of the Enlightenment), a misguided one (the alternative version of the Enlightenment), a laggard who should learn but refuses to do so (the dominant version of the nineteenth century), a truant (the twentieth-century version), or a gifted but somewhat pigheaded one (the present version). It is therefore deeply appropriate that for the last five years the main metaphor used in European discussions of Russian politics and economics has been that of *transition*.

The dimension of European identity formation along which Russia stands out is not first and foremost the spatial one. The question often asked—Is Russia located inside or outside of Europe?—has usually been answered in the affirmative, although it is hardly a yes/no question and should thus not be expected to lend itself to ready answers. To the extent that it has not, it is an easy exercise to establish examples of how countries such as Germany and Spain have also been constructed to be spatially outside Europe; one French saying has it that "Africa begins at the Pyrenees." Russia's specificity as Europe's other thus resides not along the spatial but along the temporal dimension, as the country that is perpetually seen as being in some stage of transition to Europeanization. When Russia is discussed as not yet ready for membership in, say, NATO, this representation may be offered in terms of specific contemporary practices in the area of human rights or elsewhere. Its effectiveness in present discourse will, however, be reinforced by the rich baggage of the "not yets" and "justs" of half a millennium.

Danger resides on the borders, Mary Douglas argues, and so, as long as Russia is constructed as a border case, it will also be inscribed with danger. As noted in Chapter 1, Anne Norton (1989) has suggested that identities are at their most transparent when they are at their most ambiguous and that the most rewarding place to study them is therefore in their attempted delineation from what she calls their liminars. Russia, in whatever territorial shape, by whatever name, as whatever representation, has a history as Europe's main liminar. The uncertainty of self with which its representation is associated throughout the periods given here is therefore highly interesting not only when the issue is Russia but also when it is European identity. There are uncertainties surrounding its Christian status in the sixteenth and seventeenth centuries, uncertainties about the extent to which it could succeed in internalizing what it learned from Europe in the eighteenth century, uncertainties about its military intentions in the nineteenth century and its military-political ones in the twentieth century, and now again uncertainties about its potential as a learner—uncertainties everywhere.

Once asked about the parentage of the European Economic Community (EEC), Paul-Henri Spaak answered that Stalin was its father, inasmuch as fear of the Soviet Union had provided the impetus to hang together rather than hang separately. To wheel out another and perhaps overused quotation, the first secretary general of NATO, Lord Ismay, held that the job of NATO was to keep the Americans in, the Russians out, and the Germans down. Regardless of the degree of institutionalization, then, the representation of Europe is tied to the idea of the Russian other. Since exclusion is a necessary ingredient of integration, this is in itself no problem. The temptation remains, however, to play up the alterity of Russia *in order* to increase the integration of the European self. This is an ingredient of a number of contemporary debates that have to do with the expansion of the EU and NATO, trade policy, arms control, and the like. Since these issues are tied up with half a millennium's worth of representation of Russia as barbaric, Asiatic, and so on, they seem to call for rather more sensitivity to the question of how the representation of Russia enters into them than what seems to have been shown so far. It lies close to hand to see Russia as a learner, as half Asiatic, as having despotic political institutions, as riding roughshod over its Muslim minorities. For a start, and as demonstrated in chapter 6, all these ideas and more are part of Russian representations of self as they emerge in its attempted delineation of Europe. The focus of inquiry here is too broad to allow for discussion of how representations of Europe will impinge on any one specific question of policy. In conclusion, I will therefore simply suggest that if in our ongoing representation of Russia we do not allow for more reflection of how the deeply entrenched patterns discussed here remain a more-or-less unacknowledged factor, we will add our voices to the chorus that confirms the dominant version of Russia as a learner that is forever just about to make the transition into Europe.

4

Making Regions: Northern Europe

*In short, everything which draws them [Sweden and Denmark/Norway] to-
gether, is natural. Everything which pulls them apart, is unjust and unnatural.*
— ERIK MAGNUS STÄEL VON HOLSTEIN IN 1794,
QUOTED IN BØRRESEN 1991: 14

For reasons that probably have more to do with quantity than with
quality, in the international relations literature on regions, and particularly in the noneconomic literature, "Europe" is often not included as a region. Thus the two readings of how the self/other perspective may be brought to the study of identity formation at the
Europewide level that were presented in Chapters 2 and 3 played
themselves out in a "heterologue," with texts written mainly by historians. Once one turns to regions—or, granting that Europe may
just as well be treated as a region, subregions—in addition to such
texts one must also take into consideration the existence of a cluster
of region-focused theoretical writings, as well as writings on the specific regions in question. An attempted poststructural analysis like
the present one insists on working within the concepts that are already in circulation in the extant literatures, and so the different configuration of the field of knowledge means that the readings of the
(sub)regions must necessarily be somewhat different from the readings of "Europe."

I take as my examples two regions that during the Cold War were to be found, both socially and geographically, immediately to either side of the interface between what was routinely referred to as "the West" and "the East." Although regions, like all other human collectives, are constantly defined and redefined as a number of actors engaged in a discourse that is never brought to a permanent standstill, it is particularly instructive to see how identity formation played itself out at a juncture when that East/West divide came up for representation. If, in the case of Europe, the focus was less on actors than on the representational texts, the thesis that is brought to bear here is that each actor tried to impose a definition of the region that defines the core as being as close as possible to that actor. These cores are both territorial and functional, and the way to take hold of them is through the manipulation of knowledge and power. The point here is not in any way to treat these actors as sovereign; rather, the point is to acknowledge that after the fall of the sovereign actor in politics and the sovereign author of regions, actors and authors are still thick of the ground (Neumann 1997a).

These actors engage in what, by analogy to nation building (Anderson 1983), one may refer to as region building, and so this chapter argues the case for a *region-building approach*. This approach is nothing more than the application of this book's self/other perspective to the problematique of the literature on regions. It could be argued that the nation-state simulates the archetypal principle for political organization: that of kinship. In a situation where the kinship structures themselves are of less and less political importance, the nation-state takes on the hyperreal quality of the simulacrum: The metaphorical family of the nation-state becomes more real than the family itself. If the nation-state's reality *in space* is testified to by its territory, its reality *in time* is a question of getting itself a history. That a nation-state is constructed from historical material that may never have existed or whose relevance is dubious does not necessarily detract from the reality of that nation-state once it is territorially bounded. The use of such marginal historical material does, however, throw its reality and thus identity in time into serious doubt. When an elite has formulated a political program that hinges on the existence of some nation, it is always possible, admittedly with more or less difficulty, to construct a prehistory for that nation and thus embody it in time as well as in space. This is done by identifying, and thus making relevant to the identity of the human collective in question, a host of political ties, cultural similarities, economic transactional patterns, and so on. Of course, such a political process will always be imposed on a geographical area that is already, in a number of respects, heterogeneous. The points made here is simply that these similarities and dissimilarities are processed politically by nation builders and that it is *these political actors* who decide which similarities should henceforth be considered politically relevant and which should not.

The region-building approach simply suggests that such insights should be applied not only to nations but also to regions. It is a largely neglected fact in the literature that regions are also imagined communities. The existence of regions is preceded by the existence of region builders. They are political actors who, as part of some political project, see it in their interest to imagine a certain spatial and chronological identity for a region and to disseminate this imagination to as many other people as possible. It is not suggested here that each and every aspect of nation building is replicated on the regional level. To mention but two obvious differences, region builders may not always, or even occasionally, see the forging of a region as a prelude to the forging of a political entity; nation builders, on the other hand, do so by definition. Furthermore, in the sense in which it is used here, "region building" implies the crossing of state borders and so is entangled with the question of state sovereignty in a different way than is nation building.

It was discussed in chapter 1 that a genealogical analysis of social phenomena pioneered by Nietzsche, orchestrated by Foucault, and extended into the field of international relations by Ashley, Der Derian, and others is a major source of inspiration for the present analysis. Since my ambition in Chapters 4 and 5 is to suggest a specific approach to a set of specific phenomena, namely regions, perhaps this is the time to be more specific about what this inspiration entails. As set out by Richard Ashley, a genealogical tack

> involves a shift away from an interest in uncovering the structures of history and toward an interest in understanding the movement and clashes of historical practices that would impose or resist structure. . . . a genealogical posture entails a readiness to approach a field of practice historically, as an historically emergent and always contested product of multiple practices, multiple alien interpretations

which struggle, clash, deconstruct, and displace one another. (Ashley 1987: 409–410; see also Foucault 1977a)

In the case of regions, it is actually possible to prop up this insistence on the existence of a power/knowledge nexus by means of etymological evidence that supports a conceptualization of regions as military theaters or battlegrounds:

> Certain spatial metaphors are equally geographical and strategic, which is only natural since geography grew up in the shadow of the military. A circulation of notions can be observed between geographical and strategic discourses. The *region* of the geographers is the military region (from *regere*, to command). (Foucault 1980)

Regions, then, are defined in term of speech acts and of other acts (Shapiro 1981). But instead of postulating a given set of interests that actors are supposed to harbor before their social interaction with other collectives, the region-building approach investigates interests where they are formulated, namely, in discourse. Where every region builder's goal is to make the region-building program as *natural* as possible, my approach in this chapter aims to expose its historically contingent character. Where a region has been part of a discourse for so long that it is taken as a given fact, as was the case, for example, with the Nordic region in the postwar period, this approach can show that structures that may at first sight seem to be inevitably given will only remain so as long as they are *perceived* as inevitably given.

These insights are not entirely new to the study of regions in international relations. Traces of them can be found in works written at times when upheavals have ushered in new bouts of struggle about the definition of regions. In 1968, for example, Joseph Nye stated that regions lie where politicians want them to lie (Nye 1968: vi–vii; see also Banks 1969: 338). More recently, and as discussed in Chapter 1, Ole Wæver (1992) has investigated how different actors vie with one another to impose definitions of regions such as Europe and the Baltic Sea region crafted in their own image.

Lastly, a region-building approach is not offered as an attempt to place the study of regions on an entirely new footing. It does not aim to crowd out what are arguably the two dominant approaches in the existing literature: an inside-out approach focusing on cultural integration and an outside-in approach focusing on geopolitics. Rather, it is offered as a perspective from which to enrich the ongoing debate by asking questions about how and why the existence of a given region was postulated in the first place, about who perpetuates its existence with what intentions, and about how students of regions, by including and excluding certain areas and peoples from a given region, are putting their knowledge at the service of its perpetuation or transformation. Bearing this in mind, I now turn to a discussion of what the two dominant approaches in the IR literature have made of Northern Europe, in order to use the region-building approach to criticize and supplement their findings.

INSIDE-OUT/OUTSIDE-IN: A CONTINUUM OF APPROACHES

The extant literature, diverse as it is when it comes to pinning down the main dynamics that characterize a given region, can nevertheless be arranged along a continuum, at whose extreme ends theorists concentrate wholly on factors either internal or external to the region. One example of the former was widespread during the eighteenth century, when the cold *climate* of the North, with its allegedly beneficial effects on cultural life, was used as a defining trait for a Northern region. However, more than other criteria, this one proved to be notoriously slippery and to melt away as one tried to fix the border to the south. Since the time of German romanticism, *language* has been held forth as the central cultural criterion by which to delineate human collectives. In the case of Northern Europe, this diacriticon places Finland, as well as the Saami (formerly known as Lapps) speakers of other Finno-Ugric languages situated in the extreme north, squarely outside the region. Iceland and the Faeroe Islands would be border cases: Both Icelandic and Faeroese are West Scandinavian languages, but where the other Scandinavian languages are readily mutually understandable, the archaic nature of these two sets them apart.

Analyses that are predominantly inside-out typically try to amend the wooliness of regional borders by postulating a center, a core area where the internal defining traits are *more* similar, and interaction more intense, than in the regional periphery. Bruce Russett's standard work on regions concludes along these lines (1967: 182). Where Northern Europe is concerned, the core area would be Denmark, Norway, and Sweden. Indeed, in those three countries the term "Scandinavia" is used to cover these three states only, whereas the term "*Norden*" (the Nordic region) is used to include the periphery as well. This ambiguity is reflected in English usage, where "Scandinavia" can denote either area.

Russett's work is but one example of how integration theory places itself toward the inside-out end of the continuum. In the 1950s Karl Deutsch (1957) proposed a threshold score for internal cultural and transactional variables, beyond which the region in question also becomes what he called a *security community*. For Deutsch, Nordic cooperation is an example, in fact *the* example, of a pluralistic security community, that is, one in which the institutional strategies of state formation or supranational cooperation have not been at work. According to Deutsch, then, the common cultural traits of the Nordic region have *in themselves* been strong enough for the region to transcend international anarchy.

Amitai Etzioni explains the existence of regions and regional institutional cooperation by focusing on common cultural "background variables" as well as on internal transaction data about streams of persons, goods, capital, and services. According to Etzioni:

> There is no region in Europe and few exist in the world where culture, tradition, language, ethnic origin, political structure, and religion— all "background" and identitive elements—are as similar as they are in the Nordic region. (Etzioni 1965: 220–221)

Similarly, in his standard works on Nordic integration in the postwar period, Bengt Sundelius identifies the societal level as the source of regional dynamics. However, instead of explaining institutionalization in terms of spillover, which is a mechanism that is not necessarily dependent on cultural similarity, he highlights the culturally determined similarity of the way in which regional elites perceive the extraregional environment:

> Both the scope and intensity of joint policy grew significantly prior to 1970. . . . the policy dimension of political integration has developed prior to and presumably independent of institutional growth in the region. Thus, the results or outputs of the joint processes operating in the area already show significant changes prior to the institutionalization and formalization of these joint policymaking activities. This finding leads us to question why the political elites in the countries have undertaken a major structural reorganization of the joint activities, when significant policy results were achieved prior to this change.

The answer may rest in a fear that external developments during the last ten years, such as the growth of the EEC and the enlargement of that group, would undermine the results already reached in the Nordic region. (Sundelius 1982: 186–187)[1]

This analysis is still mainly inside-out. However, its focus is not on internal factors seen in isolation, but, rather, on internal elite perceptions of the region's external environment. This line of attack can, arguably, also be found in the literature on the "Nordic balance." At first glance, the idea of Nordic balance seems to give priority to outside factors. Arne Olav Brundtland and the other authors behind it wanted to *describe*, as it were, the sum total of Nordic security policy orientations, to *name* the alleged Nordic strategies for maximizing leeway vis-à-vis their respective allies and partners, and to *explain* why the great powers did not increase their presence and thereby allowed the Nordic region to keep its characteristic low level of tension compared to the rest of Europe. The classical formulation of Nordic balance defines it as

> the notion that the stability of the Northern European area is a result of reduced great power involvement, and that comparable possibilities exist for both the United States and the Soviet Union to neutralize possible increased involvement by the other superpower, thus removing incentives for initiatives leading to increasing tensions in Northern Europe. (Brundtland 1966: 30)

For Nordic peace researchers, to criticize the idea of a Nordic balance has been something of a professional rite of passage. Their endeavors have resulted in a reading of this literature that places it closer to the inside-out end of the continuum than to the outside-in end. For example, Ole Wæver interprets it as

> a system of political dissuasion, a balance of unexploited options; and in a slightly idealized version, the theory is about how Norden (and especially Norway) kept the superpowers out by elegantly using it. . . . [The idea] has dissuaded the superpowers from increasing their military presence in Norden, because of the knowledge that such an increase would lead to a corresponding move from the other superpower. (Wiberg and Wæver 1992: 24)

Readings that foreground the action-reaction character of the idea and readings that stress its character of being primarily part of domestic discourse will place it on either side of the middle of the continuum. This area is also populated by Louis Cantori's and Steven Spiegel's framework for comparing regions. Their suggestion is to divide all regions (or what they, in the jargon of 1960s-style systems analysis, insist on referring to as "subordinate systems") into a core and a periphery. "The core sector," they write, "consists of a state or a group of states which form a central focus of the international politics within the region" (Cantori and Spiegel 1970: 20, emphasis removed). They then go on to add the influence of the international system, the relevant gestalt of which they refer to as "the intrusive system," to the internal dynamics within the region itself.

This pincer movement, whereby regions are concurrently approached in terms of dynamics working inside-out and outside-in, is further elaborated by Barry Buzan and others in the literature on what they refer to as "security complexes." According to Buzan: "In defining regional security, the principal element that must be added to power relations is the pattern of amity and enmity among states" (Buzan 1991: 189). These patterns, he goes on, exist "within some particular geographical area," presumably the region. The states that make up the region and are the bearers of these patterns together form a security complex: "A security complex is defined as a group of states whose primary security concerns link together sufficiently closely that their national securities cannot realistically be considered apart from one another" (Buzan 1991: 190).[2] Regional developments are predicated on the nature of the security complex as well as on the extent to which the global rivalry of the great powers manifests itself within the region.

Closer to the outside-in end of the continuum, there is a sizable literature in which the interests and interaction of the great powers relevant to the region take center stage. Whereas the inside-out approaches operate with a plethora of different regional actors—international nongovernment organizations (INGOs), nations, states, bureaucracies, parties, commercial enterprises, trade unions, cultural personalities—the outside-in literature tends to stress systemic factors, states, and geography.[3] Where the former tend to see regional cores as being constituted in terms of cultural factors and therefore single out Denmark, Norway, and Sweden, the latter stress geopolitical factors. For example, Johan Jørgen Holst sees the Scandinavian peninsula (Norway and Sweden) along with Finland as the regional core (1973: 1). Similarly, whereas the inside-out approaches concentrate on the naturalness of cultural criteria in delineating a region's borders, the outside-in approaches discard these in favor of natural geopolitical strategic landmarks such as mountain ranges, rivers, and bodies of water:

> Geographically, the Nordic region is located north of the Baltic Sea, Germany and the North Sea. It covers an area of almost two million square meters. While the borders of the rest of Eurasia have often been made up by rivers and lakes, the Nordic borders have most often been defined by seas and bays. (Bingen 1991: 1)[4]

Most great power military planners seem to see regions almost exclusively in these terms. One instructive example is a memo written in 1905 by a certain Captain Ottley, secretary to Her Majesty's Committee of Imperial Defence, upon the consequences of the imminent breakup of the union between Sweden and Norway:

> Once in possession of Sweden and Norway, Russia would be in a position to hermetically seal the Baltic entrances and, in alliance with Germany, might be expected to make short work of Denmark, even if Denmark was not flung to Germany as a sop to ensure her acquiescence in the Russian expansion. . . . We have to consider how this danger may best be met. In the opinion of the Admiralty the right course for Great Britain to pursue will be to endeavour to prevail on the French Government to renew, together with ourselves, our ancient guarantee of both the Scandinavian States, not merely against Russian, but against *any* foreign aggression.[5]

Ottley viewed the affairs of Denmark, Norway, and Sweden as being clearly interrelated because of geographical proximity and the possible thrusts of penetration from Russia and Germany (and, one might add, from Great Britain itself). To pioneers in geopolitical scholarship such as Rudolf Kjellén, the working of this great power triangle was indeed the drama of Scandinavian politics.

Inside-out theories tend to postulate a plethora of actors on the societal level. Outside-in theories, on the other hand, tend to concentrate on the levels of the system and of states. It would, however, be premature to conclude that the literature's resistance to clear-cut compartmentalization calls the entire exercise of classification into doubt. "Classification," writes Martin Wight, that greatest classifier in international relations, "becomes valuable, in humane studies, only at the point where it breaks down" (Wight 1991: 259).

The literature reviewed so far, although rich in insights and diverse in assumptions, can nevertheless be criticized for sharing a major oversight. Although it focuses on regions as entities whose contents and borders are in a process of change—indeed, the major disagreement is over how change occurs—the existence of a region is taken as a given. The nature and causes of the *genesis* of regions are not addressed. The best way to show up this blank spot may be to examine what is arguably the most useful of the approaches just mentioned, namely, Barry Buzan's combination of inside-out and outside-in factors in the theory of security complexes.[6]

The security complex is represented as "an empirical phenomenon with historical and geopolitical roots" and represents a "durable rather than permanent" pattern (Buzan 1991: 191). Buzan acknowledges that the empirical side of his argument "courts the charge of reification" but nevertheless goes on to state that "the reality of security complexes lies more in the individual lines of amity, enmity and indifference between states, than in the notion of a self-aware subsystem." In other words, the construct does not assert its authority as an "imagined community," a cognitive construct shared by persons in the region themselves. Rather, it is the construct of one man—the allegedly sovereign author. "The individual lines of security concern can be traced quite easily by observing how states' fears shape their foreign policy and military behaviour," Buzan maintains (1991: 191).[7]

The blank spot here is *whose region* Buzan is talking about. The most remarkable feature of his definition of a security complex as "a group of states whose primary security concerns link together sufficiently closely that their national securities cannot realistically be considered apart from one another" (Buzan 1991: 190) is the absence of a subject. Cannot realistically be considered by whom? To Buzan, the delineation of regions, understood as security complexes, is a technical question that "may be a matter of controversy." The politics of defining and redefining the region is therefore marginalized. The idea of security complexes, like all the other ideas about regions discussed above, makes assumptions about what a region is. Making these assumptions is an inherently political act, and it must therefore be reflectively acknowledged and undertaken as such.

APPROACHES APPLIED: ONE REGION, TWO NARRATIVES

This section will attempt to illustrate how one may put the two sets of assumptions toward the ends of the inside-out/outside-in continuum to work and construct two widely differing narratives of the Northern European region.

A generalized narrative of the Northern European region predicated on inside-out style assumptions would begin by elaborating the communal nature of the region's culture and history. From 1389 to 1523 the region was actually politically united in the Union of Kalmar, and for three centuries after that Denmark and Norway remained one political entity. Throughout this period, the entire region was characterized by close cultural and economic contacts. For example, the Swedish legal code of 1734, which also applied in Finland, bore a remarkable similarity to the legal codes introduced in 1683 and 1687 in Denmark and Norway. Indeed, the idea of political reunion was mooted on a number of occasions and received a groundswell of support from a wide array of societal groups from the late eighteenth century onward.

The Scandinavianist movement was particularly active in the first half of the nineteenth century and laid the foundation for the intensification of cooperation toward the end of the century. For example, 1873 saw the forging of a Scandinavian currency union, which had gradually grown into a monetary union by 1901. The currency union was, moreover, matched by a bout of spelling reforms that brought the typography of the Scandinavian languages closer into line. In 1905 the Union of Sweden and Norway broke up in a peaceful and orderly fashion, an occurrence that is still almost unique in European and indeed world history. In 1907 a Nordic Interparliamentarian Union was set up, and during the First World War the monarchs came together to signal their mutual solidarity. At this time, moreover, economic interaction rose steeply. Furthermore, the League of Nations' most successful staging of peaceful conflict resolution took place in the Nordic region, where Finland and Sweden negotiated an agreement on the status of the Åland Islands in 1921. Again, the Permanent Court of International Justice in The Hague passed what is perhaps the most wide-ranging of its rulings to be subsequently adhered to, over conflicting Danish and Norwegian claims to sovereignty over Greenland in 1933. The year before had seen the first meeting of Nordic foreign ministers. Economic cooperation between "the Oslo states" (Denmark, Norway, Sweden, and the Benelux) in the years before the Second World War foreshadowed the European Free Trade Cooperation after the war (Ron 1989). Finland moved closer to the core of the region throughout the 1930s; after all, the area had a history as part of Sweden before its incorporation into the Russian empire in 1809. After the inception of state sovereignty in 1917, the common cultural heritage proved itself to have survived as a lasting tie to Scandinavia.

Following such a sequence of events, the formation of the Nordic Council in 1952 was the logical next step for Nordic cooperation, and one that was foreshadowed by a Danish proposal of 1938. The intensification of the informal Nordic societal networks and transgovernmental telephone diplomacy, as well as successes such as the common labor market, the passport union, and the streamlining of social law are seen as further evidence of the instrumental role of cultural regional homogeneity, which is further evidenced by the shared egalitarian "Scandinavian welfare state model." Although this model is closely associated with Scandinavian social democracy, it is often argued that the model has transcended its social origins and become a part of the shared regional culture. A former Swedish prime minister from a nonsocialist party who was at this time also chair of the broadly based INGO "the Nordic Association" (*Foreningen Norden*), Thorbjörn Fälldin, put the argument this way:

> It should be pointed out that nowhere in Europe does there exist such a natural and unitary region as the Nordic one. Its 22 million people share a common culture, speak similar languages, and share the same high level of education and buying power. The Nordic region is already a natural home market. (*Dagbladet* [Oslo], 11 September 1991)

The tendency to compare the Nordic region favorably to the EC was a stock ingredient of much inside-out writing during the Cold War. Two factors were brought to the fore: the prevalence of societal actors and the absence of formal agreements. For example, in a Swedish book on European integration from 1974, one can read that

> Nordic cooperation is unique inasmuch as the main impetus behind it comes from below, and is deeply rooted in the citizenry. Contrary to the EC, the development of Nordic cooperation is not a consequence of political decisions made on the state level; neither have national

parliaments been among its main driving forces. (Lindquist and Lundgren 1974: 79)

In this view, the absence of formal agreements to prop up Nordic cooperation only goes to show its *moral superiority* compared to the EC in the past and to the EU and other regional forums now. Between friends there is, as it were, no *need* for legislation; it is adequate that sovereign governments reach informal consensus and that they then proceed to implement the decisions reached through national parallel action (Nielsson 1989). This is a very solidarist, indeed Burkean, view of international relations generally and international law specifically, and it is therefore well suited to round off this generalized inside-out narrative of the Northern European region.

The contrast between this narrative and one rooted in outside-in assumptions, which trace regional developments back to changes in the international and European order, is indeed striking. To start with, whereas the inside-out narrative would tend to treat the region as something that was there from the beginning of written history, it is hard to see how to generate a meaningful outside-in perspective for the period before the beginning of the eighteenth century. There are two reasons for this. First, it was arguably only as a result of the Thirty Years War (1618–1648) that the state system around the Baltic Sea merged with the system focusing on continental Europe and thus ceased to be a highly self-contained entity in terms of security. It is only from then onward, therefore, that it is at all meaningful to cordon a Nordic self off as an "inside" vis-à-vis an "outside." Second, it was only when Russia replaced Sweden as the dominant Baltic power that the region became the object of the characteristic triangular power struggle between Russia, Germany, and Great Britain. Before that, Sweden's status as a great power in the European state system at large, tenuous though it may have been, placed its immediate territorial surroundings on a par with other parts of the system.

The triangular outside rivalry changed the face of the Northern European region during the Napoleonic Wars. Following the treaties of Tilsit in 1807 Sweden had to cede Finland to Russia. In order to somewhat compensate Sweden for its loss and thereby solidify Russia's hold on its new acquisition, Tsar Alexander I decided that Sweden should be given the Norwegian part of Denmark/Norway. In this he obtained the support of the other great powers, and Norway duly changed hands.

The potency of outside-in factors become especially visible during wartime. The next war that had an impact on the region was the Dano-Prussian War of 1864, which effectively finished off Scandinavianism by showing that regional cooperation broke down when outside factors impinged on the different Scandinavian countries in different ways. Moreover, Denmark's defeat gave rise to differing calculations of Denmark's strength in Copenhagen and Stockholm. These differences, infused by external factors, explain why the currency union of 1873 came about; both parties thought they would be able to dominate it. Where the event of Norwegian sovereign statehood in 1905 is concerned, the outside Russian and German support for the Norwegian cause as a means of softening the region to great power pressure was important.

During the First World War, the Scandinavian states shared an interest in keeping the warring great powers at bay and in compensating for the loss of trade with the combatants by increasing trade between Denmark, Norway, and Sweden themselves. After the Great War, however, the old patterns of trade quickly reasserted themselves. This can be taken to indicate that Scandinavian cooperation had no internal dynamic but, rather, was a spurious and therefore ephemeral side effect of the uncertainty concerning the European balance of power. This conclusion can be bolstered by highlighting events that took place during the Second World War. At this time, Sweden not only failed to react to the German occupation of Denmark and Norway in 1940 but even went so far as to open its borders to regular Nazi troop transports. The number of transits made exceeded 2 million.

As a result of the turn toward a bipolar international system in the wake of the Second World War, however, Sweden was left with few alternative courses other than to pursue regional cooperation. Although its attempts to forge a Nordic Defence Union failed, it was still keen to pursue lower-level ventures in this direction.

Since the Napoleonic Wars, and also occasionally before that, Denmark and Sweden had been nonaligned states, and since 1855 the neutrality of Sweden/Norway had been guaranteed by France and Great Britain. Norway and Finland also settled for nonalliance after obtaining sovereign statehood in 1905 and 1918, respectively.

However, the different experiences of each during the Second World War changed this picture radically. In 1948, Finland, although non-aligned, entered into a Treaty of Friendship, Cooperation, and Mutual Assistance with the Soviet Union; Sweden remained nonaligned; and Norway and Denmark were among the founding members of NATO. Given the external environment and the different ways in which the states reacted to it, attempts to form a Nordic Defence Union backed by the regional great power Sweden floundered. The setting up of the Nordic Council in 1952 was, moreover, only possible as a low politics venture (cooperation on social and economic policy) that compensated for the failure of high politics cooperation (on foreign and security policy). The common interest in alleviating great power pressure remained key: "The Nordic Council was originally formed in order to balance the negative effects for Nordic cooperation of the different security loyalties emerging in 1948–49" (Andrén 1991: 291).

The Nordic region, then, could serve as a rhetorical alternative as well as a modest supplement to the closer ties to external great powers that followed as a result of changes in the shape of the international system. The intensification of Nordic cooperation in the postwar period was a function of the region's status as a Cold War buffer between East and West and, in a longer time perspective, between Russia/U.S.S.R., Great Britain and the United States, and Germany. Finland needed Nordic cooperation as a counterweight, however modest, to the pressure from the Soviet Union ensuing from lost wars and the existence of the friendship treaty. In Norway, Nordic cooperation was seen as a way of giving regional policy a profile and thus alleviating and complementing the heavy dependence on the strong sea powers, Great Britain and the United States:

> Norwegian support for the idea of a Nordic Customs Union in the 1950s can be explained as a way of mobilizing support for the country's Atlantic policy in a situation where Oslo had opposed a Nordic Defence Union in favour of NATO. Moreover, both Norway and Denmark supported the 1970 plan for a NORDEC among other things as a way of increasing domestic support for their EC policy. (Jervell 1991a: 194)

In Denmark, bilateral relations with Germany continued to play a crucial role. This explains not only postwar developments but also the lack of revanchist demands against the defeated neighboring state after the First World War—the internal factor of domestic nationalist clamoring for a reoccupation of Schleswig notwithstanding—and for the conciliatory policy ensuing after five years of German occupation during the Second World War. To Denmark, then, Nordic cooperation was a way of balancing the great power neighbor immediately south of the border.

As the 1970s drew to a close the Cold War reintensified, and the Nordic region was once again exposed to an externally generated challenge to regional cooperation. Throughout the Cold War, the area had played a double role as a grey zone for superpower rivalry and as buffer zone between the two blocs. Now changes in military technology and doctrine induced the superpowers to view it more in terms of the former and less in terms of the latter. With the end of the Cold War, however, the triangular pattern of rivalry between Russia, Germany, and the Atlantic powers reappeared as the basic determinant of Nordic regional dynamics.

These two narratives of what characterizes the Nordic region do indeed differ substantially. It is hardly surprising that different assumptions about the prevalence of inside-out versus outside-in factors give rise to differences in emphasis and conclusions. Since different assumptions may be chosen to illuminate different aspects of regional politics, however, the two perspectives and their concomitant narratives are complementary rather than mutually exclusive.

WHOSE REGION?

Due to its affinity to the literature on nation building, the region-building approach immediately reveals one crucial insight left out by the inside-out and outside-in narratives. The Scandinavianism that arose toward the end of the eighteenth century and had its heyday toward the middle of the nineteenth was not only a bona fide example of a region-building movement but also a direct competitor to less territorially inclusive nation-building projects in the area. Like the nation-building projects, the goal of imagining a Scandinavian community was served by the production of knowledge. From the 1830s onward there arose a Scandinavianist historiography, and attempts were made at standardizing language throughout the proposed region (Børresen 1991; cf. Deletant and Hanak 1988). In the years leading up to German and Italian unification, romantic intellectuals in Denmark and Sweden/Norway discussed whether or not there should be a Scandinavian state. There existed an intellectual elite with a Scandinavianist program that was in a number of cases not only region building, but also state and nation building. For example, in an 1865 book Lars Heyer discussed six possible variants of the political Scandinavia and concluded by promoting the state option (see Zorgbibe 1968). However, even before the publication of that book, the project had already suffered a severe setback. In 1864 Sweden/Norway did not make good on vague promises of support for Denmark in the war against Prussia.

At this time, moreover, the Norwegian nation-building project was gathering momentum. In 1905 the success of this project resulted in the breakup of the double monarchy with Sweden. Scandinavianism succumbed to the interests of the already existing states and to the Danish, Norwegian, and Swedish nation-building projects. It survived, however, as a region-building project with a number of traits reminiscent of a nation-building one.

The dip in production of knowledge furthering the Scandinavianist cause is a telltale sign of its retreat since the 1860s. In an examination of "Nordic" historiography from this century, Stein Tønnesson found that "only very few Nordic histories have been published. The main one is a three-volume work by Johan Ottosen, published at the turn of the century, with an introductory chapter on 'The Aryan Family of Languages'" (Tønnesson 1991: 24).

The fate of Scandinavianism presents a good illustration of the region-building point that cultural similarities are not politically relevant in and of themselves; rather, they must be politically processed to become so. The political elites of Christiania, Copenhagen, and Stockholm were much closer to one another culturally than they were to town and countryside within any one state. Inside-out approaches to regions would lean toward seeing this as an indication that the Scandinavian project would emerge victorious from its struggle with the national projects. What happened was the exact opposite. What was politically communicated as culturally relevant (such as Finnish lakes, Norwegian mountains, Danish phlegmatism) proved more important for political organization than cultural similarities per se.

The participation of the Swedish/Norwegian state in the region-building project during the run-up to the Dano-Prussian War was no isolated phenomenon. In 1794 the Swedish ambassador to Paris, Erik Magnus Stäel von Holstein, had already summed up his view of the Scandinavian states (Sweden and Denmark/Norway at that time) by stating that "in short, everything which draws them together, is natural. Everything which pulls them apart, is unjust and unnatural" (quoted in Børresen 1991: 14). The question posed by the region-building approach would be: Whence this interest in Scandinavia? Sweden had been historically dominant in the region ever since the end of the Thirty Years War. It tended, and still tends, to see Finland, Norway, and to some extent Denmark not only as a buffers against the Atlantic powers, Russia/U.S.S.R., and Germany but as an extension of the self.

In its post–great power existence, Sweden was able to hold on to Finland until 1809 and to dominate the double monarchy with Norway lasting from 1814 to 1905. When Sweden made a virtue of necessity and declared itself nonaligned after the Napoleonic Wars, one of the benefits, especially in the post–Second World War system, was the opportunity to launch itself as a *moral* great power and an *actor* with a clear profile. For example, throughout the 1950s there existed a fully fledged Swedish nuclear research program.[8] The state's profile was accentuated by the existence of what was seen as a uniquely Swedish welfare state, whose example could inspire other countries to maneuver between unmitigated market liberalism on the one hand and a Soviet-type economy on the other. The uniqueness of the Swedish model—which, it is instructive to note, was referred to as the "Scandinavian" model in the other Scandinavian states—did not, however, keep Sweden from continuing to see the region in terms of a continuation of self. A line in the Swedish national anthem goes "I want to live, I want to die in *Norden,*" that is, in the Nordic region, and not "in Sweden" as one might expect in a national anthem. Moreover, Tønnesson's examination of Nordic secondary school curricula reveals that in Sweden the country's name is frequently left out and replaced by "*Norden.*" Such an omission, he comments, would have been "unthinkable in the other countries. Only a truly self-assured central power can permit leaving out its own name" (Tønnesson 1991).[9]

Of course, the region-building approach could be used to highlight the intentions and strategies not only of societal movements and self-professed regional great powers but of any actors partaking in regional politics. For example, it was mentioned above that a 1905 brief from the British Admiralty on "the threatened dissolution of the Union between Norway and Sweden" was a good example of an outside-in analysis. The region was seen as a wrestling ground for external powers, in which Britain would try to secure its interests by prevailing on the French government "to renew, together with ourselves, our ancient guarantee of both the Scandinavian States, not merely against Russian, but against *any* foreign aggression."[10]

The region-building approach could add a few comments in the margin of this analysis. First, the "ancient" guarantee in question, presented as proof of Britain's "natural" role in the region, was but fifty years old at the time when this was written. Second, the way in which the British officer states the problem in the paragraph preceding the one just quoted is illuminating: "The idea that the kindred Norse race should ever fall beneath Muscovite domination is repugnant." The key word here is "kindred," by means of which it is once again presented as *natural* that Great Britain should take charge of the situation—indeed, that Great Britain should not only be *in* the region but that it is also in some sense *of* the region.

This mood of presentation keeps emerging in the statements of other great powers with an interest in the Nordic region. During the German occupation of Denmark and Norway during the Second World War, it was a recurrent theme that Germans and Scandinavians were of the same Aryan race. And during a meeting with Nordic ministers, Russian Prime Minister Aleksey Kosygin is reported to have asked rhetorically: "Is not really the Soviet Union a Nordic country?" (quoted in Berner 1986: 2).[11] These ways of defining a state as part of the region in question share a common structure: first the insistence that the state in question is "really" part of the region; then the conclusion that this fact should "naturally," and if possible exclusively, be given a special *droit de regard* by "the other" powers in the region.

With the waning of the Cold War, the clash of interpretations of the Nordic region was thrown out in the open for all to see. The upheaval in the international system changed the cast of actors in the struggle to define the region. The situation invited the actors to overhaul and renew their armory and to test new strategies.

The Cold War should not, however, be seen as a truce in the fight between different definitions of the region. To reiterate some of the examples given above, the Soviet Union launched an unceasing campaign to define the region in such a way that its own inclusion was secured. Denmark, Finland, Norway, and Sweden tried to entrench the region as an area of "low tension" compared to the rest of the European region. The existence of the rival region-building projects of the European Free Trade Association (EFTA) and the EC fed into the struggle to define the Nordic region. When EFTA lost in its struggle against the EC and Denmark joined the EC in 1972, the resulting overlap between the EC and the Nordic region had the effect, among other things, of strengthening Denmark's hand in the struggle for *Norden*.

The lively struggle during the Cold War notwithstanding, its discontinuation raised the heat of battle by several degrees. The EC's presence loomed larger than ever. The Soviet Union's demise as a global power caused it to renew its interest in Europe, including Northern Europe. Before long, programs for a "renewal" or "transformation" of the Northern European region were cropping up everywhere.

REGIONS AND IMAGINED CENTERS

A number of these programs took the Baltic Sea as their geographical base and were presented under labels such as the new *Hanse*, the Baltic Sea region, *Mare Balticum*, the Euro-Baltic Region, and the Scanno-Baltic Political Space. A tightly knit epistemic community of "Nordic" foreign policy intellectuals played a conspicuous role in producing the knowledge that was used to prop up these several ideas. Their battle cry was that under present postmodern conditions, state sovereignty is relativized in favor of a new European medievalism in which different political issues are settled on different political levels:

> The very first step has been a series of conferences, think tank reports, and articles in more or less scientific journals. The first steps have been taken by intellectuals, to some extent the cultural elite but in a more clearly political form. (Wæver 1991: 102)

Finally, like all other region-building projects, this one tries not only to impose its own definition of the region but also to fend off rival projects. The "Baltic discourse," Pertti Joenniemi writes, "should not be made 'realist' in a traditional sense trying to prove that cooperation around the Baltic rim fits the (narrowly conceived) security needs of the actors in the region" (Joenniemi 1991: 3).

The pledge that the Baltic Sea region will have benefits for everybody is thus qualified by excluding actors who take a "narrow," that is, erroneous, view of their interests. Such actors would presumably include, among others, Toomis Käbin, the Swedish Export Council's main adviser on Estonian affairs. The fact is that he, too, advocates a definition of the Northern European region that might be said to dovetail with the project for a Baltic Sea region: "In the same way as West Germany is now in charge of what was once East Germany," he told Sweden's leading newspaper, "it seems natural that Sweden takes over responsibility for Estonia and its development" (quoted in *Dagens Nyheter* [Stockholm], 16 September 1991). Different definitions of, and intentions for, the region obviously seem "natural" to different people. Aping the mind-set of his Swedish colleague, Vagn Jensen, the vice director of the Danish Export Council, claims to pursue "the Blue Banana—the Baltic sea is a banana, a blue one, compared with the European yellow banana" curving its way from London, around Brussels and down to Lombardy (quoted in *The Baltic Independent* [Tallinn], 27 July 1991).[12]

The economic thrust of this simian simile sits well beside the North German initiatives from Björn Engholm and his associates. As early as 1988 they had begun to advocate the forging of a new *Hanse,* an *Ostseeraum* (*Chancen* 1990). In doing so, they have drawn attention to the way in which climate, culture, and history have themselves forged a natural community:

> The close ties between the peoples [of the Baltic Sea region] are bound by the social standards, temperaments and social characteristics which in the last instance stem from the living conditions of the North: The landscape, the climate, the maritime environment and the settlement patterns. We have a stable temperament, we are not gregarious, rather a bit inaccessible, yet reliable. Our sense of social justice is well advanced. The social infrastructure of Sweden, Denmark, Finland and Norway is unique, and we do not in any way feel any resentment towards the other Baltic states. The common background of the Northern European countries covers a broad spectrum and has deep roots. What we need, is a strategy for the future. (Quoted in Wind 1992: 53)[13]

The ascription of nurture to nature, the stress on a common human *Geist,* and the forging of a "we" (self) as opposed to an other more unstable, more gregarious, more accessible, less reliable, less just, less advanced, and less tolerant—Engholm is obviously well versed in the German romantic nationalist literature.

As seen from the Russian shore, the Baltic Sea region is an opportunity to become a Northern European insider at last. The interplay of interests and intentions between the federal government in Moscow and the Russian provinces to the west is similar, yet much more fluid, than is the case in Germany. Although competition between the federal and the local levels is much less regulated by law and thus more unpredictable and unstable, the relevant agendas of Moscow and the provinces are not dissimilar. At the Moscow end, the former Russian Deputy Foreign Minister Andrey Fedorov put forward a suggestion for regional cooperation within what he referred to as the Nordic-Baltic belt (*severo-baltiyskiy poyas*).[14] The project would include the Nordic states, the Baltic states, and the four Russian political entities Murmansk, Leningrad (now St. Petersburg), Karelia, and Kaliningrad. It is instructive to note that the German *Länder* and Poland would be excluded, leaving Russia as the only great power participant.

The Russian Western provinces, on their part, have been actively pursuing bilateral contacts with neighboring non-Russian areas, among other things in order to minimize economic control from "the center," that is, Moscow. In St. Petersburg, for example, it is pointed out that the city is by far the largest Baltic city. Moreover, its mayor has put it forward as the permanent site for Nordic and Baltic Council organs: "The inclusion of Russia in the world economy can advantageously be mediated through St Petersburg," the mayor's main adviser wrote (Yag'ya 1992: 5). St. Petersburg, he continued, is a bridge "between Russia, a number of the countries of the Community of Independent States and the rest of Europe. . . . Through St Petersburg, Europe may as it were stretch its borders towards the Pacific," and for this reason "the fate of humanity to a large extent hinges on the state of affairs in the Baltic" (Yag'ya 1992: 1, 5). A definition of the Baltic Sea region along these lines would, of course, place St. Petersburg close to its geographical core and not on its Eastern periphery. In this sense, this proposed definition of the Baltic Sea region is a variant of a Russian idea that was fashionable in the

1920s and that has recently made its return. The idea, which will be presented in chapter 6, is that Russia is a "Eurasian" power and that it is therefore the natural bridge between Europe and Asia.

In Poland, the urge to define oneself as the hub of regional cooperation has surfaced in a similar way but with a different twist. At one point during the existence of the Polish-Lithuanian Commonwealth, Poles referred to their country as the land between the seas; that is, between the Baltic and the Black Seas. This image still lingers in the Polish national identity and may be what has inspired Tomasz Knothe, of the Polish Parliament's Information Bureau, to write that: "as a member of both the Hexagonal (presently known as the Central European initiative) as well as of the Baltic Sea Cooperation, Poland takes up the interesting position as the main link between the two groups" (Knothe 1992: 35).

For an actor to combine two regional projects in order to highlight its own importance is interesting. Other Polish attempts at defining the Baltic Sea region have, however, centered on ecological cooperation, which is the only functional area where there is already some cooperation between Poland and the other riparian states. Poland spent the interwar period vainly trying to build a region between Russia and Germany. These failures are still seen as a drawn-out preface to the national tragedy that took place in 1939. Echoes of this can be heard in today's political debate and lend a particular urgency to Polish region-building attempts in the Baltic Sea area as well as in Central Europe and vis-à-vis the EU, as will be discussed in Chapter 5.

Estonia and to a lesser degree Latvia share shades of Poland's traumatic memories of failed interwar attempts to forge a region that could somewhat offset German and Soviet advances (Järve 1991). Like Poland, Estonia, Latvia, and Lithuania refuse to put all their region-building eggs in one basket. Although these three states set up a Baltic Council in the 1930s, their efforts to build an image of a three-state Baltic region only date back to the second half of the 1980s. As recently as 1987, an exile Estonian remarked in a conference on "Regional Identity under Soviet Rule: The Case of the Baltic States" that

the main theme of our conference here in Kiel is "Baltic Regionalism." Permit me, then, to draw up an antithesis: To my mind the Baltic population—I am now speaking of the overall majority—has never taken part in any "regionalism," nor was it ever affected by it. This applies to the nineteenth century as well as to our own. . . . The pioneering cooperation of young exile Latvians, Lithuanians, and Estonians, which led to the Copenhagen Tribunal, to the "Cruise," [undertaken jointly by nationals from the three Baltic republics as an exercise in confidence building], and to a Baltic Futures Seminar in Summer 1985, must be commended. Hardly ever did such inter-Baltic enthusiasm exist earlier, either in the Baltic or in exile. (Rebas 1988: 101, 113; but see also Bungs 1988)

The Estonian, Latvian, and Lithuanian attempt at projecting an image of a "Baltic region" onto "the West" in the last few years of the Cold War was, however, instantly effective and makes for a nice illustration of the potential rewards of even the most superficial exercises in region building. It is equally instructive that region building among the three has come to a standstill after the resuscitation of statehood. Moreover, the three states are engaging in different and mutually contradictory strategies in their attempts to join the Nordic Council, the main institutional embodiment of the Nordic region. Although the council had accepted all three states as observers as of 1991, Estonia continued to see the option of full membership as unrealistic and possibly even counterproductive. It therefore chose an incremental approach to membership. Latvia and Lithuania, on the other hand, wanted to apply for membership without further delay and approached Tallinn with a proposal that the three nations send off a joint application. Since Estonia had engaged in more region-building activities in Northern Europe than the other two, the Latvian and Lithuanian moves may perhaps be seen as an attempt to thwart an Estonian region-building offensive that they could not match.

Estonian, Latvian, and Lithuanian aspirations to join the Nordic Council have to vie with other conceptualizations for the institutional definition of the Northern European region. The Nordic Council itself, for example, at an early stage leaned toward a structure whereby Nordic and Baltic Councils would together form a Council for the Baltic Sea Region. For example, it funded a report in which one can read that

the project *The Nordic Region in Europe* has established a reference group of researchers from the Baltic Academies of Sciences. They will follow the negotiations to establish a Baltic Council with the aim of influencing the process. They see it as an important goal to forge an organization which is compatible with Nordic Cooperation. (*Norden* 1991: 204, note 6)

It is even less surprising that the Nordic Council and this "reference group of researchers" have joined forces with the activists behind the region-building project for a Baltic Sea region mentioned at the beginning of this section and with region builders in the North German *Länder*. The upshot was that the Nordic Council arranged a series of parliamentarian conferences on cooperation in the Baltic Sea area, and in March 1992 the foreign ministers from all the states involved established a maximalist Baltic Council (that is, with participation of all riparian states as well as Norway), which after five years has already taken on a certain hue of naturalness.

Finland has been among the driving forces behind the parliamentarian conferences and has generally maintained a high region-building profile. Finland has aimed to add the Baltic and Russian areas to the Nordic region and in this way forge a Baltic region in which Finland would be centrally placed geographically. An unusually illustrative attempt at regional definition of this kind came when the entire foreign policy elite of the Swedish minority in Finland, which is concentrated in the riparian areas, published a book on Finland's future. The book suggests that Baltic cooperation should be conceived of as a two-tier system of A-members and B-members: "Nearly all Finno-Swedes would be located in the A-area. Considering the intensive Nordic cooperation, one might even include those Nordic countries that are not riparian Baltic states, that is, Norway and Iceland, in the B-areas" (Bonsdorff 1991: 105). One could hardly ask for a more explicit attempt by a citizen to format a region so that the state to which he belongs, and indeed of which he is a minority member, is given pride of place.

In Sweden, too, region-building activity has centered on Sweden as a "natural" core, with the Nordic region as an inner circle and a wider Baltic cooperation as an outer circle. In this way, Sweden has found a formula for transforming the strategy for regional domination discussed above to fit the new circumstances of the post–Cold War era. Only in Iceland and Norway has there been little region-building activity along these lines. This is hardly surprising, considering that these two states are not situated on the shores of the Baltic Sea. In Norway as the Cold War was coming to an end, the preoccupations were with preserving the Nordic region and with the widening gap between the decreasing level of tension in the Baltic Sea area on the one hand and the sustained presence of naval vessels in the High North on the other. As summed up by the Minister of Defense:

> The concern is . . . that naval competition could separate Northern Europe from the rest of Europe if it is not subjected to negotiated limitations at a time when arms control negotiations are transforming the military geometry of the Cold War. (Holst 1990: 15)

In September 1991, however, Foreign Minister Thorvald Stoltenberg owned up to the new developments and admitted that "we just have to come to terms with the fact that the Nordic region [*Norden*] is not what it used to be" (quoted in *Dagens Næringsliv* [Oslo], 21 September 1991). Norway then tried to go on the offensive with a two-pronged region-building attack. First, Foreign Ministry sources started to float informal suggestions for a "Northern region" to stretch from the Kola Peninsula to the southern shore of the Baltic Sea. The Kola Peninsula, which borders Norway to the west, harbors the world's largest naval base, and by tying this area into a regional constellation Norway hoped to avoid being left alone with Russia in the North: "A Northern region would not only be an interesting expansion of today's Nordic region, but could also become an important bridge between the EC and the north-western parts of the Soviet Union" (Jervell 1991a: 193). This region-building project was subsequently refined, and in a manner that brings to mind the Polish attempts to place itself as the link between the Northern European and Central European regions. The "Northern region" was depicted as a conglomerate of an Arctic region, a Baltic region, and North Sea region. Incidentally, the Northern region thus defined would have Norway as its pivotal axis (see Jervell 1991b).

Norway's second line of attack was to try and get a toehold, however tenuous, on the Baltic coastline. Since, as the foreign minister, Thorvald Stoltenberg, remarked in a speech at the time, "one can hardly call Oslo a typical Baltic city," Norway had to find some other way of staking a claim to Baltic status.[15] This was done by introducing what the foreign minister, in the same speech, declared to be "something entirely new in Norwegian foreign policy." The Norwegian delegation to the meeting of foreign ministers in March

1992, where the establishment of a Baltic Council was declared, included a representative of the southeasternmost Norwegian county, Østfold. The reason for the innovation surfaced during the meeting, when, in an attempt to shore up Norway's claim to Baltic status, Norway maintained that Østfold was situated "at the mouth of the Baltic Sea" (Brundtland 1992).

CONCLUSION

This examination of post–Cold War discourse on Northern Europe does indeed illustrate that the region-building approach is vindicated in holding that multiple alien interpretations of the region struggle, clash, deconstruct, and displace one another. Whereas a number of statements made by representatives of the "Nordic" states continue to acknowledge the existence of a "Nordic" region, nearly all are quick to stress that the continued existence of such a region is not contradictory to the forging of a new Baltic Sea region. In other words, the Nordic region seems to have undergone a sea change.

Of course, inside-out and outside-in approaches to regions offer a number of insights into the character of this transformation. The region-building approach would not maintain, for example, that inside-out explanations in terms of cultural affinity are necessarily incorrect renditions of history. Cultural ties between the Nordic region and the Baltic region did indeed already exist in the Middle Ages, when, for example, areas that are today parts of Estonia and Latvia were, after all, parts of Denmark and Sweden. The Kalmar Union (1389-1523) did indeed incorporate a number of these areas in a single state. During the Thirty Years War Poland did have a Swedish line of kings (the Wasa). "Tallinn," it is true, does mean "Danish city" in Estonian, and Estonian is indeed a Finno-Ugric language, not very different from Finnish and the languages of Saami minorities in the northern parts of Norway and Sweden. The presence of Baltic exiles in Sweden did make up a human link between the Nordic and the Baltic countries throughout the Cold War.

The region-building approach would not necessarily take issue with any one of these claims. It would, however, insist that these facts, or even cultural similarities as such, are not in and of themselves politically relevant. It has already been noted that the high level of cultural similarity among Scandinavian elites, and for that matter among the citizenries of the Scandinavian nations, did not in and of itself spawn a Scandinavian state. For the sake of contrast, witness the cultural similarities between the northern and southern shores of the Mediterranean, which were activated as part of a French region-building and indeed state-building project at one point, only to be deactivated later to the extent that it now seems preposterous—and certainly politically irrelevant—to mention them. Cultural differences are *made* relevant by political actors, to serve some political cause, and their activation is therefore *itself* a political act.

That begs one vital question: Is it possible to construct a region, as it were, ex nihilo? A region-building approach would suggest that the answer to this question is yes. It is always possible to find some link, some prehistory, that can be used to justify the inclusion of a certain actor in a certain region. Both Siberians living on the Pacific coast of Russia and their neighbours across the water in Japan have been mentioned as possible members of the Baltic Sea Region. It may be a more time-consuming region-building project to include these actors into the fold than to include, say, the Scots. It would certainly include harder discursive work. Given the state of the discourse on Northern Europe, it does seem more "natural," "reasonable," "fair" to include the Scots than the Japanese. Many authors would be satisfied to discuss the degree of "fairness" and so on that is involved in such decisions. But the region-building approach would insist on going to the root of things and would ask where the criteria for what is "natural" come from, who formulated them, who chose to apply them and thereby made them relevant, and who stands to gain from them.

Proponents of an outside-in analysis may perhaps go along with such a sentiment, but they would then go on to criticize the region-building approach for pouring old wine into new bottles. In the case of Northern Europe, it was only as local actors realized the need to react to upheaval on the international and European levels that the new round of region building really took off. Since external factors were thus able thoroughly to impact a region that has often served as a showcase for inside-out approaches, it is a powerful argument in favor of outside-in approaches.

Yet the analytical divide between an "outside" that is calling the shots and an "inside" that is trying to avoid being shot, should in and of itself raise suspicions about whose interests such an analysis would serve. The region-building approach would not necessarily have any principled objections to the foregrounding of great powers; after all, it is a theory based on the nexus between power and knowledge. Objections would, rather, be raised against tendencies to exclude other state and societal actors and against the reification of the "national interest."

This critique reveals the normative core of a region-building approach. Instead of adopting the accepting attitude inherent in many outside-in approaches, it insists on an unaccepting, irreverent and therefore invariance-breaking attitude. In Chapter 5, on Central Europe, therefore, the aim is not only to demonstrate the imagined character of that region but to explode the oft-heard claim that a Central European political project is an *alternative* to national projects.

5

Making Regions: Central Europe

*When Poles and Rumanians . . . argue that Russia is not of the West,
whereas their own nations most emphatically are, one feels that this is more
than an academic classification, that it is an argument born of fear or des-
peration, and that the exclusion of Russia from the "West" is at the same
time a call for support and assistance on the part of the Western nations.*
— HENRY L. ROBERTS 1964: 361

Since 1992 one of the starting points of discourse on enlargement of
the EU and also of NATO has been the need to privilege a region
now referred to as Central Europe. The term "Central Europe" has
not only become firmly entrenched as a term, but it has also con-
tributed to propelling the states that ostensibly make it up to the
forefront of the queue of EU applicant states. In its present incarnation, the discourse on Central Europe dates back to the 1950s, when
intellectuals like Czesław Miłosz reopened the question of whether
there existed a supranational identity in this area and, if so, who belonged to it (Swiderski 1988). Drawing on the region-building approach set out in Chapter 4, this chapter will demonstrate how, from
humble beginnings, Central Europe took the shape of a Cold War
appeal, issued above the heads of the local politicians, by Czech,
Hungarian, and Polish dissident intellectuals, to Western civil society. Later on, Western intellectuals took up the bugle call. With the
local Communist politicians gone and the former dissidents installed

in their still-warm seats, the discourse on Central Europe became part of the armory of official foreign policy. From there it went on to become part of the overall European discourse on the expansion of the EU and NATO. By demonstrating how this came about, this chapter also demonstrates how the European representations of Russia discussed in Chapter 3 made it possible for Central European intellectuals and politicians to play off these representations of Russia in order to forge a self that owed much of its political success to being compatible with the Europewide representations of Russia.

It is often maintained that Central Europe is a project radically different from national projects in the region, since it unites where national projects divide. This, however, is not necessarily so. Since nation-building and region-building projects are both instances of identity politics, they will necessarily have a unifying as well as a divisive aspect. The all-important question, rather, is *how* differentiation is produced. This is an empirical question, which this chapter takes to be its main focus of inquiry.

CULTURE AND GEOPOLITICS

The participants in the discourse on Central Europe seldom present their project as a region-building one. Rather, they most often set out to describe a readily observable reality, in which certain peoples inhabiting certain lands happen to share certain cultural traits. Who these people are, which lands should be included, and which cultural traits are involved are all intensely debated issues. The two first "Variations" of novelist Danilo Kiš's "Variations on the Theme of Central Europe" give us a taste of the issues involved:

> With no precise borders, with no Center or rather with several centers, "Central Europe" looks today more and more like the dragon of Alca in the second book of Anatol France's *Penguin Island* to which the Symbolist movement was compared: no one who claimed to have seen it could say what it looked like. To speak today about Central Europe as a homogeneous geopolitical and cultural phenomenon entails risks. Even if we might agree with Jacques Morin's affirmation that Europe is "a concept without borders," the facts oblige us to remove from this concept the part of the European continent, with the exception of Austria, that under the name of *Mittel-Europa* organically belonged to it. As for Bruno Bauer's thesis, also cited by Morin, that Europe is a "community of destinies," *Gemeinschaft,* I am afraid

that since Yalta and Helsinki we can speak of this only in the past tense, or the pluperfect. (Kiš 1987: 1)

In a more specific vein, but echoing Kiš's "geopolitical and cultural" criteria for delineating the region, Timothy Garton Ash defines "East Central Europe" as

> Czechoslovakia, Hungary, Poland, and the GDR. Since the terms "Eastern" and "Central" Europe are so variously used, it is perhaps worth justifying this further distinction. The term East Central Europe combines the criteria of post-1945 Eastern Europe and pre-1914 Central Europe. By post-1945 Eastern Europe one means the formally independent member states of the Warsaw pact, apart from the Soviet Union. The term Central Europe is, of course, more problematic, but for the period before 1914 it may be taken to mean those countries that, while subsumed in one of the three great multinational empires (Austro-Hungarian, Prussian-German, or Russian), nonetheless preserved major elements of Western traditions: for example, Western Christianity, the rule of law, some separation of powers, a measure of constitutional government, and something that could be called civil society. The western Ukraine and the Baltic states are thus excluded by the first criterion, while Bulgaria is excluded by the second. Romania is a borderline case. (Ash [1986b] 1989b: 250, note 10)

The discourse on Central Europe offers endless variations on the use and application of geopolitical and cultural criteria to delineate Central Europe. For example, Grzegory Gornicki writes of Europe in its entirety that

> the real centre of gravity of the continent is in Germany. The concept of *Mitteleuropa* is German, too, devised for specifically German interests and purposes. The Central Europe discussed in Warsaw, Prague, Budapest and Vienna is, nevertheless, something different. Its measuring rod is geopolitical and it embraces the countries "between Russia and Germany." (1991: 57)

He then goes on to point out that Poland is the only country that in a strictly spatial sense is situated between Russia and Germany. However, although this should be a bona fide argument for including Poland in Central Europe, Gornicki questions this by invoking the "geopolitical" criterion of *size*. Poland, he maintains, may simply be too big for Central Europe; witness the problems of cooperation during the interwar period. To this could be added the fact that only part of Poland was ever part of the Habsburg Empire, whose ghost Central Europe has been said to invoke (Ionescu 1985: 3; Matvejević 1989: 187; Kiš 1987: 2; Steger and Morell 1987). And what about the Jews, the Germans, the South Slavs, the Belorussians, the Sorbs, the Bosnians? Indeed, what about the Belgians—citizens of a buffer state if there ever was one? Belgium was indeed included in the *Mitteleuropa* project for a protectionist economic zone drawn up by Friedrich List ([1841] 1904) with inspiration from Fichte ([1800] 1979), and it is included in more recent writings on Central Europe (see, for example, Mutton 1961: vii).

The fact that the inclusion of the Belgians in this list seems unwarranted shows up the limits of this manner of discourse. The whole focus on geopolitical and cultural criteria restricts the discourse to one about the content and borders of Central Europe, as if the animal actually existed in one or more spatial dimension. However, the Cheshire Cat–like appearence and disappearence of the discourse about a region in this area over the last two hundred years should be a pointed reminder that the Central European project is first and foremost a political one. The central fact is that attempts to reconstitute the region were renewed in the 1980s. The central questions are not only *how* this was done but *why*, and why the discourse took off just then, when it had failed to do so at other occasions during the postwar era. It was all well and good to maintain, in 1986, that "Central Europe is back"; indeed, this is the opening sentence of Ash's essay "Does Central Europe Exist?" ([1986a] 1989). However, the mere sizing up and gauging of the arguments put forward by the participants and the recurring reminders that there existed some kind of moral, attitudinal, cultural brotherhood "out there" told us little about the discourse as a *political* phenomenon, and that is the concern here.

READING CENTRAL EUROPEAN REGION BUILDING

In order to grasp the political significance of this discourse, one has to consider its framework. One should not ask "How can this region be defined?" or "How can we help the participants in this discourse define their object?" but "Why do certain people, at a certain point in history, within a certain political context, try to build a region?" The point of such a region-building approach is the same that in certain quarters is held to be the point of social analysis at large, namely, not to discover the roots of our identity but to commit itself to its dissipation. It does not seek to define our unique threshold of emergence, the homeland to which metaphysicians promise a return; it seeks to make visible all those discontinuities that cross us. (Foucault 1977a: 156)

At some points this becomes abundantly clear. For example, when Gornicki described *Mitteleuropa,* quoted above, as having been devised "for specifically German interests and purposes" and then went on to maintain that "the Central Europe discussed in Warsaw, Prague, Budapest and Vienna is, nevertheless, something different," he was of course right inasmuch as the two signs are different. His implicit claim that the one is more "real" than the other, however, surely cannot be defended. *"Mitteleuropa"* and "Central Europe" are merely shorthand for conglomerates of loosely similar imagined communities, whose proponents try to convince as many other people as possible to imagine them as hard as they themselves do. Peter Glotz may be accused of a lack of understatement when he urged his fellow Germans to "use the concept of Mitteleuropa as an instrument in a second phase of détente policy" (quoted in Ash 1990: 6). Nevertheless, he can hardly be accused of pushing his social democratic policies unfairly, since this pushing *is* what politics, that is, identity politics, is all about.

These facts are certainly not lost on the more self-reflecting participants (although the level of explicit self-reflection is overall suspiciously low). To George Schöpflin, "the emergence of the Central Europe debate and the slow, halting (re)construction of a Central European identity" are significant exactly as political phenomena:

Not only does this identity offer a way out of Soviet-type homogenization in emphasizing the European qualities of the local cultures, including above all those of pluralism and democracy, but by offering individuals a second, higher tier of identity, it can help them to escape the threat of reductionism encapsulated in political nationalism. By the same token, despite all the major and minor variations that differentiate Central Europe from the West, the central Europe project is potentially a viable way of re-Europeanizing the area, of recovering some of the values, ideals, aspirations, solutions and practices that were eliminated by Soviet-type systems. (Schöpflin 1989: 27)[1]

Eric Hobsbawm remarks in *The Guardian* (London) that what he chooses to call *Mitteleuropa* "belongs to politics rather than to geography, to the realm of political programmes rather than to reality. . . . More often than not geography is the continuation of politics by other means" (11 October 1991).[2]

Different normative assessments of the project, whether it is a "Traum oder Trauma [a dream or a trauma]," make for different denotations (Burmeister, Boldt, and Mészáros 1988; Meyer 1955). Schöpflin marks his approval of the project by adopting the term "Central Europe" as it is used by most participants, whereas Hobsbawm distances himself from it by equating it with *Mitteleuropa*, which to most participants is the negation of what they are celebrating.[3]

Since region building can be seen as a kind of identity politics, in which participants try to forge an identity, it unavoidably involves accentuating similarities between self and other. Identification is as much about what one is not as about what one is. Group identity is not conceivable without an other from which the self can be differentiated. Danilo Kiš highlights the self-stereotyping involved in the Central European project when he writes that

> it seems to me that to think today of this vast, heterogeneous expanse with its many national cultures and languages as a uniform whole is largely the consequence of a certain simplification: it overlooks the differences and underlines the similarities. (A process the exact opposite of that followed by the nationalists who overlook similarities and underline differences). (Kiš 1987: 2).

However, Kiš's parenthetical comment is utterly misleading. Surely the Central European project is different from the various nationalist projects embraced by it in the sense that the line delineating the in-group encompasses more and is drawn differently. The differentiation from the others outside (and indeed inside—Communists, for example) those lines is, however, potentially of the exact same kind as that involved in any nationalist project. Surely, it is possible to follow Lord Acton and the federalist tradition and argue that an ethnically heterogeneous entity is morally superior to a homogeneous one. Kiš and Schöpflin both seem to be doing so by recommending the idea of, as it were, wrapping a Central European identity around the national ones. However, although this would ameliorate the nationalist idea of an internal ethnic other against which the in-group should differentiate itself, it would not do away with the problems involved in external differentiation.

The crucial factor is how this external differentiation between self and other is executed. What is the framework within which differentiation takes place? How is the other assessed morally? What is the proposed relationship between self and other?

The discourse is a geopolitical and cultural one. "Cultural" is a notoriously slippery word, inasmuch as it can cover concepts as different as the Polish nationalist idea of Poland as the "Christ of nations" and the modernized version of the myth of the "philosopher-king" resounding in Czech national discourse. Perhaps it is more fruitful to speak about the framework of differentiation as thoroughly modern: The grand theme that resounds in the discourse is that of human progress toward freedom. History, it is maintained, is propelling Western Europe toward an ever brighter future, and Central Europe has a legitimate place in its wake. This modernist view of history comes in two guises: Marxian, that is, the East European, Soviet-type view of history, and liberal, the Central European view of history. In other words, there are two "othefs" involved: Western Europe and the Soviet Union. The most thorough as well as the most often cited exposé of the spatial dimension of the framework within which differentiation occurs is to be found in the works of István Bibó and his student Jenő Szücz (1988).

The moral assessment of the discourse's two main "others" is a matter of no small controversy. Most participants would agree with Claudio Magris when he calls the Central European project "a metaphor of protest—against the Soviet rule over Eastern Europe and against the American way of life in Western Europe" (Magris et al. 1991: 18). However, the latter point is more often phrased as a moral rebuke to Western Europe, reproaching it for usurping the marker "Europe" and arguing that it cannot do so without losing a vital (or even "organic") ingredient of itself. This theme was sounded by Milan Kundera as early as 1980:

> As a concept of cultural history, Eastern Europe is Russia, with its quite specific history anchored in the Byzantine world. Bohemia, Poland, Hungary, just like Austria, have never been part of Eastern Europe. From the very beginning they have taken part in the great adventure of Western civilization, with its Gothic, its Renaissance, its Reformation—a movement which has its cradle precisely in this region. It was here, in Central Europe, that modern culture found its greatest impulse: psychoanalysis, structuralism, dodecaphony, Bartók's

music, Kafka's and Musil's new esthetics of the novel. The postwar annexation of Central Europe (or at least its major part) by Russian civilization caused Western culture to lose its vital center of gravity. (Quoted in Matejka 1990: 131)

This was also the thrust of the original title of Kundera's successful region-building essay "A Kidnapped West."[4] Kidnapping is not to be condoned, and especially not when it is conducted against part of the in-group, the "West." That it was the West to whom the essay was addressed and that it was not intended for perusal in that Central Europe of which it was ostensibly a discussion is borne out by Kundera's later insistence that the essay falls into that part of his production that he disowns because it was tailormade for Western consumption.[5]

This marking of Western Europe as being, as it were, outside of itself as long as Central Europe remained in the custody of the Soviet Union also reveals the very positive moral assessment of "the European idea." Indeed, most traits ascribed to Central Europe can be found in the rhetorical armory of European federalists. Moreover, the positive assessment also extends to Western Europe, warts and all. In order to highlight the broad significance of the discourse under scrutiny, one could reproduce two Hungarian contributions to the international security discourse:

> The countries of West Europe have been the "core" of the world system as the most advanced and powerful countries of the world. They almost always dominated their neighbours to the East which by the twentieth century were generally very small and, at most, semi-developed countries. Furthermore, these small countries (although many of them were packed into the Habsburg empire for several centuries) suffered from the pressures of Western modernised and industrialised states on one side and the Eastern empires (Russian and Ottoman) on the other. They have been swinging through history between long waves of Westernisation and Easternisation. After the last five decades of Easternisation, there appears once more to be a fundamental turn in the other direction and so their Westernisation begins again. (Ágh 1991: 84–85)

Again,

> For Hungary, the notion of "European identity" expresses an awareness of Europe as the "common cultural homeland," of the fact that

Europe is, despite its political division, a single cultural whole, with a diversity of links that even the Cold War years could not wholly dissever. (Kiss 1989: 145)

The controversy is not so much about the Western European other, which is perceived ambiguously as both self and other at the same time, but about the other to the east. It is not a matter of different moral assessments of the Soviet Union as a *political* entity, which is seen almost universally as morally inferior to Central Europe. It is, rather, about whether the other is simply confined in time to the Soviet political system, or whether the other is "eternal Russia." Moreover, it is about whether Russia is wholly other, or whether there is the same kind of ambiguity between self and other in the case of Central Europe and Russia as there is between Central Europe and the West.

In his essay, Kundera was very clear that the other was not simply the Soviet Union but eternal Russia: "Russia is not just as one more European power but as a singular civilization, an *other* civilization. . . . totalitarian Russian civilization is the radical negation of the modern West" (Kundera 1984: 36). For this he was reproached by, among others, Milan Šimečka (1989). Kundera's framework and moral assessment of the Soviet Union as a political entity should by now be familiar: "Doesn't the tragedy of Central Europe derive precisely from being next-door neighbours of the Soviet Union in whose brotherly embrace we gasp for breath?" Unlike Kundera, Šimečka insists on differentiating between the Soviet Union and Russia: Russia was and is culturally amorphous. Moreover, he points out the "other in self" character of the Soviet presence in Central Europe: "It was not Russia which ushered in the beginning of the end of the Central European tradition. It was Hitler" (Šimečka 1989: 158). Kundera's article, he goes on, attributes

a demonic power to the Russians. We are not too distant from the events, however, to forget that it was not the Russians who put paid to Czech culture which seemed to be evolving so promisingly to us in the 1960s. It was our lot: Central Europeans born and bred. (1989: 159)

Furthermore, Šimečka sees a "cultural duality present in almost all central European traditions," and here he seems to include Russia. The fact that Šimečka gives mainly tactical reasons for these views does not, of course, change them as insertions into the discourse.

Moreover, in a conversation with Eva Kantůrková, he repeated that "we shouldn't always concentrate on the fact that the whole of our past of Europe was placed under Soviet influence. The main thing is that our own history had made us ripe for what then happened."[6] This position elicits a very interesting response from Kantůrková, who sees his inclusion of Russia as an "act of magnanimity," and maintains that

> because of our subjugation to Sovietism, Milan Kundera has written us off as no longer belonging to the world of the living. Essentially, he drew his conclusion from the thesis that what counts is who is Master. My feeling, on the contrary, is that our particular Master has served to revive a will to be European which has been expressed in the most diverse ways.[7]

Šimečka's assignment of Russia to Europe can be seen as an "act of magnanimity" only as long as it is a rarity for a non-Russian participant to do so. The second observation to be made is that Kantůrková shows up the use made in the discourse of the Soviet Union as an other that is held to be definitely not Western and compared to which the Central European claim to Westernness can therefore be bolstered.[8]

Šimečka's position also provoked an interesting response from Mihály Vajda. Before he had read either Kundera or Šimečka's pieces, Vajda had already proposed that "Russia seems to have resolved the long-standing disputes of the Russian intelligentsia. Russia is not part of Europe. . . . Of the two major Russian traditions—a European consciousness imbued with inferiority complexes and a sense of world-saving mission based on the purity and superiority of the Russian soul—the latter seems to have gained the upper hand" (Vajda [1985] 1988a; Vajda 1988b: 76, note 17, a piece in German, claims that he wrote independently of Kundera, a claim that is curiously absent from Vajda 1989, which is an English translation of 1988b). His answer to Šimečka elaborates on this position.

Šimečka had taken his cue from the Russian Lev Kopolev's appeal to Kundera not to exclude Russia from Europe. "I do not deny that there are and were many 'European' Russians," Vajda writes. "But as long as their fate is the holocaust, imprisonment, banishment, exile, or, at best humiliation and neglect," he continues, "not even one of the finest of them can convince me that the culture or civilisation of that country as a whole is a European one." In concluding this first part of his argument, he quotes Kundera as having said about Russia that "I don't know if it is worse than ours, but I do know it is different" (Vajda 1989: 168). Vajda takes this to mean that Kundera sees Russia as outside the purview of moral judgment, and he asks rhetorically: "Is Kundera, indeed, anti-Russian? Reading, and re-reading his very elegant essay I could not find a trace of this alleged anti-Russian attitude" (Vajda 1989: 169).

Why, Vajda once again asks rhetorically, cannot Šimečka and others accept that Russia is not European? His answer is worth quoting at some length:

> The answer lies, in my view, in the false universalistic claims of European rationalism which cannot accept that the free individual (and, as a consequence, a free society) is not an inalienable feature of human beings, but *a chosen value.* . . . Just because freedom is a universal value *for us,* we contradict this main value if we judge and condemn all those who have chosen other values. Every civilization has the right to be an *other* without being conceived by us as less human, or inferior. . . . for centuries and until recent times it remained an open question which path Russia would take: a European one, or another. . . . the choice to become non-European was finally made only in the last decades. . . . Russians are incapable of tolerating another civilization, an other form of life. (1989: 170, 173)

Where the "Central European nations" are concerned, however, "there is no place for any kind of moral doubt" (171); they are bona fide Europeans. Having dispensed with these shafts, Vajda rounds off by taking issue with what he sees as the main thrust of Šimečka's piece: "Please, do not annoy the beast on our borders." This allegedly pandering attitude to the men-animals to the east is something with which Vajda will have nothing to do: "I have been trained neither as an animal tamer, nor as a politician." Truth should come first, and politics second, Vajda concludes (175).

Vajda's piece is extraordinary for two reasons. The first and less interesting is its lack of logical consistency. On the one hand, Vajda holds that the "universalistic claims of European rationalism" are false and that one cannot say whether a given civilization is worse or better than another, and he insists that "every civilization has the right to be an *other* without being conceived by us as less human, or inferior." On the other hand, he holds that Russian civilization makes up "an other form of life," states that he is no "animal tamer" who can handle the Russian "beast," and draws attention to Russian practices of "holocaust, imprisonment, banishment, exile." On the one hand, Russia is partially European, and "we" (that is, the Europeans) should therefore "confess that we want to defend all those who have chosen our civilization as against their own" (171), to add yet another quote. One of those who should be defended because he is really "one of us" is Lev Kopolev, "one of the finest of them" (that is, the Russians). According to what standard can Kopolev be "one of the finest of them" when universalistic measures cannot be used? How can one take a page like the holocaust out of the book of European historical experience and apply it to that Russian "other form of life" if values are not transferable between the two spheres? How can Russia be "an *other* [civilization]" and at the same time be held to have been partially European for centuries and still contain "Russian Europeans"? György Lukács's apprentice leaves those questions pending, and since my main concern is the discourse as such and not one of its many participants, so shall I.

The other and main reason why Vajda's position is of concern here is for its very concrete moral assessment of Russia. The text's claim to abstain from moral assessment of Russia notwithstanding, the forging of an opposite other that takes place in it is quite striking. The wording, a civilization that is "an *other*," "an other form of life," could hardly be more explicit. The spatial differentiation between Russia on the one hand and Europe on the other is also hard and fast: Ukraine is Europe, Russia is not. Where Central Europe is concerned, "there is no place for any kind of moral doubt" as to their Europeanness.[9] However, if that is the case, then why do Vajda and a number of the other participants in the discourse insist on it so doggedly?

Šimečka and Vajda's contributions are also interesting in explicitly suggesting what kinds of relationships Central Europe should maintain with its others. Much closer relations are desired to Western Europe not only by these two participants, but all around; however, there are disagreements as to what degree West European economic and political models should be copied. Where Russia is concerned, however, the quotations already produced should testify to the diversity of positions held.

1989 AND AFTER

The events of 1989 were greeted enthusiastically by those who used the term "Central Europe." In January 1990 Václav Havel once again gave voice to the idea that Central Europe was a cultural concept in search of realization when he told the Polish Sejm that

> there is before us the real historic chance to fill with something meaningful the great political vacuum that appeared in Central Europe after the break-up of the Habsburg Empire. We have the chance to transfer Central Europe from a phenomenon that has so far been historical and spiritual into a political phenomenon. We have the chance to take a string of European countries that until recently were colonised by the Soviets and that today are attempting the kind of friendship with the nations of the Soviet Union which would be founded on equal rights, and transform them into a definite special body, which would approach Western Europe not as a poor dissident or a helpless, searching amnestied prisoner, but as someone who has something to offer. (Havel 1990: 56–57)

Moreover, in keeping with the cultural image presented by most Czech, Hungarian, Polish, Slovene, and Croatian participants in the discourse, there was indeed a clear-cut difference in electional behavior between these lands and other parts of the Eastern Europe of the bygone postwar era. In these lands, noncommunists were voted into power, and a change of regime was initiated. Elsewhere, sections of the old ruling groups were voted in, and regime changes occurred much more slowly or failed to emerge altogether.

However, the Central European cooperation that should, in Havel's words, transform Central Europe "into a political phenomenon"—that is, transpose it from the realm of identity politics to institutional politics—also occurred only slowly. Two summit meetings between Czechoslovak, Hungarian, and Polish heads of state and concrete and repeated Polish and third-party initiatives notwithstanding, cooperation failed to emerge. Even where interests and strategies were perceived to dovetail, as in the case of policy vis-à-vis the EC (now the EU), cooperation among the three states did not emanate from the initiative of any one of them but had to be imposed by what was effectively the third party, the EC: "The competition among the three states to be the first to enter Europe is held in check by the Western political community's inclination to treat the new democracies of Central Europe as a unit" (Tökés 1991: 113; also see Neumann 1992).

The program of Havel the participant in the discourse on Central Europe was thwarted by, among others, Havel the president.

However, the Central European project continued to operate as a political project in the way it always had: as a moral appeal and reproach addressed to Western Europe. Indeed, this is yet again set out programmatically in the second half of Havel's contribution to the discourse, together with a new proposal for relations with that other external other, the crumbling Soviet Union. Thus it is only possible to follow Kristian Gerner halfway when he asserts that "the liberation from Pax Sovietica 1989–1990 revealed that there did not exist any 'Central Europe'" (Gerner 1991: 146). Rather, contrary to what was often implied by participants such as Václav Havel, it appeared that although the Central European project did not result in institutionalized contacts between societies or states in the area, it could still be used politically vis-à-vis Western Europe and Russia. In terms of identity politics, the project's reality was actually unimpaired by the failure of political structures to emerge; its dynamics had from its very inception lain on the interface between the imagined region and its external others, Russia and Western Europe, and continued to do so.

The attempted external differentiation of Central Europe from and at the expense of Russia continued as before. Perhaps the most concrete and striking example so far of this practice emerged in October 1991 as a self-proclaimed appeal to the EC's Maastricht summit: "Though we should do our utmost to promote democracy in the new Russia," the article starts out:

> This should not obscure the more immediate and manageable challenge of Central Europe. . . . Historically and culturally, Poland, Hungary, and Czechoslovakia belong to Europe. A Europe that contains Crete but not Bohemia, Lisbon but not Warsaw, is historical nonsense. . . . Yet where would this leave the rest of post-Communist Europe? . . . It makes plain, practical sense to start with those that are nearest and work out to those that are farthest. Poland, Hungary, and Czechoslovakia are nearest not only geographically, historically, and culturally, but also in the progress they have already made on the road to democracy, the rule of law, and a market economy. (Ash, Mertes, and Moïsi 1991: 19)

So, the three coauthors conclude: "Following the suggestion crig-
inally made by the Czechoslovak foreign minister, Jiří Dienstbier,
some of the aid to Russia and the other post-Soviet republics should
be made in a form which both enables and obliges them to spend it
in East Central Europe" (19). Moreover, all other EC concerns should
be streamlined to the overriding priority of catering to "Poland,
Hungary and Czechoslovakia": "All proposals for a deepening of the
present EC of twelve through closer integration must be workable by
extension in a community of twenty" (19). Finally, it is asserted that
all good things may come together. Privileging Central Europe will
turn it into "a magnet for Southeast Europe, for the Baltic states, the
Ukraine, and, yes, for the European parts of Russia," and the broad-
ening of the community that privileging Central Europe entails will
"help in deepening" the EC's integration process as well. All this is
presented by *The New York Review of Books* under the title "Let
the East Europeans In!," which yet again stresses that what is good
for Central Europe is good for Eastern Europe as well as for Europe.

Far from being a peripheral part of the discourse, these formula-
tions quickly found their way into the rhetorical armory of people
like the Polish minister of foreign affairs, Krzysztof Skubiszewski,
and the Czech president Václav Havel. In a *tour d'horizon* of the
state of European relations in the spring of 1992, Skubiszewski held
that

> as a consequence of the end of the Cold War, contemporary security
> relations on our continent have lost their simplicity and may be geo-
> graphically described as concentric circles progressing from the stable
> nucleus of the countries of the European Communities, the Western
> European Union and the North Atlantic Alliance, to the most unsta-
> ble peripheries. . . . The most important danger zone in Europe, with
> regard to possible military conflicts, is the area extending between
> Russia, the Ukraine, and Rumania. . . . The association of the three
> countries [Czechoslovakia, Hungary, and Poland] with the European
> Community is relevant to their security but also to that of the West:
> the hard core of Europe will comprise a bigger territory. (Skubiszewski
> 1992)

Havel, furthermore, could argue that it was very important to expand the EU and NATO since it would "give nations like ours a signal that the West truly wants us and sees us as part of the Western
sphere of civilisation" (quoted in *The Economist*, 30 March 1996).

With statements such as these, the discourse on Central Europe has come full circle. It started as an appeal by Czech, Hungarian, and Polish dissident intellectuals, issued above the heads of the local politicians, to Western civil society. Eventually, Western intellectuals responded to the plea. Finally, with the local Communist politicians gone and the former dissidents in command of the state apparatus, the arguments of the discourse on Central European have become part of the armory of official foreign policy (Neuhold 1991).

CONCLUSION

The discourse on Central Europe was and is a moral appeal to Western Europe on behalf of an imagined community born of frustration with the Soviet hegemony in Eastern Europe. As with any other sign, attempts to grasp the meaning of Central Europe without taking context into consideration are futile. Only when that hegemony started to slip was this discourse able to make the impact on the wider foreign policy debates in the West that was desired by the participants. The breakthrough here was the publication of Milan Kundera's essay in 1983 and 1984. After the regime changes in Czechoslovakia, Hungary, and Poland in 1989, the existence of the discourse provided a framework within which appeals to Western Europe for assistance and inclusion could be made. The case for seeing the project in this light is strengthened not only by the failure of institutional region building to emerge after 1989 but even more by the continued use being made of it in texts tailor-made for the European foreign policy discourse. There is a parallel to be drawn here to the three Baltic states, whose cooperation with each other is almost nonexistent but which have nevertheless been able to pass themselves off as an entity vis-à-vis third parties by availing themselves of Russia as an other (Jæger 1997).

The way Central Europe is constituted entails certain costs. Appeals to Western Europe on behalf of Central Europe are consistently made by differentiating Central Europe from a barbarous East—first and foremost Russia. As already mentioned, external differentiation is an unavoidable part of identity politics; the problem resides not in this act itself but in the qualities that most participants seemingly see a need to ascribe to Russia in order to keep them, as it were, squarely beyond the pale. The central point here is not whether or not there exist cultural differences between, say, Czechs, Hungarians, and Poles on the one hand and Russians on the other. The surprising thing would indeed be if this was *not* the case. Neither is the point whether Central Europe's search for identity vis-à-vis Western Europe is structurally similar to Russia's, whether they share a cultural debate between, as it were, Westernizers and nationalists. Csaba Kiss suggests that the Central European project is just one more bout of local Westernizing when he asserts that

> many motives may be hidden behind the discovery or rediscovery of Central Europe. During the construction of modern national culture, roughly over two centuries, writers and thinkers have been confronted by the dilemma—sometimes sooner, sometimes later—that they must expound the backwardness of their own national cultures and the differences from that European culture from which they sprang. This was how two possible solutions were formulated and these have, in effect, recurred repeatedly since the Enlightenment and romanticism. One of these is the imitation of Europe and the other is total differentiation from it. (1989: 135)[10]

To Kiss, the solution to this dilemma is exactly to seek self in other, to recognize the ambiguity of identification discussed above. He concludes by quoting Witold Gombrowicz, who said about his Polish in-group that "we cannot become a truly European nation until we separate ourselves from Europe, since our Europeanness does not mean submergence, but that we become a part of it, indeed a very particular part not interchangeable with any other" (1989: 136).

This is indeed very important, and it brings us to the central point, which is whether not only cultural but also ethnic differences should be processed politically and thus made politically relevant, which is what the Central European project often seems to do. Indeed, the language and the thrust of the Central European project are similar to those of nationalism inasmuch as they try to turn the political field into a battleground between groups that are not only culturally but more often than not also ethnically defined.

It must be reiterated that identity politics, of which the Central European project is an example, invariably involves external differentiation vis-à-vis out-groups. For that matter, the project under scrutiny here is a small-scale replay of discourses such as the ones scrutinized in chapters 2 and 3, by which "Europe" was forged by an identification process differentiating it from others such as "the

Turk" and "Russia." It is instructive to recall that some of the most avid participants in *that* debate were Russians, who bolstered Russia's claim to Europeanness by contrasting it to the barbarous Turk. As already mentioned, in 1916 the leading Russian liberal Pavel Milyukov argued that Russia was better equipped than the Sublime Porte to take care of the Straits and Constantinople because

> the presence of the Turk in Europe is incidental. They remain at the end of five hundred years as much strangers as they were at the beginning. European ideals and words, like "nation," "government," "law," "sovereign," "subject," do not apply to them. (Quoted in Riha 1969)

In the discourse that has been discussed in this chapter, it has been the Russians' turn to play the role of non-European other for groups out to boost their own Europeanness. Once again, differentiation is often made in terms stating moral superiority (civilized versus barbarian, democratic versus authoritarian) or even in terms of ethnicity. Far from being unavoidable, the choice to avail oneself of such devices to produce otherness is open to each and every *zoon politikon* (political being) dabbling in identity politics. There are a number of reasons why the West should support the forging of a multiparty system and a market economy in the Czech Republic, Hungary, Poland, and so on. The idea that they are somehow "more European" than their immediate neighbors to the east is, however, not among them.

6

Making Nations: Russia

Without railways and mechanical industries Russia cannot be considered secure in her boundaries. Her influence in Europe will fall to a level inconsistent with her international power and her historical significance.
— RUSSIAN MINISTER OF FINANCE MIKHAIL K. REUTERN
CA. 1861 TO TSAR ALEXANDER II, QUOTED IN LAUE 1963: 9

Whereas Chapters 2 and 3 dealt with the uses of the other in the collective identity formation of Europe and Chapters 4 and 5 with the uses of the other in the making of (other) regions, this chapter and the next will deal with the uses of the other in national identity formation. Recall that Chapter 4 took as its starting point the fact that a number of key theoretical insights have evolved out of the study of nation building and then proceeded to discuss the making of regions in terms of those insights. Since the making of regions has not been previously discussed in terms of how the self/other nexus has played itself out in those particular cases of identity formation, this was considered to be worthwhile. In the case of nations, however, knowledge production over the last fifteen years or so has already demonstrated a number of times over how this works theoretically and empirically. Nonetheless, for three reasons I offer this section on nation building.

First, since the main aim of the book is to demonstrate how the self/ other nexus is operative on *all* levels of European identity formation, leaving out the level that is arguably still the one to be activated in most contexts and that is still inscribed with most political significance would not be a very good idea. If that sounds a bit on the formalistic side, there is a second and crucially substantial reason: One theme that runs straight through this book is the one advertised in the subtitle, namely, how important "the East" has been to the forging of European identities. Turkey and Russia have both been othered as "the East." The representation of Northern Europe after the Cold War involved making "Northern" countries out of the formerly "Eastern" countries of Estonia, Latvia, and Lithuania. The constitution of Central Europe involved not only the representation of an "Eastern" past as a period of captivity but also as a series of attempts to inscribe relative geographical Eastern position (for example, Austria versus Slovenia, Slovenia versus Croatia, Croatia versus Serbia, Serbia versus Bosnia) with the specific political meaning of being "Eastern" in the sense of being Balkanishly backward. One possible response to this is to point out, as was done in Chapters 1 and 3, that relegating an "East" to a "West's" allegedly linear past is in and of itself an act of identity formation in terms of othering. But another response is to demonstrate how those communities that are othered in this way actually deal with it in their own discursive work. This is what I will try to do in this chapter and in Chapter 7 by concentrating on the Russian and Bashkir nations.

The Russian nation has been routinely represented as "Eastern" for almost two hundred years (see Chapter 3). The Bashkir nation, on the other hand, has tended not to be represented at all, probably exactly because it has been considered, automatically, as it were, so "Eastern" as to be socially and politically wholly *out of* Europe, although geographically it is located to the west of the Ural mountains, which have been represented as the eastern boundary of Europe. There is much talk in identity scholarship about speaking to the silences of identity formation, foregrounding what has been occluded, giving a voice to marginals. Including a discussion of Bashkortostan in a book on the representations of European identities is one way to do this.

In addition to these formalistic and substantial reasons, there is a methodological one, namely, that the inclusion of two more cases allows for the application of two more perspectives. In Chapter 2, on "the Turk," the focus was on othering as a way of drawing "Europe" together by a process of externalization in space. In Chapter 3, on

Russia, the focus was on othering as marginalization both in space and in time, as Russia was represented as hovering on the border of European identity along its spatial as well as its chronological dimension. In Chapter 4, on Northern Europe, the focus was on how state selves try to nest themselves geographically and politically as the pivot inside another regional self. In Chapter 5, on Central Europe, the focus was on how one self was forged as an attempt to tear itself off from another and othered self (the East, the Warsaw Pact nations) in order to join another (the West, NATO, the EU). In this chapter, the focus will be on how othering of Europe is *the* way in which two representations of the Russian self fight for political hegemony.[1] In the next chapter, on Bashkortostan, I will broach the issue of how representations of Russians and Tatars play on their being *both* internal and external to the Bashkir self. Different processes of identity formation are dominated by different kinds of othering, and so they call for different readings.

WESTERNIZERS VERSUS NATIONALISTS

Some in the West are trying to "exclude" the Soviet Union from Europe. Now and then, as if inadvertently, they equate "Europe" with "Western Europe." Such ploys, however, cannot change the geographic and historical realities. Russia's trade, cultural and political links with other European nations and states have deep roots in history. We are Europeans. Old Russia was united with Europe by Christianity. . . . The history of Russia is an organic part of the great European history. (Gorbachev [1987] 1988: 190)

Thus said Mikhail Gorbachev, the last secretary general of the Communist Party of the Soviet Union, in the English-language version of his book *Perestroika*. As the attempts at reforming (or rebuilding, *perestroit'*) the Soviet model exposed the vacuum at the center of the state, discourse on how what was increasingly referred to as Russia should relate to contemporary Western models—in this case pluralism and capitalism—was coming to the fore of general politics. It was as part and parcel of this process that Gorbachev raised the issue of the Soviet Union's relations with Europe and thereby also sanctioned the legitimacy of debate, a legitimacy that had been at best tenuous in the preceding sixty-odd years of Soviet discourse.

The slogan of the "common European home," which had its roots in diplomatic practice of the early 1980s, now also became central to Russian political discourse.[2] The new representations of Russian identity involved a political struggle over how to differentiate Russia from Europe (as well as from Asia; see Hauner 1990). The Russian discourse on Europe pitted Westernizers against nationalists.

The Westernizers emerged both out of the dissident movement and out of Gorbachev's entourage of reform Communists. The framework within which they represented Europe was a cultural one, stressing liberal ideas about the integrity of the individual and the limited rights of the state vis-à-vis the citizen as the common political goals of all mankind. Russia was not held to be morally superior to Europe; rather, it was seen as its potential equal and in certain respects its contemporary inferior.

For example, the writer Chingiz Aitmatov told the Congress of People's Deputies meeting in the summer of 1989 that the Soviet Union should learn a new brand of socialism from "the flourishing law-governed societies of Sweden, Austria, Finland, Norway, the Netherlands, Spain and finally, Canada across the ocean" (quoted in Brown 1990: 60). Furthermore, during the same session of the congress, Gorbachev's top adviser Aleksandr Yakovlev told a TV journalist that

> parliaments in other countries have existed for decades and they have entirely different traditions. They have written many volumes about procedural matters there. We do not have that. Of course, we must learn professionalism in the economy and politics; above all we must learn democratic professionalism. We must learn democracy, tolerance of others' opinions and thoughts. (Quoted in Brown 1990: 60)

Some Westernizers presented the need to copy and learn from the West as a question of qualifying for membership in "civilization." By formulating the preferred relationship between Russia and Europe in this way, they stressed the Russian people's *own* lack of "European democratic consciousness" as perhaps the main problem. "Civilized democracy never had a good chance in this country," Lilia Shevtsova wrote at the end of 1990 (Shevtsova 1990: 4; Heinz Timmermann quotes a TV comment by the senior official Nikolay Shishlin from 21 July 1990 to the effect that Germany could help with the "incorporation of the Soviet Union into world civilization"; 1992: 58). And in the summer of 1991, in an article with the striking title "I Am a Russophobe," Andrey Novikov wrote:

Today the question of "Westernisation" [*vesternizatsiya*] is very much in vogue. How can we become Europe in the course of three Five-Year Plans? How can we cover the path which the West spent five hundred years traversing? The answer is self-evident—not in any way. If a liberal consciousness were not able to take hold during the nineteenth century, how should it be able to do so today? And if there is no liberal consciousness, can there be any liberal democratic institutions? And if so, what are the chances for a "return" to the lap of world civilisation envisioned by those who talk about "new thinking" and the end of the Cold War? Will it take the shape of crowds of wild barbarians who, passports in hand, storm the Soviet-Polish border in order to sell off ikons for a hundred dollars? No, the wall will not be built by us, but by the West, a wall similar to the one which the Americans have built along their border with Mexico. (Novikov 1991: 14)[3]

These writers set themselves up as belonging to an endangered species of Russian Europeans, somehow managing to keep the torch of civilization aflame in the presumedly non-European twilight of Russian mass culture. Novikov takes this so far as to propose a relationship between Russia and Europe based on isolation, not because he wants it so but because he holds the non-European parts of Russia to deserve it and sees the need for Europe to impose it.

Other Westernizers, presumably seeing the political dead end into which this proposed relationship with Europe would lead, insisted on trying to replace the fading Soviet Russian identity with something else and came up with the catchword "Eurasia." For example, when asked whether Russians had not always "felt themselves to be of Europe, yet disputed everything European" in the summer of 1989, the historian Mikhail Gefter answered that "we are not a country. We are a *country of countries* . . . a centaur by birth" and therefore dependent on the development of all mankind (Gefter 1989).

Although Gefter is also a Westernizer, his argument is very different from Novikov's, inasmuch as Gefter seeks not to dissolve Russia in Europe but to carve out a new identity for it in lieu of the identity furnished by the old Soviet Communist one. Gefter was hardly alone in this undertaking. For example, the idea of a "Eurasian" destiny for the Soviet Union had already cropped up in the writings of foreign affairs specialists. In groping for a strategic goal for Soviet foreign policy to take the place of the defunct ideological struggle with the West, Vladimir Lukin came up with the formation of a European community from the Atlantic to the Urals in the West and the joining of the Pacific integration process in the east. If that succeeds, we would become the bridge between the two "Europes." It may sound utopian today, but this variant seems highly realistic to me, perhaps the only way our country may enter the upcoming Millennium in a worthy manner. (Bovin and Lukin 1989: 67)

Westernizers proposed relationships with Europe based on two different variants of partnership. Whereas some advocated a "return to civilization"—that is, a relationship with Europe in which Russia was seen as an apprentice with no clear additional and specific identity—others saw this as a poor way of rallying mass Russian support behind a program based on individual rights, market economy, and political pluralism. Instead, they evolved the catchword "Eurasia" as a proposed group identity for a Russian-based state that would secure the electorate's support for closer relations with Europe.

Although Westernizers dominated Russian discourse on Europe in the late 1980s and into the 1990s, a nationalist opposition was also clearly present. In December 1987, *Pamyat'* had already put out an appeal that maintained that

in our country these days the activity of *enemies* is becoming more obvious. They are entrenching themselves in all the sections of the PARTY, the leading force of the USSR. Dark elements in it, speculating with Party slogans and Party phraseology, are in practice carrying out a struggle with *the indigenous population of the country, and annihilating the national face of the peoples.* They are reanimating Trotskyism, in order to discredit socialism, in order to sow chaos in the State, in order to open the sluices of Western capital and Western ideology. (Quoted in Duncan 1989: 597)

In a Russian discursive setting, the internal other juxtaposed to "the indigenous population" here is immediately recognizable as "the Jews." Spelling out the anti-Semitism inherent in this appeal, Igor' Shafarevich published a piece that attacked Russia's detractors, those who see it as an Asiatic despotism populated by slaves and who hold that the Communist state was only the last in a number of totalitarian regimes. Shafarevich pointed out that the idea of the totalitarian state was developed in the West, by Hobbes and others, and not in Russia. So was the idea of socialism, which "had no roots at all in Russian tradition before the nineteenth century. Russia did not have any authors of More's and Campanella's type" (Shafarevich 1989: 171).[4] As a matter of fact, he concluded, the characteristics singled out by Russia's detractors as "typically Russian" were not Russian at all; to the contrary, they were "the price for Russia's joining the sphere of the new Western culture" (Shafarevich 1989: 171). To Shafarevich, Westernism is at the root of all Russia's problems:

> To all appearances, the Western multiparty system is an outgoing social order. It is possible to appraise its role in history highly: It came with a guarantee for civil war, for defense from government terror (but not from "Red brigades") and for an increase in material wellbeing (and the threat of economic crisis). (Shafarevich 1989: 171)

Nevertheless, Russia's detractors want to impose this system on Russia, and they want to do it in the manner of an "OCCUPATION," Shafarevich writes. People like the TV journalist Nevzorov were even more explicit:

> There is no future for perestroika, because it is too much of a Western idea. But the West cannot suppress the Russian soul. That people is yet able to work miracles, such as the Great Patriotic War. Russians fight against the enemy, be they hungry and empty-handed. The existence of the Russian people is not appreciated by everybody. That is why we must protect the culture and the Orthodox church with tanks. Otherwise they will be suppressed. We need to save our beloved fatherland. We have to do away with the democrats. Otherwise they will rob Russia. (*Rahvalent* [Tallinn], 29 May 1991)

Elgiz Pozdnyakov complains that "the disease of 'Europeanism,' of 'Westernism,' came to Russia" with Peter the Great (Pozdnyakov 1991: 46).[5] Since then, he charges, a number of Russians have seen Russia through the eyes of an outsider and not of an insider. Either these "Westernizers" have held that Russia's destiny lay with European civilization, or they have not seen a destiny for it at all. In either case, they have been wrong. Russia's particular destiny is to maintain a strong state so that it can act as the holder of the balance between East and West, a task "vitally important both for Russia and the entire planet" (Pozdnyakov 1991: 46; one notes the contrast to the representations of Russia concurrently offered in the central European discourse discussed in Chapter 5). And Pozdnyakov goes on to write that

Russia cannot return to Europe because it never belonged to it. Russia cannot join it because it is part of another type of civilization, another cultural and religious type. . . . Any attempt to make us common with Western civilization and even to force us to join it undertaken in the past resulted in superficial borrowings, deceptive reforms, useless luxury and moral lapses. . . . in nature there does not exist such a thing as a "Common Civilization." The term in fact denotes the pretention of Western European civilization to the exclusive rights to universal significance. (Pozdnyakov 1991: 49, 54)

Other nationalists presented a rhetoric that was grounded not in the need for a strong state but in the need for spiritual regeneration. For example, in 1990 Aleksandr Solzhenitsyn published a long philippic against modernity: Russia should not expend its force on being a superpower but on attaining spiritual clarity; free elections and a multiparty system were harmful onslaughts against the organic Russian nation; Russia should concentrate on restructuring its own house rather than on any common European one (Solzhenitsyn 1990).

For Russian discourse on Europe, 1992 and 1993 were pivotal years. Given that so many aspects of the political were being represented so thoroughly, the stakes were very high, and given the radical incompatibility of the two representations of the European other, the question was how the relationship between these representations would play itself out. The two extreme (and for that reason rather unlikely) possibilities seemed to be either that a monological situation would arise in which one representation swallowed the other or that there would be a civil war. What ensued instead was a twofold dialogical development. First, the regrouping of communism as a political force took the shape of infusing the nationalist representation with a number of key ideas and institutional resources out of the former Communist regime. The Russian Communist Party took the idea of a "nationally comprehended, spiritually grounded statehood" as its starting point (Zyuganov 1994: 42). This re-presentation of Russia was set out in books by the party chairman Gennadiy Zyuganov, books whose very titles underlined this nationalist starting point: *Great Power* (Zyuganov 1994); *Russia—My Motherland: The Ideology of State Patriotism* (Zyuganov 1996). Other variants of the nationalist representation were pushed to the margins of political life. The others of this representation were not only a hostile "West" but also the very forces of cosmopolitanism and globalization that it was said to have set in train and to control.

Second, 1992 and 1993 saw the end of the standoff between the Westernizing and the nationalist representations as the political strength of the nationalist representation began to work on the Westernizing representation, stripping it of what came to be known as its "romantic" tendency to hold up "the West" as an entity to be unequivocally copied. Thus, although Westernizers sat on a number of key material and institutional resources, the Westernizing representation of Russia did not crowd out the nationalist one. Of course, the European discourse on Russia discussed in Chapter 2 is one factor that may help us understand why this did not come to be: Despite Gorbachev's discursive work, Russia was not recognized as a European country in a number of key social, political, and economic contexts.

One reason why Russian Westernizers were not able to carry the day in Russian discourse has to do with the fact that their efforts to be accepted as a "normal" European country in overall European discourse came to naught. This may indeed be so, but it does not show us why Westernizing representations changed as thoroughly as they did. In order to understand that, it is necessary to understand what happened in Russian discourse itself, how it was that the nationalist representation could maintain such a strong position in discourse despite a relative dearth of institutional and material capital. The reason, I will argue, has to do with the fact that the nationalist representation came complete with references back to an unbroken and proud national history, which had been propelled by, among other things, nationalist sentiments allegedly of the same kind as those that were the stuff of that nationalist representation that presented those historical references.

The nationalist representation was able to draw on the symbolic capital in its discursive work, which first forced the Westernizing representation into a dialogue and then transformed it to make it more compatible with the nationalist representation. Put another way, there was a stiffness in Russian discourse that the Westernizing representation could not break down, and so it happened that it was itself transformed instead. Since the nationalist represention drew its strength from the narratives it told about itself and its role in Russian history, one must look to those narratives and that history, and not only to the wider European discourse, in order to understand the shift in Russian discourse.

THE REFERENCES OF THE NATIONALIST REPRESENTATION OF RUSSIA

It would be a mistake to see the Russian debate about Europe that emerged in the 1980s and the 1990s as a unique response to post-Soviet challenges. On the contrary: The conflict between Westernizers and nationalists can be traced in the samizdat writings of the 1960s and 1970s as well as in writings of the tsarist period. For example, the most striking thing about Solzhenitsyn's piece from 1990 quoted above is, arguably, its almost verbatim repetition of the views set out in the samizdat articles collected in *From under the Rubble* ([1974] 1975). Of course, even if it had been the very same article, that would in and of itself not have meant that it would have been "the same" in other respects, since its discursive context would have been brand new. Nonetheless, there is a continuity here that should be highlighted, even at the risk of overly stressing how things stay the same instead of how they change.

Solzhenitsyn's samizdat articles attacked Westernizers, and particularly Andrey Sakharov, for parroting false Western ideas about freedom:

> The West has supped more than its fill of every kind of freedom, including intellectual freedom. And has this saved it? We see it today crawling on hands and knees, its will paralyzed, uneasy about the future, spiritually racked and dejected. Unlimited external freedom in itself is quite inadequate to save us. Intellectual freedom is a very desirable gift, but, like any sort of freedom, a gift of conditional, not intrinsic, worth, only a means by which we can attain another and higher goal. (Solzhenitsyn [1974] 1975: 18)

Solzhenitsyn wanted nothing to do with Andrey Sakharov's suggestion for introducing the multiparty system. "[A] society in which political parties are active never rises in the moral scale. . . . can we not, we wonder, rise above the two-party or multiparty parliamentary system? Are there no *extraparty* or strictly *nonparty* paths of national development?" Solzhenitsyn asks, and laments that the "almost perfect" Westernizing unanimity in circles outspokenly critical of Soviet power was

> an example of our traditional passive imitation of the West: Russia can only recapitulate, it is too great a strain to seek other paths. As

Sergei Bulgakov aptly remarked: "Westernism is spiritual surrender to superior cultural strength." (Solzhenitsyn [1974] 1975: 20)[6]

Whereas this article of Solzhenitsyn's took on the West and Russian Westernizers, another contribution printed in *From under the Rubble* drew the line against what Solzhenitsyn referred to as "National Bolsheviks." "The nation," Solzhenitsyn wrote, "is mystically welded together in a community of guilt, and its inescapable destiny is common repentance" ([1974] 1975: 113).

And in case one should have thought this to be an isolated instance of nationalistic mysticism, one could cite another contribution to the same anthology, which quotes from the Bible in support of the idea that God instituted nations:

> If the *nation* is a corporate personality endowed with its being by God, then it cannot be defined as a "historical community of people" or a "force of nature and history" (Vladimir Solovyov). The nation is a level in the hierarchy of the Christian cosmos, a part of God's immutable purpose. Nations are not created by a people's history. Rather, the nation's personality realizes itself through that history or, to put it another way, the people in their history fulfill God's design for them. (Borisov [1974] 1975: 210)

Solzhenitsyn, however, does insist that not just any nationalism is worthy of support. A harsh, cold current of opinion

> has become discernible of late. Stripped to essentials, but not distorted, it goes like this: the Russian people is the noblest in the world; its ancient and its modern history are alike unblemished; tsarism and Bolshevism are equally irreproachable; the nation neither erred nor sinned either before 1917 or after; we have suffered no loss of moral stature and therefore have no need of self-improvement; there are no nationality problems in relations with the border republics—Lenin's and Stalin's solution was ideal; communism is in fact unthinkable without patriotism; the prospects of Russia-USSR are brilliant; blood alone determines whether one is Russian or non-Russian. As far as things spiritual, all trends are admissible. Orthodoxy is not the least bit more Russian than Marxism, atheism, the scientific outlook, or, shall we say, Hinduism. God need not be written with a capital letter, but *Gosudarstvo,* [that is, the State] must be. Their general name for all this is "the Russian idea." (A more precise name for this trend would be "National Bolshevism.") (Solzhenitsyn [1974] 1975: 119–129).[7]

As witnessed by Solzhenitsyn's attack on the "national Bolsheviks," today's statist nationalists also had precedents in the 1960s. Yet this internal nationalist debate between spiritual and statist nationalists has a much longer history. Traces of it can be found in the Russian semiofficial life of the 1920s, and it was a fixture of the political debate in tsarist times. In the early postrevolutionary years, spiritual nationalism was represented by Nikolay Berdyayev—whose thinking now enjoys a far from incidental revival in Russia—and other former contributors to the volume that appeared in 1909 under the name of *Vekhi* and that instantly became a common point of reference for the debate (and which also has been republished recently). Statist nationalism was represented by, among others, the original Eurasianists, a coterie of Russian émigré intellectuals.

In a closely argued book published in 1920, *Europe and Humanity,* Prince Nikolay Sergeevich Trubetskoy delivered a blistering attack against the very idea that Russia and other non-European countries should look to Europe for political and economic models. Before the revolution, Trubetskoy writes, it had been almost "organically inadmissible" for most people, educated as they were in the European manner, to grasp the idea that Russia's involvement with Europe was a historical mistake (Trubetskoy 1920: iii–iv). Europe does not equal civilization; this is merely a "formula of chauvinistic cosmopolitanism" (2). Rather, Europe is "the product of the history of a specific ethnic group," and "the so-called European 'cosmopolitanism'" should "openly be called *common Romano-Germanic chauvinism"* (5, 6). If a people opts for a Europeanizing course, Trubetskoy argues, then it has to gear its entire development toward European models and to shear off all the discoveries that do not square with this concept. Since it cannot do all these things in one step, the Europeanized people will be torn to pieces by generational and social tensions. National unity will suffer. And to what end? No matter how hard it tries, some of its specific traits will remain, and it will, "from the European point of view, always look 'backward' [*otstaly*]" (64). The result is that "only the government and the ruling political circles" will retain a national outlook, while the rest of the people will be demoralized and self-loathing (65).

This state of affairs will be aggravated by the sporadic events of the backward people mustering its forces and making a dash to catch up, trying to take in its stride developments that the Romano-Germans may have undergone over a prolonged period of time.

> The result of such "evolution" by fits and starts is indeed horrific. Every leap is inevitably followed by a period of seeming (from the European point of view) stagnation [*zastoy*], during which the results of the leap must be made to dovetail with the backward elements of the culture. (Trubetskoy 1920: 67)

The inevitable result is a cycle of "progress" and "stagnation." "And so," Trubetskoy concludes, "the upshoot of Europeanization is so heavy and horrible that it cannot be considered a good, but a bad thing" (1920: 69–70).

The differences of opinion and emphasis between the spiritual and the statist nationalists in the 1920s echoed the debate between Nikolay Danilevsky and Vladimir Solov'ev in the 1880s. Danilevsky presented his views in another recently republished volume, *Russia and Europe,* which he sums up in the following manner:

> . Throughout the book we have presented the thought that Europe is not only foreign to us, it is indeed hostile. Europe's interests cannot be ours, but not only that: In most cases they will be in direct opposition to one another. That does not yet mean that we could or should break off all our dealings with Europe and cordon ourselves off from it by means of a Chinese Wall. That is not only impossible, but would actually have been positively harmful. Dealings will have to be close, yet they must not be intimate, hearty, as if between kindred. Where political relations are concerned, the only rule must be an eye for an eye, and a tooth for a tooth—tit for tat. Yet even if it is impossible to cut ourselves off from European affairs, it is yet fully possible, useful, and even obligatory to relate to them from our specific, Russian point of view. That must be our only criterion by which to judge: How is this or that happening, this or that thought, this or that important personality going to influence on our specific Russo-Slav goals? Are they going to hurt them or to benefit them? Happenings, thoughts, and personalities that are of no value we must treat with the utmost indifference, as if they took place or lived on the moon. . . . What stands in our way, however, we must fight in all ways possible, whatever the consequences for Europe itself, for humanity, for freedom, for civilization. (Danilevsky [1869] 1888: 480–481)

Solov'ev retorted that Danilevsky was mistaken in ascribing Europe's hostility to Russia in terms of the envy of a dying culture upon beholding its successor. Rather, Europe's hostility is to a large extent of Russia's own making, provoked by things like Danilevsky's book:

> Europe looks at us with hostility and fear because they understand that the Russian people are a dark and elementary power, whose spiritual and cultural preconditions are frightfully small but whose aspirations know no boundaries. In Europe nothing sounds louder than the clamor of our "nationalism," which wants to smash Turkey, smash Austria, rout Germany, and conquer Constantinople, and, when the time is right, even India. But when asked what we intend to give to humanity in exchange for what we are going to destroy, which spiritual and cultural values we will contribute to world history, then we will have to keep silent or mutter some meaningless phrases. (Solov'ev [1888/1891] n.d.: 137)

Russia, Solov'ev continues, should grasp that its relations with Europe are fraternal. Instead of railing against Europe, it should confess its sins and put its own house in order. Bearing in mind history's intention, it should brace itself for the path toward spiritual perfection. Indeed, since the early Russian nationalists adapted German romantic nationalist thinking to their own uses, there has existed a tension between those who have focused on the divine strength of the people and those who have focused on the strength of the state (Schelting 1948; Walicki 1975; this distinction may be even older; cf. Cherniavsky 1958). Thus for the revamped Russian Communists to splice together a representation of Russia with explicit references to both these traditions and to put it to good discursive work despite the aggressively nonspiritual history of the Communist movement itself is indeed no mean feat.

THE REFERENCES OF THE WESTERNIZING REPRESENTATION OF RUSSIA

Turning now to the precedents of today's Westernizing representation of Russia, one is immedediately confronted by the question of how to categorize Stalinism. From Bukharin and Trotsky onward, anti-Stalinist Communists have insisted that Stalin was certainly no Westernizer, that he was, rather, an Asian despot, a Ghengis Khan. Bukharin, for example, attacked Stalin's program of superindustrialization as a policy "in line with old Russia" and referred to it on a number of occasions as being "Asiatic." Stalin himself he privately referred to as a "Genghis Khan" (see Cohen 1974: 291). This representation is present in contemporary discourse: For example, Evgeniy Starikov (1989) argues that Stalin's Asiatic paternalistic model for society crowded out a European one based on a civil society.

The Stalinist representation of Soviet Russia and the Soviet Union, on the contrary, put itself forward not as "Asiatic" but as the epitome of European thinking. Yet there is a passage in that basic statement of Stalinism—the Short Course of the Party History—that explicitly states that Stalinists saw themselves as fighting Westernization inside the party. According to the Short Course, the Bolsheviks tried

> to create a *new* Party, to create a party of a *new type,* different from the usual Social-Democratic parties of the West, one that was free of opportunist elements and capable of leading the proletariat in a struggle for power. In fighting the Bolsheviks, the Mensheviks of all shades, from Axelrod and Martynov to Martov and Trotsky, invariably used weapons borrowed from the arsenal of the West-European Social-Democrats. They wanted in Russia a party similar, let us say, to the German or French Social-Democratic Party. They fought the Bolsheviks just because they sensed something new in them, something unusual and different from the Social-Democrats of the West. (Short Course [1938] 1948: 171–172)

E. H. Carr has indeed suggested that the Bolsheviks were the "Westernizers" of the party and the Mensheviks the "Slavophiles" and has drawn up the following catalogue of examples of how this internal social democratic debate proceeded:

> A Menshevik journal which appeared spasmodically in Petersburg after the 1905 revolution dubbed the Bolsheviks "Slavophilizing Marxists." Plekhanov, as well as the Mensheviks, denounced Lenin's attitude towards the peasantry as non-Marxist and a revival of *narodnik* heresies. In 1912 the Menshevik Axelrod was preaching the need "to Europeanize, i.e. radically to change, the character of Russian social-democracy, . . . and to organize it on the same principles on which the party structure of European social-democracy rests"; and Lenin angrily retorted that "the notorious 'Europeanization' about which Dan and Martov and Trotsky and Levitsky and all the liquidators talk in season and out of season" was "one of the chief points of their opportunism.". . . Axelrod was like "a naked savage who puts on a top-hat and imagines himself for that reason European." (Carr 1958: 18)

At the very least, one may note that Communists of all shades invested large amounts of energy in presenting themselves as the true Europeans—indeed, in Stalin's case as the only true European. One also notes that Carr, in his catalogue of examples, refers to the late-nineteenth-century debates between Marxists and populists as paradigmatic of the debate between Westernizers and nationalists. This is not entirely accurate, inasmuch as many populists, too, saw themselves as Westernizers in at least some senses of that word. For example, someone like Nikolay Ivanovich Sieber, a Marxian scholar, could hardly have been clearer in his insistence on the necessity of Russian industrialization for individualization when he wrote in the early 1870s that "we shall have no sense in this country until the Russian *muzhik* is cooked up in the factory boiler" (quoted in Kindersley 1962: 9). But the populists, who still preferred their peasants raw, also argued in terms of European precedents. Writing in 1869, for example, Petr Tkachev maintained that individualism, as espoused by Russian Westernizers, was first formulated by Protagoras and the Sophists, the ideologists of the urban, bourgeois civilization of Athens. Against this individualism, he set the anti-individualism of the Sparta celebrated by Plato (Walicki 1969: 41–45). Tkachev's thought is interesting not least for its choice of comparative case. At this time, ancient Greece was almost universally held to be not only the "proto-European" phase of history but also the cradle of European civilization as such. By choosing this particular point of reference for a comparison of Russia and Europe, Tkachev is able to present his own program as a European one.

The debates between Marxists and populists were preceded by the debates between liberals and "Russian socialists." There exists an almost paradigmatic exchange of letters between Aleksandr Turgenev and Aleksandr Herzen from the early 1860s, in which Herzen held that Russia was a cousin of Europe, who had taken little part in the family chronicle but whose "rustic charms were fresher and more commendable than her cousins'" (Hertzen 1968: 1747). Turgenev begged to differ: "Russia is not a maltreated and bonded Venus of Milo, she is a girl just like her older sisters—only a little broader in the beam" ([1862] 1963: 64–65). Indeed, both Herzen and Turgenev saw the relationship in terms of family metaphors, but when it came to degree of kinship and to relative desirability, they parted ways.

And in 1847–1848, Vasily Botkin and Herzen were already discussing the pros and cons of industrialization and the need for an indigenous working class in Russia. Botkin, a tea merchant, prayed that "God give Russia a bourgeoisie!," only to be met with a counterprayer from Herzen: "God save Russia from the bourgeoisie!" Vissarion Belinskiy, in a letter to Botkin, declared that "so far all I have seen is that countries without a middle class are doomed to eternal insignificance" (quoted in Gerschenkron 1962: 164–166).

THE SYSTEM OF NATION STATES AND THE RUSSIAN DEBATE

Since Anderson published his book on nations as imagined communities in 1983, his idea that nationalism is a modular phenomenon has been attacked, first and foremost from a postcolonial standpoint by Chatterjee (1986, 1993), but also on ontological grounds. For example, Christoph Ullock has charged that

> Anderson's relegation of the South to being "perpetual consumers of modernity" is part of a much deeper problem. By insisting upon the "ineradicable" nature of past "modular" forms, Anderson unwittingly takes *all* of the *imagination* out of *all* imagined communities! The shift from a focus on the *productivist* and *aesthetic* underpinnings of the emergence of the national form to an emphasis on the *circulationist* character of the national idea paradoxically results in the removal of *all* imagination from the process of imagining community. At an even more elementary level, while Anderson's initial discussion of nationalism involves a metaphysics of *becoming,* sensitive to the effect of spatio-temporal change upon the imagination, by the end of the book, his discussion of nationalism is imbued with a metaphysics of *being,* incapable of recognising how recent changes in communication and transportation technology might impact upon processes central to imagining community. (1996: 427–428)

What is at stake in this debate is clearly how to place the relative emphasis: on the way in which each nationalism builds on its predecessors or on the specificity of each particular nationalist representation. A similar tension makes itself felt in a parallel debate inside the discipline of international relations about what impact the system of states has on the making of regime type and foreign policy of each particular state (Gourevitch 1978; Bull and Watson 1984). On the one hand, the system of states does exert systemic pressure on each of its parts to adapt a variant of the regime type which is hegemonic at any given point in time. On the other hand, each regime, however strongly molded by this structural pressure, must also be grasped in its specificity.

Without privileging being over becoming or universalism over particularism, structural pressure must be acknowledged as being one of the strongest and perhaps *the* strongest context that may help us understand the continued centrality of Westernizing and nationalist representations in Russian discourse on Europe as well as in overall political discourse. Russia's political and economic backwardness—that is, its low degree of functional differentiation of power between politics and economy and between state and society—meant that the country continuously had to face up to the challenge posed by the more highly differentiated and therefore more efficient political and economic order in Western Europe. I avoid the word "advanced" here because of its normative and modernist connotations: In its starkest and most immediate form, the challenge had to do with Russia's need to maintain an economic base that would make it possible to sustain its military power and thus its role in international politics. Inasmuch as Western European models were seen to be more efficient in performing this than was the Russian model, it meant that Russia's strength relative to that of Western European states was in decline, and so the question of what was to be done was deemed to be unavoidable. At the risk of repeating myself, let me once again point out that this is not an argument in favor of the determinism of material, structural factors. It is simply to point out what some of the important contexts of Russian discourse were and to suggest that structural pressure made it easier—but of course in no way inevitable—for some rather than other representations to dominate discourse.

The pressure for each state to borrow from the most effective models available in order to maintain the economic base for its political and military power was and is acknowledged by some participants in Russian discourse and was and is contested by others. If interstate competition is one context that may further our understanding of *why* Russian discourse on what to do about allegedly more efficient Western models is a recurrent theme in Russian history since the formation of an international system, it also suggests the broad layout of options available to the participants. On the one hand, one would expect one group of participants to find the solution to the problem in copying Western models, and one would expect them to carry on an internal debate about which variant of the Western models should be copied, and to what extent and at which speed it should happen. On the other hand, one would expect to find a group of participants who would either deny that the Western models are indeed more economically effective or would maintain that economic effectiveness should take a back seat to other concerns. Cursory glances at the way Europe was discussed in Turkey and Japan during the last century makes one question whether the Russian debate is as unique as certain Russianists would have it. (Again, that is of course not in any way to contest that it is as unique and as specific as any other set of discourses.)

Of course, the possibility always exists that some new idea may emerge and spawn a specifically Russian model for economic and political organization. It would indeed be an overstatement to conclude that the inventory of the debate is given once and for all. Yet it is difficult to see how this can happen in any other way than by negating some aspect of thinking that could be referred to as "European." Russians are too caught up in Russia's relationship with Europe to think entirely independently of it. When a contemporary, antimodern romantic nationalist like Solzhenitsyn rails against Western civilization, he does so within what is routinely referred to as *European* literary genres like the novel and the essay, availing himself of European-developed media like the newspaper, in a public debate upheld by conventions developed in Europe, in a formal language with its roots in Europe, availing himself of linguistic archaisms in the way pioneered by German romantic nationalists. In short, it is the fate of Russians and others who have wanted to forge a non-European, antihegemonic debate that such debates cannot fail to maintain ties to Europe, if only inversely so, because of the very fact that they are patterned as attempts to negate the European debate and therefore remain defined by it. Globalization means that "Europe" may be nowhere, in the sense that it no longer has one and the same center in all contexts, but it also means that "Europe" is everywhere, in the sense that discursive elements like the ones mentioned are permeating more and more discourses.

Faced with the more efficient European economic model of industrialization, Slavophiles insisted that Europe had paid for it by its spiritual death, whereas Russians had retained a richer spiritual life and were therefore morally superior to Europe. Furthermore, Slavophiles hinted that the greater European military prowess was due to the inherently violent nature of European states, whereas the Russian state was peace loving by comparison and therefore less effective militarily but more advanced morally. In today's debate, an argument similar to the former is made by Solzhenitsyn, who, following early Slavophiles and also Dostoyevsky, argues that the Russians are morally superior to people of the West because they have grown spiritually as they have been faced with hardships, such as communism, which have not been present in the West. Shafarevich writes that the West may be richer than Russia, but that it is more prone to economic crises. The two former associates are still at one in insisting that Western economic models are morally inferior to their own vision of a Russian, old-style village economy because the latter is ecologically sounder.

Westernizers cannot shift the ground of moral comparison in the same way: For them, the moral assessment rests to the degree to which the *Rechtsstaat* (civil society and individual rights) are in place and are functioning. Consequently, Europe tends to be regarded either as morally superior to Russia (if viewed synchronically) or as morally equal to Russia (if viewed diachronically). After all, according to Westernizers Russia is steadily developing along the same lines as Europe developed and is therefore of a kind with it, practically as well as morally. The proposed relationship with Europe is, therefore, also of a kind: Russia should be an apprentice copying European models.

One classical formulation of this was made by Turgenev when he held that Russia was a girl no different from her older European sisters, "only a little broader in the beam." Setting aside the anthropomorphization (which was hardly out of character for a nineteenth-century constitutionalist but which would, if only for its organic connotations, certainly have been out of character for a contemporary Westernizer) this insistence that Russia is just like Europe, only a little slower and a little less subtle, is quintessential to the Westernizing representation and during 1992 was the assessment made by the Russian state under Yeltsin's leadership.

Yet in contemporary Russian discourse there exist different ideas about which European models should be copied and also about how fast it is possible to proceed. The former issue shall not be addressed here. Where the latter is concerned, the view has gained ground among Westernizers that Russia is not a little but a lot slower and less subtle than is Europe, indeed so much that it may never catch up. This old worry—first aired by people like Pyotr Chaadayev back in the 1830s—appears in the contemporary writings of Shevtsova and Novikov. The problem for someone like Novikov is that his analysis of Russia's relationship with Europe—that the latter would be vindicated in building a wall to keep out backward Russia—is hardly going to cut much ice for the Westernizing representation in Russian discourse on Europe. It is not an idea that heeds Herzen's warning to the Westernizers of his day that they would have no broad public appeal before they addressed the questions raised by the Slavophiles, or Dostoyevsky's weighty dictum that "in Europe we were hangers-on and slaves, whereas we shall go to Asia as masters. In Europe we were Asiatics, whereas in Asia we, too, are European. Our civilizing mission in Asia will bribe our spirit and drive us thither" (Dostoyevsky [1876–1881] 1954: 1048). However, one reading of Gefter's, Lukin's and other Westernist texts, which argue that Russia should not copy European models at a breakneck pace and that discourse on Europe should be complemented by a discourse on Asia, would be that Dostoyevsky's cynical dictum is indeed being heeded.

The most acute participants in Russian discourse on Europe have acknowledged the structural pressure exerted by Western hegemony and predicated their thinking on it. Herzen, Trotsky, and Trubetskoy all acknowledged that Russia could not simply disregard Europe's dynamism. Yet, characteristically, except for communism, Russian discourse has not been able to produce any models that could take the place of the European ones. Although Trubetskoy drew up an impressive and depressing catalogue of the disadvantages for Russia of copying European models—the humiliation conferred on it by Europe's arrogance in usurping the term "human civilization" for itself, the handicap incurred by competing on somebody else's home turf, the imbalance caused by Russia's recurrent breakneck attempts at catching up and the concurrent split between a Westernized elite and the nation's people—his alternatives to further copying were far from equally impressive.

Westernizing representation has shed its romantic aspect. "The West" is no longer unequivocally something to be copied, and there is no longer an expectation that Russia can become part of Europe as the result of one or two five-year plans. As so many aspects of Russian politics and society have changed since the advent of perestroika, however, the centrality of Russian discourse on Europe has only increased. It is this lingering centrality, and not the uniqueness of each of the constellations of representations of which it is made up, that I wanted to highlight in this reading of Russia in terms of its European other.

7

Making Nations: Bashkortostan

[Chairman of the Supreme Soviet Murtaz Gubaydullovich Rakhimov] has an immense throng of new settlers (78 percent of the whole population, mainly Russians and Tatars) behind him who will not hesitate to slaughter half of the defenseless Bashkirs (as has already happened in 1918–1920) at any least attempt of secession. Tatars have invariably been rendering the most active assistance to Russian colonizers to exploit Bashkir people and bloodily suppress their national movement.
—From the additional remarks to an appeal to the United Nations by the Committee of the *Bashkir People's Center Ural*, September 1991, quoted in Guboglo 1992b: 231

In Chapter 3, I showed how Peter the Great launched a successful campaign to re-present the eastern geographical border of Europe from the Don River to the Ural Mountains. Two nations whose lands thus became part of Europe are the Bashkirs and the Tatars. Bashkortostan is one of six republics of the Russian federation. It occupies an area of 3,214,000 square kilometers in the middle Volga and South Ural, usually labeled the Volga-Ural region.[1] Tatarstan, which neighbors Bashkortostan to the west, is another. Of the 4 million people living in Bashkortostan at the time of the last census in 1989, 22 percent identified themselves ethnically as Bashkir, 39 percent as Russian, and 28 percent as Tatar.

The particularly intense social and political changes in the Russian state formation in the early 1920s and again in the early 1990s made an intensification of Bashkir nation building possible. This chapter discusses how a Bashkir self has been formed in contradistinction to Russian and Tatar others. Representations of "Russia" have focused both on Russia as a state formation inside which the Bashkir nation resides and on Russia as the Russian nation, self-ascribed members of which have made up a substantial part of the population of what used to be called Bashkiria and has since October 1990 been known as Bashkortostan. Similarly, representations of Tatarstan have focused both on the political entity of Tatarstan, which in a number of contexts is the most resourceful of the six Volga-Ural republics, and on the Tatar nation, some members of which represent Bashkirs as a variant of their own ethnic group. The two major others of the Bashkir self are, in other words, both represented as both internal and as external.

Whereas in discussing the making of the Russian nation much contextual knowledge could be taken for granted, I should not think it would offend anyone to suggest that this is not the case where Bashkortostan is concerned. This chapter will therefore present Bashkortostan region building in terms of a systematic catalogue of first the diachronic and then the synchronic diacritica by means of which the ethnic boundaries between the Bashkir self and its others have been marked.

DIACHRONICS: AL-BASHKIRD, BASHKIRIA, BASHKORTOSTAN

Bashkir nation building started around the turn of the century and culminated in the years 1917–1920, only to intensify once again during recent years. In writing a history for the Bashkirs, nation builders have reaped a rich harvest from various written sources. Etymologically, the ethnonym has been traced to the writings by foreign visitors to the Volga-Ural region as early as the tenth century A.D. Describing his voyage to Volga in 922, Ibn-Fadlan mentioned in his diary that after having crossed the Kandjaly River he reached a "Turkic land of al-Bashkird." A century and a half later Makhmud al-Kashgari enumerated Bashkirs, along with Kirgiz and Tatars, among twenty main Turkic peoples. He also made a comment that the dialects of Kirgiz, Oguz, and others are "pure Turkic ones," the Bashkir tongue being "very close to them" (Yuldashbaev 1972: 5–6).

Another source on the early history of Bashkirs are the *shejere*, or genealogies, which existed originally as a genre of oral folk literature and were written down in the sixteenth century or later. *Shejere* are attached to particular subgroupings of Bashkirs, often described as tribes by Soviet ethnographers. It is on the basis of data extracted from these genealogies that a number of Bashkir scholars of the beginning of the twentieth century could publish articles on the problem of the formation of a Bashkir nation. To be divided in a number of minor subgroupings ("tribes") was a specific feature of all nomadic and seminomadic peoples of Turkic origin. As far as the Bashkir are concerned, the several dozen subgroupings have habitually been classified into four large territorial groups, namely the southeastern, northeastern, southwestern, and northwestern.

However, at the beginning of the century there also existed a strong Tatar Pan-Turkic movement in the area; the movement took on added significance following the flux in political regime around 1917. For example, a May 1917 article in the Tatar Orenburg newspaper *Vakyt* held that "to call Bashkirs and Tatars different names taking into account merely differences in dialects, which as a matter of fact prove very insignificant, is to divide one and the same nation in an arbitrary way" (quoted in Yuldashbaev 1972: 27).

The 1972 book from which this quotation is taken went on to argue that all the specific features of the Bashkirs, if any, are not sufficient to treat them as a separate ethnic group. This representation echoed the one made by members of a Tatar delegation that met Lenin in March 1920. They maintained that essentially there are no important distinctions between Bashkirs and Tatars, the only remarkable one being a slight difference in spoken language. The problem had erupted into the open during the third Bashkir *kurultai*, or assembly, in December 1917. An ultimatum to the *kurultai* was issued by the Muslim Committee, stating that Bashkir representatives tried to keep Tatars and other Muslims from fulfilling the mandate given them by their electors and that they were "outraging the sacred traditions of other nationalities" (Guboglo 1992: vol. 2, 85). Bashkirs fought back, the *kurultai* actually issuing a warning to the effect that "if stubborn Tatars should attack the leaders of the Bashkir movements, Bashkirs will not be responsible for the security of Tatars in Bashkiria" (quoted in Guboglo 1992: vol. 2, 87).

SYNCHRONICS: INSTITUTIONALIZING THE BASHKIR NATION

Rail Gumerovich Kuzeev (1987) has done a historical survey of Bashkir "tribes" by tracing the habitat of forty-seven subgroupings at the beginning of the century. Due to the constraints of Soviet discourse, similar inquiries into what he refers to as the "tribal" structure of the Bashkirs during Soviet times could not be undertaken. There are hints, however, that the "tribal" structure remained of importance. Indeed, increased visibility of a "tribal" structure is part and parcel of contemporary Bashkir nation building. To give but a few examples, a number of articles dealing at length with the history and culture of particular Bashkir "tribes," such as Yurmata, Usergan, Kipchak, and Tabin, was published in Ufa in the early 1990s. Most of these articles have been about Yurmata. Besides publications on the history of this "tribe," an independent social organization called the Yurmata Union was established in 1990 in the city of Ishimbay, in the center of Yurmata "tribal" territory (*Bashkortostan* [Ufa] 23 July 1991; interview with Yurmata Union Vice President M. Ismagilov in *Bashkortostan* [Ufa] 28 January 1990). When a festival specifically of Yurmata folk art was organized in August 1992, newspapers hailed it as an event of great historical significance. Proposals for convening a special congress of the Yurmata have also been circulated (*Bashkortostan* [Ufa] 14 August 1992).

Being associated with particular areas, Bashkir "tribes" claim the right to be the exclusive managers of land within their primordial territories and attempt to deny that right to other groupings inside Bashkortostan. All non-Bashkir residents in "tribal" areas are considered to be newcomers and aliens, that is, others who do not have the same attachment to the land as do local Bashkirs. In trying to tone down this aspect of ethnic conflict, Bashkir nationalist leaders maintain that under current circumstances, the idea of private ownership of land is irrelevant for Bashkortostan. This stand sets the economic program of Bashkir nation builders somewhat apart from those of other national movements throughout the former Soviet Union. Instead of being oriented toward privatization and a market economy, it aims to prop up the idea of "tribal" ownership of land.

Whereas self-ascribed Russians make up 39 percent and self-ascribed Tatars 28 percent of the population of Bashkortostan, the percentage of people calling themselves Bashkir is only 22 percent. In Bashkortostan, the percentage of Russians started to increase in the 1970s, but this trend was subsequently reversed. The percentage of Bashkirs has also gone down but this is because of an increase not in the number of Russians but, rather, in the number of Tatars. At

the time of the last census, in 1989, Bashkiria and most other republics did not have a titular nation that constituted an absolute, or
even a relative, majority (although in Tatarstan the Tatars were a
relative majority; Tatars 48 percent, Russians 43 percent).

The status of Bashkirs as only the third largest ethnic group in
Bashkortostan (as well as the existence of neighboring Tatarstan and
of a Tatar nation of nearly 7 million people spread all over the former Soviet Union to which the Tatars in Bashkortostan can look for
ethnopolitical inspiration and support) make Bashkir nation building a delicate undertaking. The project of contemporary Bashkir nation builders, like that of their precursors in the wake of the events of
1917, is in danger of being undermined by a competing Tatar nation-
building project. Whereas in the years leading up to 1917 Tatars
drew on Pan-Turkish representations, that has not happened now to
the same extent. Pan-Tatarism, however, is still around.

In Bashkiria, the first ethnic group to avail itself of the new possibilities for mobilization opened up by the weakening of the Soviet
Union were ethnic Tatars. In March 1988 Tatar activists in Ufa decided to establish a club of Tatar culture, which was later transformed into the Tatar Social Center (TSC), now the leading organization of ethnic Tatars in Bashkortostan. A program and a charter
were passed by the first *kurultai* of the TSC in January 1989. In April
1992, the first issue of the TSC Tatar newspaper *Jidegen* emerged
(Guboglo 1992: vol. 2, 140–141). Another, more radical social organization of Tatars in Bashkortostan is the Tatar Democratic Party
"Idel-Ural" (TDP), registered in March 1991. *Idel-Ural* is also the
name of the Tatar newspaper published by the group, and it signals
the organization's program: The term was coined by the Tatar socialist Galimjan Sharaf at the beginning of the century. "Idel" was the
ancient Turkic name for the Volga. Thus "Idel-Ural" is a Pan-Turkic
way of denoting the Volga-Ural region, and it was in widespread use
in the period 1917–1920 (Zenkovsky 1960: 157 et passim). The
third and most radical main Tatar association in Bashkortostan is
the Union of Tatar Youth Asatlik (UTY), which published its program in November 1990 (Guboglo 1992: vol. 2, 193–196).

The Bashkir ethnopolitical organizations were founded, among
other reasons, as a countermove to the formation of Tatar organizations. The principal one is the Bashkir People's Center Ural (BPC),
which held its first congress in December 1989. An immediate and

central demand was to make Bashkiria a constituent union republic of the U.S.S.R., and not just an autonomous republic within the Russian Socialist Federative Soviet Republic. In electing such a platform, it placed itself squarely in the mainstream of latter-day Soviet ethnopolitics, in which union republics began to demand independence whereas other territorial units went for a one-notch upgrading. Marat Kulsharipov, a leading local historian, became the BPC's second president. His professional status was also typical of the situation in the Soviet Union at large, where historians everywhere busied themselves with producing knowledge from "national" viewpoints (Deletant and Hanak 1988).

In February 1991 the BPC was able to hold a second congress; each of its delegates was elected by 1,500 persons of Bashkir nationality. As a result nearly 1,200 representatives of various regions of Bashkortostan participated along with Bashkir delegates from other republics of the U.S.S.R.—not a small feat of ethnopolitical mobilization. In order to underline historical continuity with earlier Bashkir ethnopolitical movements, the second BPC congress decided to pass itself off as the fifth All-Union Congress of Bashkirs, three Bashkir *kurultai* held in 1917 serving as the first in the alleged series. The BPC shared the ambition of calling an assembly with a direct mandate from the nation and with the pretense of continuing the struggle of interwar national movements with the Estonian and Latvian congresses organized previously in these Soviet republics.

Among the resolutions adopted by the all-nation second BPC congress was one called "Bashkortostan, Republic of Peace," which stated that

> for centuries have the Bashkir people struggled for their native land and for Russia. Nevertheless their taking part in fighting was not aimed at annexation of alien lands or robbery of other peoples. The Bashkir nation has never been an aggressor or oppressor of any nation. From time immemorial Bashkirs loved peace and stood firmly for it. In today's unstable situation when many peoples are under threat of military aggression and bloodshed [the document was drafted after bloody events in Tbilisi, Baku, and Vilna], Bashkirs reaffirm their will for peace and are ready to contribute for peacekeeping and security. It is starting from the principles that (1) the congress acting on behalf of Bashkir people declares Bashkortostan a nuclear free zone [and a zone free of chemical weapons]; (2) the congress informs

all the persons in charge of the U.S.S.R. and Russian federation Ministries of Defense and Internal Affairs that all problems in the republic must be solved by peaceful means only. The use of weapon against citizens must be prohibited. (Quoted in Guboglo 1992: vol. 2, 185)

The sixth (or third) congress of the BPC was convened in Ufa in December 1991 and managed to cover a broad menu of topics. It also adopted a declaration establishing a new social association named the Bashkir People's Assembly, which was set up to achieve the BPC goal of building a democratic independent Bashkortostan, in accordance with the right of the Bashkir nation to self-determination. This declaration increased the temperature of Bashkortostan politics by several degrees (Guboglo 1992: vol. 2, 157–168).

The declaration of the BPC demanding an independent Bashkortostan did not come as a bolt from the blue but, rather, had been precipitated by statements from an organization close to the BPC, the Bashkir People's Party (BPP), founded in November 1990. A third political body close to the BPC is the Bashkir Youth Union (BYU), which was formed in May 1990. Its first congress in November 1990 declared that

> apart from interests of classes, sex and age groups, religious and corporative organizations, there are also interests of nations, which proved to be of greater importance on the contemporary developmental stage of the Soviet society. That is why in all aspects of our activities, be they ecological problems, economics, social or juridical ones, we are according priority to the interests of our own nation. (Quoted from Guboglo 1992: vol. 2, 185)

Thus the structures of Tatar and Bashkir national mobilization mirror each other, with each having a broad-based center, a somewhat more radical supporting organization, and an attached radical youth organization. Of course, the two movements feed off one another. To give but one example, here is a not unrepresentative characterization of one Tatar leader, the chair of the TSC Farid Yaushev, by the chair of the BYU Renat Baimov:

> His intention is to turn Bashkiria into a Muslim republic, himself becoming head of the state. He is an insane lad who is not all there. He is suffering from megalomania and it is our responsibility to send him to a mental hospital. Or, better, to evict him from Bashkortostan. (Quoted in Guboglo 1992: vol. 2, 184)

DIACRITICA

The reproduction of Bashkir and Tatar ethnicity in Bashkortostan involves the maintenance of and creation of new social boundaries. At least six such loci stand out. They are religion, what is referred to as "tribal" activity, language, demographics, territory, and historical figures.

Religion

Religion is not represented in a way that foregrounds the dichotomies of Christian/Muslim or Sunni/Shi'ite. Tatar activists stress the fact that Sunni Islam is a shared religion and that this should have political consequences. This representation of religion casts it as a Pan-Turkic political factor, which makes it resonate inside the shared pool of historical knowledge of the first decade of the century. Resonances are, however, different for the two ethnic groups, and hence religion becomes a diacriticon. The Bashkir activist's accusation that his opposite number intends to "turn Bashkiria into a Muslim republic," points in the opposite direction from Pan-Turkism: It stresses that religion should not be relevant for the political regime in Bashkortostan. The locus is, then, directly linked to the question of state agency by the activists themselves. Interestingly, Bashkir representations of Tatar religious life highlight the *backward-looking* character of representations that make religion central to politics. It may be noted that the contemporary European representations of "the Turk" discussed in Chapter 2, as well as of Muslims generally, tend to foreground "Muslim fundamentalists" as one key "Eastern" feature. This relegation of religion as a political category to the past is something that one may also find in Bashkir othering of Tatars.

"Tribal" Activity

The material indicates that this is a straight binary opposition: From an ideal Bashkir point of view, one is either a member of a "tribe" *and therefore* Bashkir, or one is not a member and therefore a non-Bashkir. Tatars seem not to have claimed such membership. Once again, this locus is bound up with state agency, inasmuch as it is activated not only in a folkloristic guise but also in the debate about ownership of land. The debate about how, and to what extent, to phase out state ownership of land has brought to the fore the possibility of private ownership, but it has also been animated by the idea that Bashkir "tribes" may acquire the status of juridical persons.

Language

Bashkir "tribal" activity is a locus that invigorates Bashkir nation building by reinforcing a boundary between Bashkirs and Tatars that is seemingly treated all around as relatively clear-cut. Language, on the other hand, is a locus where the boundary is far less clear. Indeed, the spectrum of dialects or vernaculars of spoken Bashkir merges with that of spoken Tatar to the extent that during the 1989 census, no less than 216,000 Bashkirs—that is, about one-fourth of the entire number in the republic—gave Tatar as their native language. The vast majority of these are residents of the western and northwestern regions of the republic, those bordering Tatarstan.

Contemporary Bashkir nation builders play down or even deny this state of affairs, declaring themselves against "any attempts to divide the Bashkir nation into two parts, contrasting those in the western and northwestern area to the bulk of the Bashkir population" (Guboglo 1992: vol. 2, 124; *Yashlek* [Ufa] 8 December 1990). The linguistic situation is given special attention, with articles treating "the western dialect" denying its close ties to Tatar (for example, Mirdzanova 1989: 15). Thus, despite the almost unanimous tendency of residents of western Bashkortostan to consider their language Tatar, modern Bashkir linguists are treating it as a separate dialect of the Bashkir language.

Tatar experts are inclined to reach a different conclusion. For example, in reviewing a book by Daria Ramazanova on the formation of Tatar dialects in northwestern Bashkiria, Kh.Fattah reproaches Bashkir philologists for their attempts to divorce their speculative views from the objective historical context. Any endeavor to treat Tatars of western Bashkortostan as "northwestern Bashkirs" and their colloquial language as a "northwestern Bashkir dialect" is considered void. The book by Ramazanova, the reviewer concludes, is "a convincing answer to these ungrounded claims" (Kuzeev 1987: 29).

There also exists scholarship that tries to resist the ethnopoliticization of the locus of language by attempting to demonstrate how mixed and transitional the spoken dialect of western and northwestern Bashkirs is (Garipov 1988). The dialects in question show characteristic features of both the Bashkir and Tatar languages, so they may well be attributed to either of them (Safiullina and Galiullin 1986, esp. 285–289). These voices try to make it harder to delineate relevant boundaries. However, from what one knows of clashes involving German and Dutch, Swedish and Norwegian, Serb and Croat, Russian and Ukrainian, and so on, such an attempt to redirect attention to similarities of inventory may even be counterproductive. As argued in Chapter 1, since it is so hard to establish a linguistic boundary that both parties can invest with political meaning, linguistic closeness may actually sharpen conflict in these cases compared to cases such as Swedish and Finnish or Russian and Tatar.

The situation is once again further complicated by the ethnopolitical invocation of state agency. Bashkir activists insist on making Bashkir the state language in the republic. The demand, voiced by the BPC as early as 1989, grows out of a feeling that the Bashkir language has been neglected for decades and is now only rarely, if ever, used in an official context. Although the remedy is contested and the demands voiced may smack of crisis maximization, the definition of the situation, that something has to be done in order to guarantee that the Bashkir language will remain in use, seems to be widely accepted. Sociological surveys suggest that some 99 percent of Russians, 70 percent of Bashkirs, and only 62 percent of Tatars in Bashkortostan have a perfect command of their mother tongue. Among Bashkirs who have a perfect command of the Bashkir language, there is a widespread feeling that speaking Russian is more prestigious: 65 percent thought so in 1979, and by 1989 the figure had actually risen to 72 percent. Urbanization has certainly played a role here. Asked if the use of Russian is a threat to the survival of Bashkir, as the BPC maintains, 42 percent of Bashkirs, 42 percent of Tatars, and 20 percent of Russians said yes. Not more than 34 percent of Bashkirs support the idea that all the residents in the republic must have a good command of Bashkir; 4 percent were opposed, and 54 percent thought it should remain a matter of personal choice. Whereas BPC leaders have declared that only a person with a perfect command of Bashkir should be allowed to run for the presidency, only 8 percent of Bashkirs polled supported the idea that a good knowledge of the Bashkir language is indispensable for high officials (Khairullin 1992: 59). Such sociological data are, of course, inadequate, yet in lieu of fieldwork-based data about the microlevel, they will have to do.

The campaign to make Bashkir the state language immediately came in for heavy Tatar criticism. In December 1991 the BPC tried to confront some of the criticism by presenting a fourfold plan. First, in order to "save Bashkir from extinction and provide social protection" for the titular nation of the republic, Bashkir should be made the state language. Second, Russian should be designated as a medium of interethnic communication and would also be well suited for drawing up international agreements as well as for routine business correspondence. Mottoes on the state emblem should be both in Bashkir and Russian. Third, Russian, Tatar, and Bashkir should all be "languages of information," to be used in newspapers, on television, in business correspondence, and in advertisements. Fourth, any language may be a "language for cultural functions," to be used in fine arts, education, and also the media (BCP resolution on language, quoted in Guboglo 1992: vol. 2, 159–160).

These proposals, not to mention the heavily interventionist philosophy informing them, did nothing to quell Tatar protests. Tatar organizations continued to back the idea of three state languages. For example, the Department for Tatar Philology at the Bashkir State University adopted a resolution that also complained that the committee on language status formed by the Supreme Soviet did not represent ethnic groups in a balanced manner, thus eschewing the principle of equal rights (Safin, in Guboglo 1992: vol. 2, 241). Language, then, is a key locus, where ethnopolitical mobilization is pitched toward state agency by means of a campaign to make Bashkir the single (as it were, the sovereign) state language.

Demographics

During the last four decades, the percentage of ethnic Bashkirs in all the cities of the republic nearly doubled. This was largely due to urbanization. The demographic situation has itself become a locus of Bashkir-Tatar clashes. Since the beginning of the 1970s, 400,000 Bashkirs emigrated to other regions of Russia. Although there also exists a huge Tatar diaspora throughout Russia and the former Soviet Union, the Tatar population in Bashkiria/Bashkortostan continued to grow at a steady pace. Thus the first congress of the BCP in 1989 already stated that "the progressive reduction of [the Bashkir] population of the republic became an obvious obstacle to the consolidation of the Bashkir nation" (quoted in Guboglo 1992: vol. 2, 112).

Indeed, a meeting held by the BPC in May 1990 demanded that the Council of Ministers put an end to the immigration of people from other republics with no roots in Bashkiria. Tatars from Central Asia were mentioned specifically, and the wish was pronounced that these people should not receive apartments if they nevertheless should arrive.

On the initiative of the sixth congress of the BPC, the Supreme Soviet of the republic created a special committee on the demographic situation. However, as an ethnic Tatar was made head of the committee, the BPC protested. Some extremist leaders of the BPC adopted the slogan "Bashkiria for Bashkirs" and insisted on the compulsory deportation of non-Bashkir residents in order to achieve a higher proportion of Bashkirs in the republic. A petition to the United Nations argued that

> without a full-scale or partial repatriation of colonizers irrespective of time of their arrival, it is impossible for indigenous nations that have turned into minorities in their own native lands to handle the situation and to realize their full national rights. The international community has had adequate experience in this respect: When Western states were granting independence to colonial countries, all the colonists had to be repatriated, although their forefathers had moved in centuries before. Russia must not be made an exception from the rule. (Quoted in Guboglo 1992: vol. 2, 154)

Not surprisingly, there immediately developed a reaction to this publication, and the BPC was accused of national chauvinism. A month later the chair of the BPC was forced to explain that the leadership of the BPC had not agreed to some key points of Baishev's text, which it alleged had been published without the approval of BPC officials. He maintained that no single document of the BPC had ever touched upon the need for deportation of non-Bashkirs. Be that as it may, the position clearly exists within the ranks of Bashkir nationalist leaders.

The BPC's official position, however, is that the Bashkirs are the only nation indigenous to the area, that all other ethnic groups are later migrant communities. This is the main strategy by which Tatar and Russian rights are rebuffed: "There is no other nation except Bashkir that is indigenous to Bashkortostan. Attempts to question this fact contradict regulations of international law" (manifesto on the contemporary state of the Bashkir nation quoted in Guboglo 1992: vol. 2, 135).

That these are highly idiosyncratic representations of global de-colonization experiences and also of international law is not the point here, since the points of view are those of the Bashkirs and the Tatars. The globalization involved here seems, however, to be crucial. Whereas it was a recurrent theme in the discussion of boundary inscription in the three former loci that ethnopolitical activity latched onto state agency, there is here an added dimension of activating global discourses and harnessing them to ethnopolitical activity. Representations of global regulations are used as local arguments.

Territory

The invocations of state agency and global agency also pop up in the next locus to be discussed here, namely, territory. Tatar ethnopolitics has not only foregrounded their local numerical strength but has also tried to involve neighboring Tatarstan in the local political process. Debates about irredentism and other forms of territorial re-allocations between political units have been rife. For example, in February 1991 the TSC maintained that the 1922 decree enlarging the territory of Bashkiria by adding the Ufa region was passed without consulting the local population and should therefore be canceled (Safin, in Guboglo 1992: vol. 2, 228). The Ufa region has an unusually high percentage of Russians. If the Ufa region were to be excluded from Bashkortostan and instead included as a separate Ufa oblast of the Russian federation, this would leave Bashkortostan without a major city, something that may be seen by some to weaken the nation. It would, furthermore, boost the percentage of Tatars in Bashkortostan and hence strength the Tatars in the remaining area relative to both the Bashkirs and the Russians. Bashkir reactions were sharp. If the anti-Bashkir activities of the TSC did not stop, the BPC maintained, then they would propose the return to Bashkortostan of its former Menzelinsk county, an area now part of Tatarstan but still mainly populated by Bashkirs (resolution by the Fifth Bashkir Congress, quoted in Guboglo 1992: vol. 2, 112). The TSC was not deterred, however, and continued to push the idea of seceding the Ufa region. In October 1991 a TSC delegation went to Moscow to meet Yeltsin and allegedly presented the idea to the chairman of the Supreme Soviet of Russia (Safin, in Guboglo 1992: vol. 2, 235).[2]

Irredentist activity is carried out using imagery like that of "the Berlin wall": Organizers of a traditional Tatar feast, *sabantui*, held on the border between the two republics in June 1991 named the border river, the Ik, "the second Berlin wall." When two months later a treaty was signed by Bashkiria and Tatarstan, Tatar activists praised it as a "treaty against a Berlin wall." In order to work further dents in this "wall," all the main Tatar organizations—the TSC, the TDP, and the TYB—have floated ideas for dual citizenship for Tatars (Safin, in Guboglo 1992: vol. 2, 243). That this is deemed to be powerful rhetoric locally shows how global discourse permeates the local one.

Historical Figures

A final locus is historical figures. Tatars regularly regard deceased distinguished poets, whom Bashkirs claim as their own, as Tatars. There is scrapping over prerevolutionary intellectuals such as Miftakhetdin Akmulla and even over Shaykhzada Babich, who, as one of the official documents of BPC puts it, "being the classic of Soviet Bashkir poetry devoted his life to stigmatizing Tatar chauvinists." Indeed, even the person referred to by Bashkirs as "the father of Bashkiria's autonomy," the social revolutionary Akhmed-Zaki Validov, has been called a Tatar scholar by Tatar activists (see Guboglo 1992: vol. 2, 114). Boundary maintenance, then, regards ethnic groups that are conceived of as consisting of the dead, the living, and the not yet born (the case could thus be made that this is a discourse that should be subsumed under the locus of demographics, but again, microlevel data concerning the experiences of locals would be needed to further illuminate this taxonomical question).

According to Fredrik Barth and as mentioned in Chapter 1, the point of studying ethnicity is to "bare the processes involved in the reproduction of ethnic groups" (1994: 11), starting with an analysis of actor ascription, but also analyzing to what extent "people's choice[s] of diacritica"—that is, how differences are inscribed so as to make a difference for ethnicity—are arbitrary or not. Barth has come to believe that "the selection of such diacritica is far less haphazard than I may have indicated in 1969" (1994: 16). Indeed, the striking thing about this list of diacritica is how *familiar* it all is from other cases in the former Soviet and Yugoslav republics and from other studies of ethnopolitics in settings where the possibility of presenting an ethnic group as a nation is available.

Barth, furthermore, foregrounds the role of the state and suggests it be treated as a "specifiable third player" in processes of boundary formation. He suggests that a taxonomy of states according to regime type would benefit analysis. This foregrounding seems to amount to an implicit critique of anthropology for not having taken this level seriously enough.

In the light of the presented material, Barth's exhortation to see the state as a "third player" must be modified in two respects. The first one concerns a well-worked theme, namely, the choice of which ethnic groups are seen as significant. There exist a number of ethno-political movements in Bashkortostan in addition to the Bashkir and the Tatar. Examples include the German *Einheit*, the Jewish *Shtern*, and Russian ethnopolitical organizations such as the People's Party Free Russia and Free Russia. However, the principal non-Bashkir and non-Tatar movement is the Democratic Youth Union of Bashkiria (DYUB; formerly the Youth Union of Bashkiria). Although DYUB is not explicitly an ethnopolitical organization, its members are pre-dominantly Russian, or they describe themselves as Russian speakers (*russkoyazychnye*), that is, by means of a locus already ethno-politicized, namely, language.

The DYUB and Free Russia backed Tatar initiatives in favor of three state languages. The two ethnic groups were also united in their critique of a new secondary education curriculum of July 1993, which reduced teaching in history, civic education, and Russian in favor of Bashkir and allocated thirteen hours per week to the teach-ing of the culture of Bashkortostan but only one to the history of the world. Thus the existence and local activities of these groups im-pinge on the already ongoing boundary-inscribing activities of Bashkir and Tatar actors.

There are also the cases where a not yet tapped potential for this kind of activity exists. For example, should Russian speakers begin to participate in local religious discourse, which is already a locus of ethnicity, it would probably bring to the fore the fact that some are Christians. This could, in turn, bring to the fore the existence of a group of Christian Bashkirs locally known as the Nagaybak. Num-bering some tens of thousands, these Christians trace their history back to groups Christianized about a thousand years ago. A stan-dardization of their spoken language was attempted in the 1920s as part of the Soviet drive for a flowering of national groups. For the time being, however, most Nagaybak give Bashkir as their language (Svanberg 1992: 97).

It is hardly surprising that there exists a plethora of ethnic groups and that the possibility exists that they will reproduce themselves in a multiplicity of ways, which may indeed also lead to new groups appearing: This seems to me to be the essence of Barth's project. Therefore, this first point is of ethnographical interest, but it has little or no bearing on Barth's suggestions for how to pursue the study of ethnicity.

It seems to me that a second point is relevant in this respect, however. It concerns the conceptualization of the state as *one* player. The discussion so far bears out the importance of regime flux for ethnopolitics: The beginnings of Bashkir nation building took place at a time when the Russian empire was in flux and took off as the empire was being replaced by the Soviet state. I lack data on the situation in the beginning of the 1940s, when there was another case of state flux. Yet when the Soviet Union itself enters a new period of flux, which among other things involves the introduction of glasnost, sanctioning the existence of ethnopolitics, there is immediate mobilization and increased boudary-inscribing activity. These activities include direct attacks on state symbols: The BYU tore the flag of the Russian federation down from the building of Bashkortostan's Supreme Soviet in the autumn of 1991. In April 1992 a group of BYU members placed a tent in Ufa in front of the monument to Salavat Yulaev, a Bashkir national hero, and announced a hunger strike aimed at winning the abrogation of the federal treaty and the signing of an equitable bilateral treaty with the Russian Federation instead. There were also demands for the resignation of the Supreme Soviet and the Council of Ministers because of the way they had handled relations with the Soviet state level.

Three distinct yet concentric levels of administrative competence are thus involved—Bashkortostan, the Russian Federation, the Soviet Union—and it may not be that fruitful to treat the state as a single actor. Indeed, much of the interest of the case is due to the more inclusive level's weakening and disappearing, thus furthering the first level's room for maneuver and even its chances of ridding itself of the second level. The general point here is that although Barth calls for a taxonomy of regime, meaning "the state's policy-making core," the analysis may also hang on a different aspect of regime type, namely, whether and to what extent a state is unitary or federal. The point is, then, that one must take into consideration not only the *existence* and the *regime* of the state in the sense of state agency as such but also the number of *levels* of state organization and how these levels interact and differentiate state agency. In order to do so, one must examine Soviet national policy, which institutionalized ethnic groups by naming political units after them.

SOVIET NATIONAL POLICY AND BASHKORTOSTAN

The Bolsheviks who grabbed power in the Russian empire in 1917 not only acknowledged the importance of the national question for politics but unequivocally embraced the principle of national self-determination (for example, see Lenin [1914] 1975). However, as Finland, Georgia, Poland, and indeed a host of other territories tried to slip away from Moscow's rule under this banner, the Bolsheviks stressed that striving for national self-determination under conditions where the alternative of proletarian internationalism was available could be nothing but bourgeois nationalism. Thus, whereas in theory the principle of national self-determination remained, it lost its unequivocality by being in practice subordinated to proletarian internationalism. Yet the category "nation" continued to be acknowledged as politically relevant. Unlike what was the case, for example, in China, the official ideology of Soviet communism found itself bound up with a myth of national self-determination that extended to allowing secession and the creation of different sovereign states. This notion was drummed into people's heads for decades without any legal possibility of realization. On the contrary: Attempts to put this principle into practice were treated as manifestations of bourgeois chauvinism and punished. Yet by this very practice, the regime consecrated nationalism as a political alternative to communism, if only negatively so. The fact that repression of "bourgeois nationalism" was necessary at all gave the lie to Lenin's idea that following a flowering (*rastsvet*) of nations, they would start coming together (*sblizhenie*), and finally merge (*sliyanie*).

There always hovered a whiff of assimilatory politics around this Leninist program, suggesting that among the ethnic groups of the Soviet Union, some were more equal than others. The role of the Russians as a *Staatsvolk* was played out on top of an entire hierarchy of ethnic groups. Nations were awarded some kind of institutionalized existence within the state structure, as a union or an autonomous republic. Of course, because of the party's dominance in the political order (the party was *not* federalized), this autonomy was heavily circumscribed; nevertheless, it played a certain role. Ethnic units of a lower status were often given autonomy within the confines of a union republic. National groups were groups whose main part lived beyond the borders of the U.S.S.R. The muddled character and built-in power discrepancies of this classificatory scheme invited groups to explore national identity further, so that arguments for classificatory "upgrading" could be found. Indeed, this also applied to the ten national territories (*natsional'nye okrugi*).

This point was enforced by the failure of the classificatory scheme to take up the ambiguities of the embodiment of nations in their spatial dimension. Bolsheviks unreservedly rejected the idea of national-cultural autonomy promoted by Austrian Social Democrats at the beginning of the twentieth century. Instead, the territorial approach to the solution of the national question was adopted despite the fact that ethnic boundaries are not clear-cut and stable. It was in an attempt to substantiate this approach that Stalin developed his "Marxist" theory of nations, with a unified territory being one of the defining features of a nation. To mention but one example of the problems this entailed: Since they lack territorial unity, Jews were deprived of the right to be considered a nation (but in a backhanded move, a Jewish autonomous republic called Birobidzhan was set up in an area almost totally void of Jews in the Far East, on the border with China). Moreover, the territorial imperative dictated the naming of a titular nation in all autonomous administrative units. This could not but happen at the expense of other ethnic groups in the same region. Second, it was unclear what happened to members of the titular nation who lived outside "their" autonomous unit.

Additional trouble was fostered by the habit of creating joint autonomous units. In the 1920s the *Narkomnats* (the people's commissariats for national affairs) wanted to reduce the number of ethnoterritorial units. Where the case of Bashkortostan is concerned, it was only by chance that a "Tatar-Bashkir Soviet Socialist Republic" did not come into existence in the years immediately after the Revolution or as a part of the rationalization drive in the 1920s. What can be witnessed now is the breakup of Checheno-Ingush, as well as the ongoing dissolution of Karachayevo-Cherkess and Kabardino-

Balkaria. Moscow's idea of availing itself of two titular nationalities was a split-and-rule tactic carried out under the guise of "merge and rule." Examining the process of establishing boundaries between republics, some have concluded that the proclaimed principle of territorial attachment of nations had been deliberately violated in such a way that some regions predominantly populated by one ethnic group appeared to be included within the territory of another (for example, Connor 1984: 302).

Nagorno-Karabakh seems to be a striking example from outside the Russian federation of a case of border definition contrary to local desires: Despite a local vote in favor of unification of the area with Armenia, a sudden visit by Stalin resulted in autonomy for Nagorno-Karabakh within the Azerbaijan union republic. However, others have attempted to demonstrate that as regards autonomous republics and oblasts, very few units on the level below would have to be transferred to a neighboring ethnic unit in order to achieve an "optimal" correspondence between administrative and ethnic borders (Schwartz 1990; Kolstoe 1994: Ch. 4).

The discourse about nationality set up, perpetrated, and guarded by the Soviet state in its early years seems crucial in forming the thrust of local Bashkortostan politics in an ethnopolitical direction. This point has been argued forcefully by nonanthropologists, who have looked at the case not from a local standpoint but from a Moscow-based one:

> In the 1920's, the Bashkir dialect that was the least related to the Tatar language served as the basis for developing a Bashkir written language. With Russian, this dialect was declared the "state language." This legislation was unusual because Lenin is known to have repeatedly expressed fundamental objections to declaring an official state language and, to this very day, nowhere in the USSR is the Russian language called the official state language. The Bashkir "state language's" purpose was to breathe life into a Bashkir national identity distinct from the Tatar national identity—to a certain extent, this strategy probably succeeded. (Simon [1986] 1991: 43–44)

Furthermore, Stalin, as commissar for nationality policy, played a key role in supporting Validov's attempts to set up a separate Bashkir republic during the critical phase in early 1920 (Zenkovsky 1960: 204, and Stalin quotation, 310, note 36). Tatar leaders kept their distance from these developments. "All this time, while the Bashkir Republic was experiencing its trials and tribulations, the question of creating a Volga Tatar state had been held in abeyance," Richard Pipes writes. He continues:

> The Tatars had played a considerably more important role in the Communist movement than the Bashkirs, and their ambitions were proportionately greater. The idea of an autonomous state, which satisfied the Bashkir nationalists, did not gratify Tatar intellectuals educated in the reformed schools, who had been associated in 1917 with the All-Russian Moslem movement and were steeped in the atmosphere of Moslem radical proselytism. The Tatar Communists were none too eager to speed the cause of a separate Tatar autonomous state. They preferred to wait for the termination of the Civil War, when, they hoped, it would be possible to establish a single Volga-Ural republic, and to resume their activities on an all-Russian scale. Their leader and ideologist at this time was a remarkable Volga Tatar Communist, Mirza Sultan-Galiev. (Pipes 1964: 168)[3]

The seemingly less ethnically based idea about a "Soviet man" (*novy chelovek,* literally, "new man") that the Soviet state tried to impose in the postwar period did not have the expected result of merging ethnically based communities. Bashkir nation builders are very clear as to the ethnic conception that underlies their idea of nationhood. As part of the general parade of sovereignty claims by ethnic groups within the Soviet Union, autonomous republics such as Abkhazia and Bashkortostan tried to obtain status as full union republics. In the case of Bashkortostan, the claim was first made in economic terms. However, in a message to the chairman of the Supreme Soviet of the Russian federation of August 1990, the BPC was already focusing specifically on the institutional ramifications of such a move, and the Supreme Soviet passed a number of draft versions of a declaration on state sovereignty. Whereas some drafts predicated the claim on the "people of Bashkortostan" or the "multi-national Bashkirian people," the BPC draft chartered an ethnically based project by stating that "the Bashkir Soviet Socialist Republic is created on the basis of the natural and undeniable right of the Bashkir nation to self-determination and state sovereignty" (quoted in Guboglo 1992: vol. 1, 126).

Thus an ethnic conception of "the people" emerged to do away with a political, nonethnic one. Although the political conception led a subterranean existence even in the BPC draft, which remarked that "citizens of all nationalities embody the subject of sovereignty," the emphasis on civic virtues and a conception of citizenship open to all comers was clearly being marginalized by the Bashkir nation-building project. Nonethnic citizens should have rights not under a law binding all citizens but only to the extent that the "republic-making Bashkir nation" decided to confer rights on them (BPC draft declaration, quoted in Guboglo 1992: vol. 1, 127).

The upshot of the BPC's insistence on making Bashkiria a full union republic was of course that it thereby would leave the Russian Socialist Federative Soviet Republic. It was, as it were, no coincidence that the right of Bashkiria to have a separate army, security forces, customs service, and currency was emphasized and the goal of a neutral international status proclaimed.

Representatives of non-Bashkirs were not amused by the BPC's ideas. A Russian Ufa-based group appealed directly to Yeltsin, urging him to treat Bashkir sovereignty with circumspection. The TSC came out against the idea of investing Bashkir sovereignty only in one nation. Russian and Tatar organizations both called for a referendum. Nevertheless, the Bashkir ethnic conception of "the people" carried the day, and a declaration of sovereignty was finally adopted by the Supreme Soviet on 11 October 1990. The name of the republic was changed to Bashkortostan (Baškortostan). According to the text of the declaration, the republic remained a member of both the U.S.S.R. and of the Russian federation. This was not acceptable to the BPC, which started to accuse the Supreme Soviet and its chair, Murtaz Gubaydullovich Rakhimov, of subservience to Moscow.

The BPC decided to reach out to the world for support. In February 1991 the BPC declared its participation in the organization for unrepresented peoples, arguing that the Bashkir nation had not succeeded in getting rid of its colonial status.[4] In May 1991 the BPC's Marat Kulsharipov called an Ufa mass meeting, which proceeded to issue an appeal to the U.N. secretary general, the U.S. president, the leaders of several other countries, and all the parliaments and governments of the world, requesting moral support to the Bashkir nation in its aspiration to create a sovereign republic equal in rights with full union Soviet republics. The issue was proposed by the meeting for inclusion on the agenda of the next session of the U.N. General Assembly (Safin, in Guboglo 1992: vol. 2, 231).

In September 1991 the BPC followed up by issuing an appeal to the United Nations. It is worth quoting at length from the additional remarks attached to the appeal. Chairman of the Supreme Soviet Rakhimov, it was argued,

> has an immense throng of new settlers (78 percent of the whole population, mainly Russians and Tatars) behind him who will not hesitate to slaughter half of the defenseless Bashkirs (as has already happened in 1918–1920) at any least attempt of secession. Tatars have invariably been rendering the most active assistance to Russian colonizers to exploit Bashkir people and bloodily suppress their national movement. Russian and Tatar chauvinists attacked Bashkirs during the preparation of the declaration on state sovereignty of the Bashkir republic. After that anti-Bashkir groups intensified their large-scale activities, laying absurd and shameless claims right up to ridiculously accusing Bashkirs of oppressing other nations. . . . Bashkirs are not in a position to surmount independently the menacing obstacles in their way. They need substantial practical help from outside. It is the United Nations that could lend Bashkirs its support. To be firm in rendering assistance, the United Nations needs, first and foremost, to give up an erroneous theory of Russia as a single state. (Quoted in Guboglo 1992: vol. 2, 231–232).

CONCLUSION

The breakdown of the tsarist Russian empire at the end of the First World War and then of the Soviet Union destabilized the state formation inside which Bashkirs lived, and so made it possible for local nation builders to apply the globally produced knowledge about "nations" and apply it locally. In both cases, the hard discursive work that went into the forging of a self for the Bashkir nation was carried out in direct opposition to other projects of identity formation. After the 1917 revolutions, the alternative projects were a Pan-Turkic one and a Soviet one. After the coming of perestroika, the alternative projects were a Tatar nation-building one and a Russian federal one. Three homogenizing moves are part and parcel of the Bashkir forging of self: First, the Soviet period of political history is bracketed so that the Bashkir nation-building projects of the late 1910s and early 1920s and the late 1980s and early 1990s may be represented as one continuous political effort. The numbering of the *kurultai,* or congresses, so as to span the two periods is only one obvious example of a multifaceted process that permeates everyday Bashkir life. Second, a similar homogenization across time is imposed on the Pan-Turkic project of the late 1910s and early 1920s and the Tatar nation-building project of the late 1980s and early 1990s on the one hand, and on the Soviet project of the late 1910s and early 1920s and the Russian federal project of the late 1980s and early 1990s on the other. Third, yet another homogenization is imposed so that these alternative projects may be unequivocally represented as *consistently* nation-building projects, that is, projects of the same kind as *and therefore* diametrically opposed to the Bashkir nation-building project. What happens, then, is that Bashkir nation builders consistently background all the other possible representations of political selves that are imbricated in the nation-building ones. And this is done in order to foreground a representation of two others—a Tatar one and a Russian one—which are unequivocally nation bulding and hence unequivocally in competition with their representation of the Bashkir self. Out of the rich political raw material of two very different political contexts and two very different human collectives, the Bashkir nation builders are able to forge a single representation of nation-building Russian and Tatar others, a representation that *necessitates* the forging of a specific Bashkir self, namely, that of a Bashkir nation that can pick up the ethnopolitical cudgels of nation-building competition.

As I have demonstrated, some of the metaphors in terms of which this is done are drawn from local history. One may read them as globally "circulationist" in the sense that they inscribe with political meaning diacritica that are of a type that has previously been used in other nation-building projects: language, religion, fathers of the nation, and so on. That does not make them any less local. It remains a question of intellectual temperament whether one wants to emphasize the modular quality of nation building, as Anderson does (1983), or whether one wants to emphasize its unique quality, as Ullock does (1996). More intriguingly, however, some of the metaphors used are circulationist not only in the sense that they are of this or that type but also in the sense that they forge direct ties between local phenomena and phenomena elsewhere. Two examples that stand out are the Tatar nation builders' representation of the strengthening of the political border along the river Ik delineating Tatarstan from Bashkortostan as a "Berlin Wall," and the Bashkir nation builders' representation of Tatars as Muslim fundamentalists. Both these meta-phors take part of their political potency from general European po-litical discourse, in which "Berlin Wall" was perhaps the most widely used metaphor to represent the East/West divide of the Cold War and "fundamentalist" is part and parcel of representations of "East-ern" political movements throughout the "Muslim world" (Tunander 1995). The fact that these metaphors may be effectively used must mean that the symbolic economy inside which they have a life must also have a certain presence locally. And that must mean that Bashkir and Tatar nation-building discourse is nested in a discourse in which certain traits are marked negatively as "Eastern."

In Chapters 2 and 3, I demonstrated that representations of Eu-rope were forged in terms of Eastern others. If this chapter cannot demonstrate as convincingly that representations of "Easternness" are central to the forging of a Bashkir self (and also of a Tatar self, for that matter), it has at least demonstrated the presence of such representative moves. At what is in European discourse often rep-resented as the Eastern geographical border of Europe, "the East" retains a negative social marking. "The East," furthermore, is used as a social marker independently of geographical placement: That Bashkortostan lies to the geographical east of Tatarstan does not keep Bashkirs from representing Tatars as "Eastern." "The East," then, is not necessarily spatially east; it may also be a social signifier cut loose from its geographical moorings. If a human collective wants to represent a "Western" or "European" self, it needs an "Eastern" or "Asiatic" shadow, but that shadow need not necessar-ily fall to the geographical east.

8

Conclusion: Self and Other after the Death of the Sovereign Subject

Identity requires difference in order to be, and it converts difference into otherness in order to secure its own self-certainty.
— WILLIAM CONNOLLY 1991: 64

The conclusion to Chapter 7, that "the East" has been cut loose from its geographical point of reference and has become a generalized social marker in European identity formation, is one that may also serve as an initial conclusion to the book as a whole. "The East" is indeed Europe's other, and it is continuously being recycled in order to represent European identities. Since the "Eastern absence" is a defining trait of "European" identities, there is no use talking about the end of an East/West divide in European history after the end of the Cold War. The question is not *whether* the East will be used in the forging of new European identities but *how* this is being done. It is the main empirical claim of this book to have outlined how this discursive move materializes in the forging of all-European, regional, and national identities. Edward Said's work on how the scholarly discourse of "Orientalism" developed and how it informed other discourses was preoccupied with "the East" as "the Orient." This book has investigated knowledge production in a much more generalized setting than that of scholarly discourse, and it has demonstrated that "the East" is not just to be understood as "the Orient." The use of "the East" as the other is a general practice in European identity formation.

Even if this conclusion holds some empirical interest, however, it must also be criticized for still being a structuralist summing up of analogue discourse in terms of a digital metaphor. In other words, it still has not really faced up to the theoretical challenge issued by Richard Bernstein in his argument that

> despite all the professed scepticism about binary oppositions, there has been a tendency in many "postmodern" discourses to reify a new set of fixed oppositions: otherness is pitted against sameness, contingency against necessity, singularity and particularity against universality, fragmentation against wholeness. In each case it is the former term that is celebrated and valorized while the latter term of these oppositions is damned, marginalized, exiled. (Bernstein 1991: 310)

Theoretical perspectives, too, have their uses, and an application of a self/other perspective like the one presented in this book must be expected to point up the *limits* of that particular perspective. The rest of this conclusion will, therefore, be preoccupied with identifying the limits of the self/other perspective on identity politics. What is attempted, in other words, is to demonstrate how far theorizing along what was referred to in Chapter 1 as "the Eastern excursion" in identity scholarship has proceeded.

Since this theorizing falls into two related but different perspectives—one poststructuralist and one constructivist—between which the readings presented here are precariously sandwiched, this exercise in self-reflection will fall into two parts. It will start with an investigation of how "the political" is conceptualized in poststructural readings. I argue that poststructuralism remains a structuralism inasmuch as it reads intentionality out of its analyses. Furthermore, its emphasis on the unique, context-bound instantiation of identity, which is perhaps its main strength, is also its most crippling weakness because it does not leave much room for an analysis of the social process of identification. The best poststructural takes on this process are arguably the ones drawing on the idea of "quilting."[1] In accordance with the poststructuralist reading out of intentionality, however, this process is conceptualized as an affair between a subject and an order, and not as an affair between a subject and an other. Poststructuralists, therefore, do not have an intersubjective take on the process of identification. Not least for political reasons, it is crippling for poststructuralism not to be able to proceed beyond this limit. Without a take on how to forge politically implementable stories of self, poststructuralists may bar themselves from constructive intervention into the political field.

Having identified the limit beyond which poststructuralism may not be able to advance the self/other perspective, I turn to the other main branch of constitutivist scholarship, namely, constructivism. This perspective does have a take on intentionality, and by drawing on the idea of "recognition" it is able to understand identification not only as an affair between a self and an order, as can poststructuralism, but also as an affair between a self and an other, understood as subjects. The problem, however, is that constructivism seems to confer on the subject rather more intentionality than it may be able to carry. The limit of this self/other perspective, then, is that it does not really begin to try to slink out of the political problematique surrounding sovereignty. Sovereignty remains foundational to this allegedly antifoundational perspective.

The main point of identifying the limits to poststructuralist and constructivist perspectives on the self/other nexus, however, is definitely not to privilege constructivism over poststructuralism but to identify a theoretical challenge that is common to both. Having bettered constructivism in killing off the sovereign subject, poststructuralist analyses should nonetheless be able to account for the subjects that are still there. Shorn of their sovereign status, subjects need to be inscribed with a new status. If poststructural scholarship contents itself with merely proclaiming the death of subjectivity, it condemns itself to a more marginal political position than what I think is its due.

POSTSTRUCTURALISM AND THE POLITICAL

In order to criticize the poststructural themes and presuppositions that I find problematic I choose as my vehicle a short, programmatic text on identity politics that comes complete with references to Schmitt, Derrida, and Connolly and an attack on Habermas. In addition to these telltale markers, the author of the text is Chantal Mouffe. Her work on discourse analysis has been central to much of the work on identity, including the present book and other efforts of what was referred to in Chapter 1 as the Copenhagen school of international relations. Reading her text symptomatically should involve only the inevitable problems that always arise when a representative sample has to be chosen.

Mouffe starts off by evoking the distinction elaborated by French poststructuralists between *the political,* which describes the ineradicable and ever-changing dimension of antagonism and hostility that characterizes human interaction, and *politics,* which, taking note of the permanent antagonism characterizing the political, seeks to establish a certain order and to organize human coexistence (compare Critchley 1992). One sees how this may be used to further illuminate the meaning of the main empirical finding of this book. I should like to suggest that the ordering of self as "Western" and other as "Eastern" in European identity formation is one way of organizing European politics. This is not a point with which Mouffe concerns herself, however. She proceeds, rather, from her general characterization of politics to lambasting liberal understandings of it for misunderstanding the very nature of the political, arguing that the liberal view

> which attempts to keep together the two meanings encompassed by the terms "politics"—that of "polemos" and that of "polis"—is totally foreign to liberal thought; that, incidentally, is the reason why liberal thought is powerless in the face of antagonism. (Mouffe 1994: 108)[2]

Politics, she argues, is constituted by its outside (its *extérieur constitutif,* for example Europe's "East"), and inevitably bears the marks of its own exclusions. In standard poststructuralist fashion, Mouffe then proceeds to suggest that the way to alleviate the impact of this inevitable exclusion is to celebrate how, since the "we" is constituted by its outside, that "we" must also somehow *be* that outside:

> On a general philosophical level, it is obvious that if the constitutive outside is present inside every objectivity as its always real possibility, then the interior itself is something purely contingent, which reveals the structure of the mere possiblity of every objective order. This questions every essentialist conception of identity and forecloses every attempt conclusively to define identity or objectivity. Inasmuch as objectivity always depends on an absent otherness, it is necessarily always echoed and contaminated by this otherness. Identity cannot, therefore, belong to one person alone, and no one belongs to a single identity. We would go further, and argue that not only are there no "natural" or "original" identities, since every identity is the result of a continuing process, but that this process itself must be seen as one of permanent hybridization and nomadization. Identity is, in effect, the result of a multitude of interactions that take place inside a space whose outlines are not clearly defined. (Mouffe 1994: 109–110)

Mouffe draws two conclusions for political practice, one about the unwanted and in any case impossible forging of a European self and one about democratic politics in general. On the former, she writes that

> contrary to what is popularly believed, a "European" identity, conceived as a homogeneous identity which could replace all other identifications and allegiances, will not be able to solve our problems. On the contrary, if we think of it in terms of "aporia," of double negative, as an "experience of the impossible," to use Derrida's words from his *L'Autre cap* [*The Other Heading*], then the notion of a European identity could be a catalyst for a promising process, not unlike what Merleau-Ponty called "lateral universalism," which implies that it is inscribed in respect for diversity. If we conceive of this European identity as a "difference to oneself," as "one's own culture as someone else's culture," then we are in effect envisaging an identity that accommodates otherness, that demonstrates the porosity of frontiers, and opens up towards that "exterior" which makes it possible. By accepting that only hybridity creates us as separate entities, it affirms and upholds the nomadic character of every identity. (Mouffe 1994: 111)

Where the inevitability for one human collective of somehow being its other is concerned, Mouffe is in the company of Derrida and also of Kristeva, whose book *Strangers to Ourselves* (1991) is a celebration of this exact point. This point is also made, however, by someone as decidedly nonpoststructuralist as Paul Ricoeur, who elaborates it at book-length in his *Oneself as Another* ([1990] 1992).[3] Mouffe uses this insight to stress that democratic politics must maintain a politics of antagonism centered on certain traditional identity nexuses in order to foreclose the possibility that other identities may be inscribed with paramount political meaning and thus may be made the defining foci of essentialist identity politics:

> Unclear dividing lines block the creation of democratic political identities and fuel the disenchantment with traditional political parties. Thus they prepare the ground for various forms of populist and antiliberal movements that target nationalist, religious and ethnic divides. When the agonistic dynamism of the pluralist system is unable to unfold because of a shortage of democratic identities with which one can identify, there is a risk that this will multiply confrontations over essentialist identities and non-negotiable moral values. (Mouffe 1994: 109)

Quite so. However, one has to add a dimension that has been at the core of Mouffe's earlier work (Laclau and Mouffe 1985), namely, that exactly because class distinctions (in the old Marxian sense of collectives defined by their relationship to the means of production, not in a Bourdieuan sense) are evaporating as possible identities, political space is opening up for the plethora of social identities around which social movements have congealed over the last twenty-five years or so. And it is exactly as a reaction to this mushrooming of the number of available identities, which cannot easily be strung together in one overarching narrative of self, that there is the kind of rush to defend the story of self that revolves around the nation that was discussed in Chapters 6 and 7. Any advance of the processes of globalization as well as of European integration may also fuel counterdiscourses that celebrate and essentialize nations, regions, Europe:

> We live in a time of recognizable *global* danger that (while it presses in exactly the opposite direction too) provides cultural impetus to rethink the strategies of identity and difference through which contemporary states define and cope with otherness. (Connolly 1991: 45)

That is to say, the very same condition that makes it possible for identities to proliferate and that makes some people celebrate this, also sparks an impulse toward denying the possibility of multiple and imbricated identities in favor of celebrating essentializing grand narratives of a certain self. Mouffe's succinct piece draws on a standard poststructuralist representation when it presents itself under the title "For a Politics of Nomadic Identity." Identities, poststructuralists argue, are context-bound instantiations, and so they cannot be stable. As an ontological presupposition, I should like to endorse this line of argument. That, however, does not in any way change the fact that political discourse consists, among other things, of essentializing representations of identities. The ontological possibility of upholding a context-traversing self aside, such selves certainly exist as what anthropologists call "folk models," that is, representations that circulate in cultures and make it possible for its members to make sense of their world (Hóly and Stuchlik 1981). Of course, these essentializing representations do not become any less real for being imagined. To demonstrate by means of some variant of discourse analysis that a self cannot remain consistent across different contexts, as I have

done in the previous chapters, is an effective way to show their con-
tingency, but it is *not* a way to kill them off.[4]

I should like to refer to Peter Winch's ([1964] 1987) celebrated
analysis of witchcraft among the Azande here. In order to study
Azande social life, which revolves around representations of witches,
Winch argues persuasively that the anthropologist should defer
the question of whether witches "really" exist. There is a parallel
between studying witches and studying the identities of political
human collectives here. If one wants to work on the inside of the
concepts that hold a human collective together, and that is indeed
what poststructuralists want to do, then one should bracket the
question of the ontological status of the representations that hold
that human collective together. The question of the ontological impossibility of context-traversing selves, then, must not be mixed up
with the epistemological question of how to study struggling representations of selves.

Perhaps this observation may, to most readers, border on pointing out the obvious, but perhaps my next contention will prove more
challenging. This step of the argument concerns the levels not of ontology and epistemology but of political practice. As a sympathetic
reader of Mouffe's work has remarked:

> The thesis of Laclau and Mouffe that "Society doesn't exist," that the
> Social is always an inconsistent field structured around a constitutive
> impossibility, traversed by a central "antagonism"—this thesis implies
> that every process of identification conferring on us a fixed socio-
> symbolic identity is ultimately doomed to fail. The function of ideo-
> logical fantasy is to mask this inconsistency, the fact that "Society
> doesn't exist," and thus to compensate us for the failed identification.
> (Žižek 1989: 126–127)

I should like to take issue with the salience of this observation. Of
course, any identity is "ultimately" doomed to give up the ghost.
The narratives that uphold a certain identity, however, will now typically present themselves as stretching over periods of several hundred years, and there is no dearth of texts that try to uphold a number of these narratives. The question is what those of us who would
like to combat essentializing representations of human communities
should do in the meantime, except for analyzing them and then wait-
ing for them to peter out. The question, put at its sternest, must be:

What if the poststructuralist insistence on celebrating "nomadic identities" lays the field open for essentializing narratives of self?

THE NEED FOR "AS IF" STORIES

On the basis of, among other things, the readings of European identities presented above, I should like to offer the proposition that once a politics conceived of in terms of "nomadic identities" comes up against a politics based on a narrative of context-traversing selves, the celebration of nomadic or multiple identities may easily lose out. Mouffe's attack on the idea of a context-traversing European self and her stress on the need for a hybridized European identity can be said to be warranted and timely, but only because attempts at telling a story of a context-traversing European self are so weak for the time being. Once such stories come to the fore in European discourse, Mouffe's political practice may well be scuppered. This can already be seen in the way she circumvents the issue by foregrounding the case of European identity rather than, for example, French identity, for which there certainly *are* stories of context-traversing selves in circulation and for which Mouffe's recommendations therefore look rather less convincing.

Mouffe must recognize this problem, inasmuch as she cites Carl Schmitt to the effect that the political derives its energy from the most diverse sources and "every religious, moral, economic, ethical, or other antithesis transforms into a political one if it is sufficiently strong to group human beings effectively according to friend and enemy" (quoted by Mouffe 1994: 197). This quote invites the reading that a political program will group human beings the more effectively the more antitheses it is able to group around one central self/other nexus. Rather than arriving at a situation where essentializing narratives will "ultimately" die out due to their built-in instability, as Laclau and Mouffe explicitly argue that they will, essentializing narratives will *win* over nonessentializing ones. This will happen exactly because they are able to group more identities around that central self/other nexus that is represented as being of essential political importance. The fact that these essentializing narratives will necessarily undergo transmutations in the process is not the point here, since this observation about their ontological impossibility will not bar them from being represented in a politically effective way.

I draw two conclusions from this, one on the level of practice and one on the level of epistemology. Where practice is concerned, in order to be effective in the political field, one simply cannot put the self under erasure but must have what I will refer to as an "as if" story to tell about it. The struggle to deny the impossibility of having a context-traversing identity is a key part of contemporary political life—indeed, it is not least the vitality and centrality of these struggles that make it worthwhile to study identity politics in the first place.

I have arrived at this view not only through my work on this book but also because of my participation in negotiations of one European national identity, namely the Norwegian one.[5] Over the last thirty years or so, these negotiations have mainly revolved around Norway's institutional relations with the EU. The key question has been to what extent stories of national selves have been compatible with the institutional integration and identity hybridization that EU membership would allegedly entail. In the negotiations of national identity, every attempt to put forward arguments in favor of nomadic, multiplex, hybrid political identities only had the effect of amalgamating the dominant story of self, which held that the Norwegian national self was under attack by the evocation of other identities as well as of a European self. Thus attempts at playing pluralist politics lost out to nationalist politics.

Another, much more fatal example is the case of Bosnia-Herzegovina in the 1990s. Once nationalist essentialist stories of self began to dominate, the only partially effective political counterstrategy was to be found in the representation of an alternative story of self that, being inevitably an "as if" story, stressed that different ethnic groups had "always" lived together peacefully and that a splitting up of the community along ethnic lines would be a break with "tradition." Those who, for whatever reason, held back from participating in any representation of these stories of self altogether were quickly left with no political space whatsoever. Without an "as if" story to tell about the self of the human collective whose identity they wanted to represent, they were left politically inefficient. As shown above, far from being coincidental, this was an immediate consequence of the hegemonic form that identity politics takes in the Europe of the 1990s and that makes it necessary that an "as if" story of self be part of any political practice that wants to be immediately effective.

For Mouffe, who takes an interest in French politics, there should be a lesson here. Attempts to combat the National Front, which issues their challenge in the form of an essentialist story of a context-traversing French nation, must first and foremost take place in the form of an alternative "as if" story of a French self, and *not* only on the obviously less effective level of a politics of nomadic identity. If, as Laclau, Mouffe, and Žižek argue, the function of ideology is to mask the impossibility of upholding a context-traversing self, then political interventions must not only take the form of analyzing other people's fantasies but also of fielding one's own. The question remains whether Mouffe has adequately heeded her own exhortation to forge a politics that can order the antagonism that inevitably characterizes the political, or whether she in some degree is guilty of the same inadequacy for which she lambasts liberals, namely, powerlessness in the face of antagonism.

Where epistemology is concerned, in order better to understand the forging of essentialist and "as-if" narratives of self, a case can be made for following anthropologists and sociologists in evolving a difference between context-bound identities on the one hand and context-traversing ones on the other. This is the task to which I now turn.

IDENTITY, SELF, IDENTIFICATION

The *Oxford English Dictionary* (the *OED*) gives as one of the meanings of identity "the sameness of a person or thing at all times or in all circumstances, the condition or fact that a person or thing is itself and not something else." If one reads "thing" to include human collectives, this definition suggests that identity and self are the same thing. To Mouffe, who sees no need to engage the possibility of context-traversing selves, "identity" is all there is, and so there is no need to challenge existing usage.

The etymologies of the two terms "identity" and "self" are intertwined. Identity comes from the latin *idem*, the same, and the *OED* shows that it was first used in the sense of *"Personal identity* (in *Psychology*), the condition or fact of remaining the same person throughout the various phases of existence; continuity of the personality" in the works of the English empiricists. Locke and Hume used the term "identity" to cast doubt on the unity of the self (Gleason 1983: 911; Ricoeur [1990] 1992: 125–128). As the term "identity" started its meteoric rise as an analytical term in the U.S. social sciences in the 1950s, however, "identity" tended to be used not as a term with which to dissipate a unity but, on the contrary, as a term with which to rebundle something that was seen as being in need of rebundling. To psychologists like Erik Erikson, for example, identity was lodged "in the core of the individual," and this "core" was something that had to be guarded against all kinds of crises. At the same time, symbolic interactionists like Erving Goffman, who had been theorizing "the self" since the outbreak of the Second World War, seemingly for no particular theoretical reason abandoned the term "self" for the term "identity" (Gleason 1983: 914–918).

As collective identity formation became an anthropological and sociological growth industry in the early 1990s, however, one saw an ever more marked tendency to separate the two terms. Two examples will suffice. Drawing inspiration from Anthony Giddens, the anthropologist Marianne Gullestad makes the following distinctions where individuals are concerned:

> I define the modern *self* as the continuous and processual effort of the individual to bring together his or her various roles, identities and experiences. *Roles,* on the other hand, are the dynamic aspects of the individual's various positions in the social structure, while *identities* are those qualities with which the individual identifies and of which he or she desires social confirmation. Some identities are directly tied to social roles, while others, such as national and ethnic identities, can be aspects of several roles. Modern people construct many fleeting and situation-specific identities, but they usually strive for a more or less coherent and continuous image of the self. (Gullestad 1996: 1–2)

The sociologist Charles Lemert draws a similar distinction between "self" and "identity" on the level of human collectives. Furthermore, he uses this distinction as a taxonomic device, insisting that the two terms are favored by two different groups of theorists. On the one hand, he writes, Charles Taylor, Anthony Giddens, and others brood over the threatened unity of the self. On the other hand, Judith Butler, Gayatri Chakravorty Spivak, and others "use 'Self' much as others use the phrase 'former Soviet Union' to refer to a once evident thing that has lost empirical salience"—and mostly they do not use "self" at all, but "identity" (Lemert 1994: 101). He then puts forward the following observation:

"Self" and "identity" may refer to different, rather than identical, events. Overall, the proposition, if it is a proposition, is fraught with theoretical amd political trouble. This, almost certainly, is why willingness to consider it in the first place is still another point of demarcation between the two groups. The first group tends to assume "Self" and "identity" are at least good enough identicals that their differences, if any, may be ignored. The second group tends to allow (and sometimes insist on) the difference but without making philosophical noise over it. This may be why the second group writes, and speaks, outside official philosophical and theoretical language. (Lemert 1994: 103)

Bearing in mind that it was Locke and Hume who began to question the unity of the self, it is of course wholly unwarranted to equate the philosophical tradition with attempts to salvage it. That notwithstanding, it is a fair point that at present, theorizing that takes place along what was called in Chapter 1 the philosophical path has rallied around the self, whereas theorizing that comes out of the "Eastern excursion" has shown a proclivity for identity. I suggest with Lemert and Gullestad, then, that we need one term for context-bound identities and another term for (the ontological impossibility of) context-traversing identities. The former may simply be referred to as identities, and the latter as selves. In terms of this distinction, my criticism of what one may call Mouffe's instantiationist poststructuralism may be reformulated as follows: A "politics of nomadic identity" as suggested by Mouffe stops at the level of identities—the only metaphoric move that is suggested in order to string identities together is that of a nomadic trek. And even so, that metaphor suggests a tighter stringing together of identities and a rather more path-dependent scripting of self than Mouffe may actually intend, since nomadic treks are usually quite fixed in their general outline. That aside, Mouffe's poststructural abhorrence of presence across contexts bars her theorizing from reaching the level of the self. Her very ontological presuppositions make it impossible for her to forge a theory of the self as anything other than an "as if" story, and that is fine. My criticism, to repeat, is directed at the unwillingness to tell those "as if" stories.

I would like to suggest that the making of selves is a narrative process of identification whereby a number of identities that have been negotiated in specific contexts are strung together into one overarching story. The making of selves is dependent on the raw material of available identities. The forging of selves, then, is a path-dependent process, since it has to cram in a number of previously negotiated identities in order to be credible. Furthermore, even ruling out the emergence of new situations in which new identities will have to be negotiated, it is a never-ending process, since there will always exist more identities than can easily be accommodated in a coherent story of self, however minimalist a definition of "coherent" is needed. Indeed, this is one of the reasons why "for a state to end its practices of representation would be to expose its lack of pre-discursive foundations; stasis would be death" (Campbell 1992: 11).

With reference to Chapter 4, let me illustrate with an example from the making of a self for the region of Northern Europe (*Norden*). The dominant story of the Nordic self stresses that Nordics close ranks against others in times of crisis. During the Second World War, however, Norway was occupied by Nazi Germany, whereas Sweden was neutral. In order to get to Norway by land, the occupation forces had to travel through Sweden. Although almost 2 million such transports took place during the five years of occupation, the Swedish government consistently professed ignorance of them. Finland, furthermore, was allied with Germany, Norway was ruled by a government headed by the Nazi Vidkun Quisling, and as late as 1942 a Swedish general advocated that Sweden should join the war on Germany's side. All this is to say that, as Nordic identities were negotiated during and after the Second World War, a staunchly anti-Nazi identity was hardly the effortless winner in these clashes of representation. Nonetheless, the identity of having been staunchly anti-Nazi during the Second World War is routinely pressed into service when the dominant narrative of the Nordic self is being represented. Other and competing identities of "the Nordic" from the same period, in which Germany and other others played rather different roles in the process of identification, are not necessarily even denied or suppressed; rather, they are treated as politically irrelevant. In being an example of how one identity ("anti-Nazi during and before the Second World War") out of a number of possible ones is forged *post festum* and then strung together with other identities that it is fashioned to sit well with to make up a coherent story of self, this is of course also an example of Nietzsche's point that it is not what people remember in common that makes them a people but, rather, what they decide to forget. And in case one should counter that the example is far-fetched because Nazi activity by Swedes, Norwegians, and other Northern Europeans was not all that rampant, there is the additional example of the dominant story of the Austrian national self, which also identifies itself as having been "anti-Nazi during and before the Second World War."

It is a point not without a certain irony that there *does* exist post-structural theorizing that may be used to illuminate this process whereby identities are strung together as a self, if only the proposed distinction between self and identity could be accepted. I am thinking about Slavoj Žižek's reading of subjectivization, which is mediated from Lacanian and Kripkean work. Žižek starts off with the process of "naming," understood as originating in a mystical "primal baptizing." The repeated use of a name itself—for example "Bashkortostan," "Central Europe," "Europe"—is the only regularity to be observed in what is in all other respects a free play of signifiers:

> It must be part of the meaning of each name that it refers to a certain object *because this is its name,* because others use this name to designate the object in question: every name, in so far as it is part of common language, implies this self-referential, circular movement. "Others," of course, cannot be reduced to empirical others; they rather point to the Lacanian "big Other," to the symbolic order itself. Here we encounter the dogmatic stupidity proper to a signifier as such, the stupidity which assumes the shape of a tautology: a name refers to an object *because this object is called that*—this impersonal form ("it is called") announces the dimension of the "big Other" beyond other subjects. [There exists] a necessary constituent of every "normal" use of names in language as a social bond—and this tautological constituent is the Lacanian master-signifier, the "signifier without signified." (Žižek 1989: 93)

Drawing on another Lacanian idea, Žižek then stresses that the arrival of a master signifier imposes sameness retrospectively by "quilting." By means of a metaphorical backward embroidery stitch, the master signifier—for example, "Bashkortostan," "Central Europe," "Europe"—strings together the previously free-floating signifiers:

> The *point de capiton* [nodal point] is the point through which the subject is "sewn" to the signifier, and at the same time the point which interpellates individual into subject by addressing it with the call of a certain master-signifier ("Communism," "God," "Freedom,"

"America")—in a word, it is the point of the subjectivation of the signifier's chain. (Žižek 1989: 101)

Jenny Edkins (1996) has aptly summed up the political implications of this process: Quilting, she observes, is a performative, ideological operation that has to be authoritarian simply because discourse itself is by its very nature authoritarian. When previously free-floating signifiers are "quilted" by the master signifier, the master signifier can only perform this task by being itself empty, a lack without meaning, and by imposing itself in what Lacan refers to as a nonfounded founding act of violence. In order to clarify this, reference is made to Žižek's comparison of the moment of quilting and Habermas's insistence on the idea of an ideal speech act:

> In Lacan the master signifier distorts the symbolic field in the very process of establishing it (temporarily) as a discursive field. Without this distortion, the field of meaning would disintegrate: the role of the paradoxical element is constitutive. As Žižek puts it, the Master is an impostor—anyone who finds him or herself at the place of the constitutive lack in the structure will do—but the place he or she occupies cannot be abolished. It can only be rendered visible as empty. For Habermas, in contrast, disturbances or distortions of rational argument are contingent; discourse itself is inherently non-authoritarian and prejudices can be gradually removed to reach an ideal situation of a rational exchange of views. For Lacan, if the structural role of the master signifier is suspended, this leads to a state of undecidability. (Edkins 1996: 7)

Even if this theorizing of subjectivization may be applied to collective identity formation (or rather, to stick to the suggested distinction between identity and self, to the formation of self) in order to do away with the problem of instantiationism, it does not solve what I have referred to as the other main limit of poststructural scholarship on the self/other nexus.[6] This is the theoretical status of the collective subject. The limit that Žižek imposes in this regard is explicit, inasmuch as I could quote him above to the effect that "others, of course, cannot be reduced to empirical others." In poststructuralist texts, the other disappears as a subject. The other is either conceptualized as a lack—witness, for example, how the analyses of Russia as Europe's other and Europe as Russia's other in Chapters 3 and 6 above do not really touch base—or the other is conceptualized as a randomized Lacanian big other pictured as the point at which the signifier and the signified meet.[7] This limit of poststructuralist perspectives may be referred to as the limit of lack of intention. It is a limit that poststructuralism has willfully and gladly taken with it from structuralism (see Jameson 1972).

CONSTRUCTIVISM AND THE POLITICAL

Having investigated the limits of a poststructuralist perspective on the self/other nexus (or, to stay in the suggested terminology, the identity/other nexus) and having located them in an insistence on limiting their investigations and political applications of identity as they are instantiated in specific contexts, as well as in a bracketing of intention, I now turn to an investigation of the limits of the other main constitutivist perspective on self and other, namely, constructivism. Once again I should like to launch the investigation by means of a symptomatic reading. I choose one of the few monographs on the question of European identities yet to appear, namely, Erik Ringmar's analysis of what some of us (understandably to the astonishment and amusement of others) consider to be the live and apposite question of why Sweden went to war in 1630.

Ringmar offers a theory of action that is quite explicitly formulated as a critique of the epistemology of those social scientists who "have accepted the modern mythology of the transcendental self— the notion that there is a 'real' or 'true' self which is given prior to, and independently of, social interaction" (Ringmar 1996a: 190; also Neumann 1997b). Thus, his point of departure is also a presupposition of the ontological impossibility of a context-traversing self. With reference to what Paul Ricoeur ([1988] 1991) refers to as narrative identity, however, Ringmar argues that there is no need to discuss whether a self exists or not in purely ontological terms, since

> it is simply not possible to say what an actor would be "in him-, her- or itself," since he, she or it can only come to exist as acting, as preparing to act, or as just having acted. . . . *Actors exist in stories and nowhere else*, and stories are governed by narratological, not ontological, requirements. . . . We can never come up with a conclusive answer to the question of what we—or anyone else for that matter— "really are," but this does not for a moment stop us talking about what we or others *are like*. (Ringmar 1996a: 74–75)

This, he argues, has immediate repercussions for how one represents collectives such as states, since states may, for example, be intentional, interest-driven actors "provided that we tell stories which identify them as such" (Ringmar 1996a: 75). Thus states and other human collectives are talked into existence by forging identities for themselves along a temporal and a spatial axis:

> From the perspective of the story's participants, the directedness of narrative can be understood in terms of the *intentional* aspect of action. To be a conscious human being is to have intentions and plans— to be trying to bring about certain effects—and the link between intention and execution is always rendered in narrative form. In this way story-telling becomes a prerequisite of action: first we attach metaphors to our unfathomable selves, to the situations we are in, and then we go on telling stories about ourselves and our situations thus understood. We tell ourselves what kind of person we were/are/ will be; what kind of a situation we were/are/will be in; and what such people as ourselves are likely to do under these particular circumstances. In this way, and in this way only, can we come to formulate notions of interests. (Ringmar 1996a: 73)

Stories, then, link up their narrating selves with present and future gestations of it, and they make a place out of space by peopling that space with others in relation to whom the self can be seen to exist. Ringmar refers to this as mapping discursive space by charting a geography of affection (1996a: 128). These "others" are the *setting* to the stories, as well as being themselves story-telling entities. These "others" about whom the self tells stories and who tell stories about the self are thus a *constitutive part* of story telling. They are key *audiences* of the stories, and as such they participate actively in the formation both of identity and interests, making both these concepts relational: "In order to find out whether a particular constitutive story is a valid description of us, it must first be tested in interaction with others" (Ringmar 1996a: 80). Confirmation of stories of self cannot be given by just anybody, but only by those others whom the self recognizes and respects as being of a kind with itself. The others in this set are referred to as "circles of recognition." To a state, the circle of major importance will therefore be made up of other states.

An instance that is worthy of particular theoretical attention is of course the one in which others deny recognition to the self's constitutive stories. In this case, the storied self has three options: to accept stories told of it by others, to abandon the stories that are not recognized in favor of others, or to stand by the original story and to try to convince the audiences that it in fact does apply. "Thus while the first two options mean that we accept the definitions forced upon us by others, the third option means that we force our own definition upon someone else" (Ringmar 1996a: 82, see also 185). And typically, the way to do this is to *act,* to fight; for example, to go to war. Ringmar actually veers into the heroic mode when he outlines the occasional necessity to act.[8]

Ringmar strongly insists that there are "formative moments," periods when new metaphors are launched, when individuals and groups tell new stories about themselves, and when new sets of rules emerge through which identities are classified. His example of such a "moment" is Sweden between 1520 and 1630, so these moments can be rather long. There are moments, however, that are nonformative, since Ringmar insists that at least until Nietzsche came around, identities were not there on the line to be negotiated but there simply to be used instrumentally:

> It is not possible to *live* if one perpetually questions one's own identity, and by mid-seventeenth century people's attention soon turned to different concerns—identities were once again there to be *used* rather than to be worried about. . . . man and state became unquestioned— and unquestionable—parts of a necessary social order. (Ringmar 1996a: 15)[9]

Ringmar, then, insists that he does not operate with any concept of a transcendental self, but only with a storied self; stories of self are, he insists, not stories of who "we" are but of what we are like. A narrative theory of self has been substituted for Mouffe's poststructuralist instantiationalism. On this argument, the concept of narrativity allows Ringmar to have what I argued that Mouffe and poststructuralists did not, namely, a take on "as if" stories of a state self as negotiated by its alleged members. But he is only allowed this at a rather hefty price: When it comes to asking whose stories are scrutinized, Ringmar is unabashedly state centric. That, of course, can easily be put right by investigating not only the stories of those who hold state power, but also other and competing stories of self that exist as a constitutive element of a certain collective. It would not, furthermore, harm Ringmar's story too much to take out his insistence on certain moments being formative and others not. The two major limits of this perspective on the self/other nexus lie elsewhere.

First, intentionality comes to carry an enormous amount of explanatory weight in this scheme. Not only is it seen as constitutive of an actor that he, she, or it is intentional, but it is also assumed that certain stories of self can be willfully forced upon others in the form suggested—that is, without becoming hybridized or creolized during their negotiation. The implication of this makes up the second major problem, which is that in this scheme of things, self and other become discrete and thus reified entities. At this point, a constructivist may cry foul and insist that these categories are only reified "in the stories," so that their status is somehow "only" narrative and not ontological. Such an argument would hardly carry much weight, however, inasmuch as all constitutivists insist that stories cannot be extricated from overall discourse. Thus Ringmar's constructivist take on identity politics has the "as if" story of self that is lacking in poststructuralist scholarship, but he acquires it only at the cost of a very heavy, to a poststructuralist certainly overblown, insistence on the power of intentionality. Exactly this insistence on intentionality, however, allows this constructivist perspective what a poststructuralist perspective has refrained from evolving, namely, a theorization of the process of identification as an affair between a subject and an other, and not only between a subject and an order.

At this stage in the argument, however, dedifferentiation of the much too neat categories of "poststructuralist" and "constructivist" threatens to set in, inasmuch as much work that announces itself as poststructuralist has actually *also* insisted on maintaining the idea of an acting subject. It is hardly a coincidence that among this work there are swathes of feminist and postcolonial texts. These are texts written, among other things, in order to strengthen, as it were, with the *intention* of strengthening, a political subject as feminist or postcolonial. And in this undertaking, the term of recognition has *also* been put to discursive work. For example, Gayatri Chakravorty Spivak discusses this in her essay on the subaltern study group, which goes about changing the history of colonialism by replacing the grand history of a change in mode of production from feudalism to capitalism by a number of small histories about confrontations, physical (insurgencies, rebellions, and so on) as well as semiotic (changes of sign-systems). One of the main points is to recover a sense not only of these "insurgencies" as challenges to the raj but also of the identifications that informed these moves. Lemert's citation of Spivak as an example of one who is interested in "identities" rather than "the self" may still be apposite: Spivak's interest is not in any cumulative process whereby one attempts to forge the series of invocations of identities together in a story of the self but only in the instantiations of identities as such. Thus the question arises as to the interaction of the collective identities of the raj and those of the subalterns. According to Spivak, the group consistently suggests

> that subaltern consciousness is subject to the cathexis of the élite, that it is never fully recoverable, that it is always askew from its received signifiers, indeed that it is effaced even as it is disclosed, that it is irreducibly discursive. It is, for example, chiefly a matter of "negative consciousness" in the more theoretical of these essays. . . . One view of "negative consciousness," for instance, sees it as the consciousness not of the being of the subaltern, but of that of the oppressors. Here, in vague Hegelian limnings, is the anti-humanist and anti-positivist position that it is always the desire for/of (the power of the Other) that produces an image of the self. If this is generalized, . . . it is the subaltern who provides the model for a general theory of consciousness. And yet, since the "subaltern" cannot appear without the thought of the "élite," the generalization is by definition incomplete—in philosophical language "non-originary," or, in an earlier version of "*unursprünglich*," non-primordial. (Spivak 1987b: 203)

Since recognition is the *act* of a subject, there will be no recognition if the subject is dead as an analytical category. Constructivism has an answer to this problem, but a poststructuralist may argue that the cure is worse than the disease, inasmuch as it seems to confer on the subject rather more intentionality than it may be able to carry.[10] The limit of a constructivist self/other perspective, then, is that it does not really begin to try to slink out of the political problematique surrounding sovereignty. Sovereignty remains foundational to this allegedly antifoundational perspective.

Perhaps takes such as Spivak's point to a possible way in which to transcend the limits both of poststructuralist instantiationalism and lack of intention, and constructivist tendencies toward reification and perhaps even voluntarism. Spivak's work is a reminder that *both* these two attempts at constitutivist analysis are informed by similar literatures, namely, those that have evolved out of what I have referred to throughout this book as the "Eastern excursion."

In a celebrated passage in his book on Orientalism, Edward Said acknowledged his debt to Foucault, one of the pivotal figures in bringing the theorizing along the Eastern excursion to the fore in general social theory. He did it among other things by taking issue with Foucault's bracketing of intentionality and subjectivity:

> I do believe in the determining imprint of individual writers upon the otherwise anonymous collective body of texts constituting a discursive formation like Orientalism. . . . Foucault believes that in general the individual text or author counts for very little; empirically, in the case of Orientalism (and perhaps nowhere else) I find this not to be so. (Said [1978] 1985: 23)

The investigations of "the East" as Europe's other that make up the main portion of this book point in the same direction: It is *not* only in the case of Orientalism that individual texts make a difference. It need not be voluntarist to argue that individual texts matter. Individual poststructural and constructivist texts have different insights into the self/other nexus to offer, and they have different limits to push. Their differences of presupposition, although tangible, should not be allowed to sap the strength needed for the common undertaking of strengthening constitutivist scholarship against heavy mainstream opposition. If the subject is killed off, it allows for empirical work that may brilliantly demonstrate the ontological point that any identity formation involves a representation of the self/other nexus that "maintains our relationship with that which we necessarily misconstrue, and which exceeds the alternative of presence and difference" (Derrida 1992: 20). On the level of practice, the limit of such work may be that, once essentialist stories of selves are being told about a certain human collective, it may be impossible to counter this story without recourse to some alternative story of self. Such stories will have to be "as if" stories, and they can only be told in terms of subjectivity. Conversely, the task of investing self and other with a new status of subjectivity without falling back on the category of sovereignty remains to be tackled.

The stakes are high. The readings of Europe's "Easts" in Chapters 2 through 7 demonstrate above all how a quickening of the pace of discursive work characterizes that period that may be referred to as the end of the Cold War. "Identity requires difference in order to be, and it converts difference into otherness in order to secure its own self-certainty" (Connolly 1991: 64). If essentializing stories of European selves should come even more strongly to the fore in political discourse, it has a rich array of identities on which to draw. As far as I can see, political opposition on the level of nation-states, regions, and the EU has already begun to take the shape of rallying around essentialized communities that are presented as threatened and hence in need of being secured. Difference is already being turned into otherness. "Eastern" others of all varieties are being put to good use in ethnopolitical undertakings on all the three levels discussed in this book. The political need for "as if" stories by dint of which one may counter these challenges to diversity is already pressing. Zygmunt Bauman has recently remarked that "if the *modern* 'problem of identity' is how to construct an identity and keep it solid and stable, the *postmodern* 'problem of identity' is primarily how to avoid fixation and keep the options open" (Bauman 1996: 18). This may be too complacent. If there is still a need to field "as if" stories about collective selves that can combat essentialist stories of self, and if there is at the same time a need to remind oneself and everybody else that these stories are indeed "as if" stories that really cannot be fixed, then it seems that we still face Bauman's two challenges concurrently.

Notes

1. USES OF THE OTHER IN WORLD POLITICS

1. Major contributions in addition to the works mentioned specifically in the text include Ashley and Walker 1990, Bartelson 1995, Campbell 1992, Connolly 1991, Der Derian 1987, Der Derian and Shapiro 1989, Doty 1993, Katzenstein 1996, Lapid and Kratochwil 1996, Lipschutz 1995, Milliken and Sylvan 1996, Ringmar 1996a, Weldes 1996, Wendt 1992, Wæver et al. 1993, Wæver, Holm, and Larsen forthcoming.

2. Johannes Fabian (1983) has discussed what he calls "chronopolitics," by which he means the projection by ethnographers of universal time onto universal space, so that other cultures may be depicted by them as "allochronic," and by implication, anachronistic—overtaken by "the West." I certainly would not like to present a chronopolitical analysis and suggest that *all* collective identities necessarily have to relate to "world time."

3. One notes the affinity between Norton's concerns and those of Simmel. One notes that Lacan's psychoanalytical analysis inspires Julia Kristeva. One notes that categorizations invariably break down.

4. Gayatri Chakravorty Spivak has drawn the immediate implication for social analysis in her remark that if one defines oneself as an outsider, then one consecrates an inside that is not worthy of being consecrated as such. One has, she went on, "to break down these distinctions, never once and for all, and *actively* interpret 'inside' and 'outside' as texts for involvement as well as change" (1987: 102).

5. In Bakhtin's own terms, there may also be relationships between texts, and one may thus have a dialogue even with an author long dead. As

everyone who has ever been infatuated knows, however, there are certain dimensions of relationships that simply cannot be maintained in this way.

6. According to Simon Critchley, Derrida's essay "Violence and Metaphysics," written in 1963, was "the only extended analysis of Lévinas's work to appear in either French or English during the 1960s, and it has largely determined the reception of Lévinas's thinking, particularly in the English-speaking world" (1992: 11). A sigh in Derrida's essay prefigures Kristeva's discussion of the dialectical and the dialogical in Hegel: "Lévinas is very close to Hegel, much closer than he admits, and at the very moment when he is apparently opposed to Hegel in the most radical fashion. This is a situation he must share with all anti-Hegelian thinkers, and whose final significance calls for much thought" (Derrida 1978: 99). Clearly, Derrida is also implying himself here. This kind of self-reflection on how the other about whom one writes is implied in the constitution of the writer is, unfortunately, rare in the discipline of international relations.

7. This is more complicated, however, since "God is not simply the 'first other', the 'other par excellence', or the 'absolutely other', but other than the other, other otherwise, other with an alterity prior to the alterity of the other, prior to the ethical bond with the other and different from every neighbour, transcendent to the point of absence, to the point of a possible confusion with the stirring of the *there is*" (Lévinas 1989: 179). The passage from the other to divinity is "a second step" (246), which need not concern us further here.

8. Todorov's point about the separateness of what takes place along the axiological and the epistemic axes is paralleled by Zygmunt Bauman's (1992) suggestion that there is no necessary affinity between how humans order social space cognitively and morally: People who helped refugees from the Holocaust at their own peril (moral spacing) were not necessarily informed by a "cognitive spacing" that suggested that they would do so.

9. I leave the entire business of whether comparing othering practices ethically is possible given Campbell's stated epistemology; it seems to me that Connolly is right in asserting no less than five times over that it is (1991: 60) and that Andrew Linklater is wrong in holding that it is not (1990: postscript).

10. Lévinas enters IR literature for the first time in Campbell and Dillon 1993, where he is lauded.

11. The discipline may also run the risk here of repeating an argument that has already been made better elsewhere, as when Zygmunt Bauman argued that "in a world construed of codifiable rules alone, the Other loomed on the outside of the self as a mystifying, but above all a confusingly ambivalent presence: the potential anchorage of the self's identity, yet simultaneously an obstacle, a resistance to the ego's self-assertion. In modern

ethics, the Other was the contradiction incarnate and the most awesome of stumbling-blocks on the self's march to fulfilment. If postmodernity is a retreat from the blind alleys into which radically pursued ambitions of modernity have led, a postmodern ethics would be one that readmits the Other as a neighbour, as the close-to-hand-*and*-mind, into the hard core of the moral self, back from the wasteland of calculated interests to which it had been exiled; an ethics that restores the autonomous moral significance of proximity; an ethics that recasts the Other as the crucial character in the process through which the moral self comes into its own" (1992: 84).

12. One notes that in a constructivist perspective, everything must necessarily be what most people make of it.

13. "'Strong' liberals should be troubled by the dichotomous privileging of structure over process, since transformations of identity and interest through process are transformations of structure" (Wendt 1992: 393). The agency-structure debate that has dominated theorizing in the discipline for some time now should make a discussion of what structuration is superfluous here. Suffice it to reproduce a programmatic quote from the *locus classicus* of structuration theory: "There are no universal laws in the social sciences, and there will not be any—not, first and foremost, because methods of empirical testing and validation are somehow inadequate but because, as I have pointed out, the causal conditions involved in generalizations about human social conduct are inherently in respect of the very knowledge (or beliefs) that actors have about the circumstances of their own action. . . . Consider, for example, theories of sovereignty formulated by seventeenth-century European thinkers. These were the result of reflection upon, and study of, social trends into which they in turn were fed back" (Giddens 1984: xxxii–xxxiii).

2. MAKING EUROPE: THE TURKISH OTHER

1. "Frank" and variants thereof were, incidentally, the terms of choice used when representations were made by the other; see Maalouf 1984.

2. The parenthesis was added to the 1590 and 1596 editions.

3. Bernard Lewis, Tanner Lectures, Oxford University, 26 February 1990.

3. MAKING EUROPE: THE RUSSIAN OTHER

1. Given the question at hand, the point is not the legitimacy of drawing such parallels but the simple fact that similar parallels between, say, a sixteenth-century ruler such as Elizabeth I and a twentieth-century ruler such as Margaret Thatcher are not a staple of scholarly debates about British policy. When such parallels are drawn, they are likely to be offered in a light-hearted and frivolous spirit, very different from the matter-of-fact tone in

which they may be found in a number of scholarly Russianist works. The matrices of the discussions are simply different.

2. As where most other matters are concerned, there is a marked difference between Russian and European historiography on this point. Sergej Platonov, for example, refers to the "gracious kindness . . . in matters of etiquette" ([1925] 1972: 19) displayed by Ivan IV toward foreign guests.

3. Life was cheap, and Christians were not really that tender-hearted. Suffice it to give an example of how Muslims and Christians ganged up, "alwaies laugheng," to go man-hunting: "Being one daie in the streate, there came certein TARTARIENS into the towne, and saied that in a litle woodde not past iii miles of there were about an cth horcemen of the Circasses hidden, entending to make a roade even to the towne, as they were wonte to do. At the hearing whereof I happened to be in a fletchers shoppe, wheare also was a Tartarien merchaunt that was come thither wth SEMENZINA [a drug], who, as soone ahe hearde this, rode vp and saied, why go we not to take them? Howe many horses be they? I answered, an c. Well, said he, we are five, and howe many horses woll you make? I answered, xl. O, qd he, the Circasses are no men, but women: let us go take them. Wherevpon, I went to seeke Mr. Frauncs, and tolde him what this man had saied. And he, alwaies laugheng, folowed me, asking me wheather my hert serued me to go. I answered yea; so that we tooke or horses and ordeyned certein men of ours to come by water. At about noone we assaulted these Circasses, being in the shadowe, and some of them on sleepe, but by mishappe a litle before or arryvall, our trumpett sowned: by reason wherof many of them had tyme to eskape. Nevertheles, we killed and tooke about xl of them. But to the purpose of these valiaunt fooles, the best was that this Tartarien wolde needes have had us folowe them still to take them: and seeing no man offer unto it, ranne after those that were eskaped himself alone" (Barbaro [1487?] 1873: 17).

4. A most useful collection of early English travel writing, including the trendsetting accounts of Richard Chancellor, Giles Fletcher, and Sir Jerome Horsey, is available as Berry and Crummey 1968.

5. In order to avoid the impression that Russia was unique in this sense, it must be added that this period, like the succeeding one, did not insist on hard and fast lines between Europe and non-Europe, and certainly not between Europe and Russia. Russia was constructed as being ambiguously Christian and ambiguously European, but it was not alone in being so. To quote but two examples furnished by Venetian travelogues from the end of the fifteenth century: Ambrogio Contarini wrote about the Mingrelians of the Caucasus that "they are Christians, and worship according to the rites of the Greek Church, but they have many heresies." While staying in the houses of Pangrati, king of Georgiana, who is described as a despot, Contarini and his entourage were "much annoyed by the Georgiani, who

were as mad as the Mengrelians" (Contarini 1873: 118, 119). And to the homeward bound Josafa Barbaro, the feeling of hitting upon territory familiar to him and his assumed contemporary reader appeared as he was leaving not Muscovy but Poland: "Being departed out of Polonia wthin iiij iorneys, we finde Frankforth [on the Oder], a citie of the Marquis of Brandenburgh, and so we enter into Allemaigne: whereof I neede not to speake, bicause it is a countrey in maner at home and knowen well enough" (Barbaro [1487?] 1873: 35).

6. Availing himself of an anachronistic metaphor, Serge Zenkovsky comments that "Ivan III was the first Russian ruler to begin the struggle for a window on Europe in the Baltic area" (1972: xii) and that Tsar Alexis (1645–1676) had already made "efforts" in this direction.

7. "Utinam sit, ut apud illos agat, quod tu apud Aethiopes! Si tanta Imperii illius moles regeretur ad morem culturioris Europae, majores inde fructus caperet res christiana; sed spes est, paulatim evigilaturos. Tzar Petrus agnoscit vitia suorum et vellet barbariam illiam paulatim aboleri."

8. Of course, this also implies that those around the Baltic knew more about Muskovy-Russia than they did about areas further south and that the construction of Russia as a military threat was more widespread. Following Poltava, Sweden was the most hostile of all and even initiated two inconclusive wars of revenge, in 1741–1743 and again in 1788–1790. As Matthew Anderson formulates it: "The systematic exploration and description of Russia in the eighteenth century was the work of Swedes or the Russians themselves, and above all of russified Germans—Messerschmidt, Müller, Gmelin, Pallas and others" (1958: 87). It is, therefore, hardly surprising that at the time, one of the most vituperative diatribes against Russia, *Du péril de la balance politique de l'Europe,* which appeared in Stockholm in 1789, was ascribed to Sweden's King Gustav III himself (or that they seem to have been penned by the Prussian ambassador to his court; see Anderson 1958: 154). The pamphlet, which argued that Russia, after its military success in the north, would also strike in the south, also appeared in English and German.

9. As Hans Lemberg (1985) and also Michael Confino (1994: 514–517) show, this took rather longer than Larry Wolff (1994) seems to suggest, with the shift having been effected only at the time of the Crimean War. It should be added that on the discursive evidence reproduced here, Lemberg's argument that the idea of Russia as Asiatic was a nineteenth-century German one, coinciding with a shift in the perception of it as Eastern rather than Northern, must be firmly rejected.

10. "The categories of ancient history that identified the barbarians of Eastern Europe, in Peyssonnel and above all in Gibbon, not only corresponded to the impressions of contemporary travelers, but also entered directly into the emerging social science of anthropology, most fundamentally

in Herder's discovery of the Slavs. For although the Slavs were only one barbarian people among many in the enumerations of Peyssonnel and Ségur, they were to become the essential ethnographic key to the modern idea of Eastern Europe" (Wolff 1994: 286).

11. Of course, the level of generality I've chosen works to the detriment of focusing on spatial variation at any one point in time. For example, Naarden suggests that, even in the first half of the nineteenth century, when Russophobia reached a height in other parts of Europe, it was absent in Holland (1992: 32).

12. The Testament was republished by, among others, Louis Napoleon and Hitler, see McNally 1958: 174. For further bibliographical discusion of the hoax see Groh 1961: 323–326. A dissenting view of its origin is presented by Wittram 1973: 57, who sees it as a fruit of the travels of d'Eon to St. Petersburg around 1755–1960.

13. Letter from Prague dated 1 September, reproduced in Balfour 1922: 79–81.

14. Edward Brennan (1992) ascribes the same view to L'abbé Guillaume Raynal and mentions that the chevalier de Corberon saw the existence of two peoples in Russia.

15. In 1848 (for example, *Neue Rheinische Zeitung*, 12 July), Marx had indeed advocated a military attack on Russia and called it a revolutionary necessity; Hammen 1952: 35.

16. According to an interview in the early 1980s with Sir Ian Jacob, military secretary to the War Cabinet: "When [Churchill] first saw the proposals for the occupation of Germany, and the Zones, he was absolutely horrified. He said: 'Are we going to let these barbarians right into the heart of Europe?' And he wanted to avoid that if he possibly could. Oh no, he was under no illusions about Stalin and . . . CHARLTON: But 'barbarians' he said? JACOB: Barbarians, yes" (Charlton 1984: 43).

17. In this they could draw on views widely held during the war. For example: "A report by the [British] postal censorship authorities in March 1942 stated that 'The majority of writers seem to pin their faith almost entirely on the Russians—"the chaps who don't talk but keep on killing Huns"'" (Bell 1990: 88).

18. Another marginal representation that may be briefly mentioned is Geoffrey Gorer's (for example, Gorer and Rickman 1949). Although sticking to the dominant representation that Russians were authoritarian and so on, by way of explanation he added the psychological rider that this was because they had all been so tightly swaddled as babies. This representation survives at the margins of discourse. In an article originally published in 1990 in the *Journal of Psychohistory*, it is argued that Russian political life is caused by the persistent lagging behind of Russian child-rearing practices as compared

to European ones. Lenin, one is told, was swaddled as a child and Stalin was beaten by his mother and father, whereas Gorbachev had a happy childhood. In the answer to the question whether "Soviet democracy" will prevail, one is told that "unfortunately, child-rearing progress has been very uneven in the Soviet Union and Eastern Europe. Tight swaddling, regular whippings, and abusive parenting remain common in many of the Soviet republics and in many areas of Eastern Europe even today. . . . What this lingering pattern of child abuse means is that the success of democracy in the Soviet Union and Eastern Europe is far from guaranteed" (deMause 1991: 182–183).

19. A triumphalist version has Russia going broke because of the strains imposed on it by the arms race. A Marxist version foregrounds how the present Russian leadership "sells out" by adapting to an encroaching world economy. Neumann 1996 stresses the perceived importance of adopting the most efficient economic and political models available for purposes of state competition in the international system.

4. MAKING REGIONS: NORTHERN EUROPE

1. Sundelius (1982) begins to amalgamate inside-out and outside-in approaches by indirectly introducing external factors.

2. Buzan again follows Cantori and Spiegel 1970 by characterizing "the Nordic area" as a "distinct sub-region" (see Buzan 1991: 199–200), and Deutsch 1957 in labeling it a security community (see Buzan 1991: 218).

3. One notable exception concerns economic theories of regions, in which outside pressures of capital accumulation and innovation are often held to be met not only or perhaps not even primarily by states but also by firms. In the literature on the Nordic region, however, a focus on the size of the home market and the subsequent enhanced ability to compete, so familiar, for example, in the literature on the European region, has largely been absent. This fact, as well as the failure of the Nordic countries to forge a customs union during the Cold War period, may be taken to support the view that Northern Europe is a subregion of Europe, as this very way of denoting it indeed suggests.

4. One notes the geopolitical ancestry of the term "Eurasia."

5. Public Record Office (PRO), CAB 17/59, "The threatened dissolution of the Union between Norway and Sweden (Naval aspects of the question)," 12 May 1905. I thank Mats Berdal for directing me to this source.

6. This critique is a reading of Buzan's *People, States, and Fear*, 2nd ed. (1991: 186–229), which declares itself to be the most authoritative statement of the theory (see 228, note 9).

7. Still, he admits that the delineation of the complex itself "may be a matter of controversy."

8. There was, moreover, hardly any discussion of the matter (Agrell 1985, esp. 192–226). The fact that Sweden during the immediate postwar years possessed one of the largest European aircraft fleets seems to illustrate the same point.

9. "I am convinced," Swedish Prime Minister Carl Bildt exclaimed to the National Press Club in Washington in February 1992, "that one of the most prominent features of the European decade that the 1990s will be, will be a revival of the importance of the Northern European region. And in this revival Sweden, as the largest and most centrally located of the Nordic countries, will play a pivotal role."

10. PRO, CAB 17/59.

11. In his Murmansk speech of 1987, Gorbachev also came close to availing himself of this move.

12. Incidentally, in the interwar period Swedish foreign trade with Estonia, Latvia, and Lithuania made up approximately 1 percent of total foreign trade.

13. The circumstances that allow Engholm's use of the pronoun "we" are, first, that the quote is from an article in a Danish publication and, second, that Engholm is readily recognized as a Danish name.

14. From a conversation with Andrey Fedorov, Moscow, 15 June 1991. Excerpts printed in Ny Tid (Helsinki), 7 November 1991.

15. Speech to a seminar organized by the Storting's Nordic secretariat and the Nordic Association, Oslo, 4 April 1992.

5. MAKING REGIONS: CENTRAL EUROPE

1. However, although Schöpflin contends that "all identities are to an extent constructed," he fails to recognize that cultural differences do not necessarily make a difference in themselves; only when they are politically processed and thus charged with political meaning can they play that role. Indeed, it is a truism that phenomena are simply not political before they enter the political field.

2. It ought, perhaps, to be pointed out that the two quotations contradict each other. Moreover, the Marxian insistence on separating "political programmes" from "reality," false consciousness from "objective factors," is diametrically opposite to the tack taken here, where discourse is held to constitute reality.

3. This central issue is highlighted, for example, in Schwarz 1989 and Rupnik 1990. "Eastern Europe" seems to be the term used to denote the area in its degrading geopolitical incarnation, prostrate before the Soviet Union. "Mitteleuropa" is used less consistently to evoke the same image, but with Germany in the role of predator. "Central Europe," on the other hand, is the term used to denote the cultural achievement of the area, achievement

that has ostensibly peaked when Russia and Germany have been kept at bay. The central exception to this generalization is György Konrád, who asserts that there "exists a dream about *Mitteleuropa* [*Közepeuropa*]. It demands a certain breeding, historical insight and philosophical open-mindedness. . . . Most integrated, most Middle European, is that people which does most for its own and its neighbours' honour. . . . A Middle European is one who regards the bifurcation of Europe as neither natural nor final" (1991: 20). However, when the journal *Cross Currents*, whose the subtitle is *A Yearbook of Central European Culture*, ran a translation of this essay, it was as "Is the Dream of Central Europe Still Alive?" (1985). And thus Konrád, too, was pressed into service. Whether he minded is quite another matter; elsewhere, he writes that "the ground is shaky beneath the Russians' feet, too, simply because they are here in Europe and not at home in the Soviet Union" (Konrád 1985: 5).

4. This is a translation of the French title; it was published in the United States as "The Tragedy of Central Europe" in *The New York Review of Books*, 26 April 1984.

5. See Kundera's postscript to the Czech version of his novel *A Joke* (1991). This might also explain why he did not want to oblige when Schöpflin and Wood wanted to reprint his essay in their anthology; see Schöpflin and Wood 1989: 140.

6. One aspect that Šimečka does not bring up but that is clearly relevant here is the strong Pan-Slavist tradition that has made off-and-on appearances in this part of the world. Banać 1987 attacks Kundera from the Pan-Slav angle.

7. The first two quotes are from "Things'll Get Better! (Won't They?): Eva Kantürková in Conversation with Milan Šimečka," part I, *East European Reporter* 2, no. 1 (1986): 11 and 13, respectively. The third quote is from part 2, *East European Reporter* 2, no. 3 (1987): 20.

8. Two can play at this game, however. Reacting to another piece by Kundera, Joseph Brodsky wrote in the *New York Times* (reprinted as Brodsky 1986) that "the sad truth about him [Kundera] (and many of his East European brethren) is that this extraordinary writer has fallen an unwitting victim to the geopolitical certitude of his fate—the concept of an East-West divide. . . . Having lived for so long in Eastern Europe (Western Asia to some), it is only natural that Mr. Kundera should want to be more European than the Europeans themselves." Like Kantürková, Brodsky subsumes "Eastern Europe" under another regional umbrella to make his point, which happens to be diametrically opposite to hers.

9. Interestingly, as a Hungarian Vajda makes no mention of Romania in the article. Would he classify it as wholly other, or as a Central European other? Or would some other category have to be invented, Balkan perhaps,

or the sui generis category "trans-Danubian"? I thank Charles E. King for translating the last for me from Paleologu 1991, chapter 3, where it is maintained that Romania is not a Balkan country but a trans-Danubian one.

10. The struggle between these two tendencies has also been observable further West: "Many Germans developed a conception of culture and politics according to which the Germans were deeper, and had a more inner-dictated concept of culture, and a more organic attitude towards society and state. This was compared with the individualistic, superficial Western democracies. At the same time, however, Germany was seen as distinct from the mysticism and despotism of the East (Russia, Asia and the like). Thus the ideology of the culture in the middle, the culture in-between the excesses of the West and the excesses of the East" (Wæver, Holm, and Larsen, forthcoming). This description of German debates also fits the Central European one, and the Russian discourse visited in Chapter 6 of this book as well, for that matter.

6. MAKING NATIONS: RUSSIA

1. This perspective, whereby a wide range of representations will be subsumed under the two headings of "Westernizers" and "nationalists," is warranted on the level of generality chosen in this book. A book-length study of Russian discourse on Europe over the last two hundred years that avails itself of a more finely gridded classificatory scheme is available in Neumann 1996.

2. The very expression "common European home" first emerged during a visit by Leonid Brezhnev to Bonn. This was reported in *Pravda* (Moscow) 24 November 1981 and commented on in the following day's edition of *Pravda* in an article entitled "Evropa: nash obshchiy dom"; see Sodaro 1990: 281. Gorbachev first used it in a speech to the House of Commons reported in *Pravda* 19 December 1984; see Adomeit 1990: 243.

3. By calling his article "I am a Russophobe" Novikov cocks a snook at Igor' Shafarevich, whose article "Rusofobiya" will be discussed later in the chapter.

4. An editorial introduction to Shafarevich's article states that "the article was written in the beginning of the 1980s; however, the reader may convince himself that it has not lost its relevance." Thus the journal *Nash sovremennik,* in which the article was published, explicitly threw its support behind the article.

5. Pozdnakov's article was originally presented at a conference at the Moscow State Institute for International Relations (MGIMO) in April 1991. Inconsistent English spelling retained.

6. Sakharov's reports stressed that "a feeling of Great Russian nationalism and a fear of becoming dependent on the West is combined, in a signifi-

cant section of the Russian people and the nation's leadership, with a fear of democratic reform. Once they land on fertile soil, Solzhenitsyn's errors may become dangerous" (Sakharov [1974] 1977: 301). He writes that "I also find myself far from Solzhenitsyn's views on the role of Marxism as an allegedly 'Western' and anti-religious teaching which perverted a healthy Russian course of development. In general I cannot comprehend this very separation of ideas into Western and Russian. In my opinion the only division of ideas and concepts in a scientific, rational approach to social and natural phenomena can be in categories of right and wrong. And just where is this healthy Russian course of development? Has there in fact ever been even one moment in Russia's, as well as any country's history, when she was capable of developing without contradictions and cataclysms? . . . I object primarily to the attempts to partition off our country from the supposedly pernicious influence of the West" ([1974] 1977: 294).

7. A variant of nationalism even closer to the spiritual end of the spiritual-statist continuum is Dmitriy S. Likhachev's. Likhachev was actually able to have such ideas published openly even during the Soviet period: "Today, we perceive Europe as our own" (1980: 33), and he wants a relationship with Europe based on cooperation rather than isolation or *Kulturkampf.*

7. MAKING NATIONS: BASHKORTOSTAN

1. I should like to extend a word of thanks to Mikhail Kryukov for research that has gone into this chapter.

2. At the same time, and sometimes in a manner contradicting the main thrust of Tatar initiatives, Tatar activists in Bashkortostan emphasized their status as a people in diaspora. For example, representatives of the Tatar community in Ufa have appealed for a referendum on reunification of the regions in Bashkortostan populated by Tatars with Tatarstan.

3. Sultan-Galiev is a key figure in Russian-Muslim relations generally. As leader of the "right wing" of the Tatar Communist Party, he saw the weak link in the capitalist chain as lying in the East and not in the West, and he thought that Communists should permeate the Islamic East *in cooperation with* local religious and nationalist leaders. Having served Soviet ends in Muslim territories, Sultan-Galiev ended his days in Stalin's camps. From June 1923 onward "Sultan-Galievism" became Stalinese for "Muslim bourgeois nationalism," and local Muslim leaders were condemned to death for it throughout Soviet Muslim territory (Pipes 1964: 171f.; Heller and Nekrich 1986: 154f.).

4. The organization's Tartu coordinative council is in charge of dealing with the rights of unrepresented nations on the territory of the former U.S.S.R., with priority being accorded to Russia.

8. CONCLUSION: SELF AND OTHER AFTER THE DEATH OF THE SOVEREIGN SUBJECT

1. Žižek, who has done more than anyone else to apply Lacanian and Althusserian approaches to identification to the study of politics, would probably object to this particular act of naming and insist that one cannot call both him and Lacan poststructuralists; see Laclau's foreward to Žižek (1989: xii).

2. This, Mouffe argues, is because "liberal thought employs a logic of the social based on a conception of being as presence, and which conceives of objectivity as being inherent to things themselves. This is why it is impossible for liberal thought to recognize that there can only be an identity when it is constructed as a 'difference,' and that any social objectivity is constituted by the enactment of power" (1994: 108).

3. "*Oneself as Another* suggests from the outset that the selfhood of oneself implies otherness to such an intimate degree that one cannot be thought of without the other, that instead one passes into the other, as we might say in Hegelian terms. To 'as' I should like to attach a strong meaning, not only that of a comparison (oneself similar to another) but indeed that of an implication (oneself inasmuch as being other)" (Ricoeur [1990] 1992: 3).

4. This, of course, is a much elaborated point in the literature on nation building, where Anderson (1983) had already criticized Hobsbawm's reading of the invention of tradition not only for wanting to install *another* invention once the old one had been exposed but also for equating the exposure of the imagined character of a certain nation with a diminution of its reality.

5. A reading of these negotiations is being made available as Neumann forthcoming.

6. Neither does the related bid suggested by Louis Althusser, namely, the political concept of interpellation, which "can be imagined along the lines of the most commonplace everyday police (or other) hailing: 'Hey, you there!'. . . The hailed individual will turn round. By this mere one-hundred-and-eighty-degree physical conversion, he becomes a *subject*. Why? Because he has recognized that the hail was 'really' addressed to him, and that 'it was *really him* who was hailed' (and not someone else)" (Althusser 1971: 163). As pointed out by, among others, Paul Hirst (1981), the Althusserian notion of interpellation points up the set-piece problems of structuralist accounts in all their varieties, since it ascribes a certain agency to structures while locating structures to a presocial field. In addition to this old problem, one may add the one I noted earlier, that the other has really been assassinated as a subject, inasmuch as Althusser has made the hailer into a policeman—that is, an individual whose role as a subject is simply that of executor for the order. One notes that Lévinas's framing of the issue of how "the other" con-

fers an ipso facto responsibility on the self simply by *presenting his face* is subject to the same problem: In Lévinas, "the other" is simply a speck of God, not an individual. Whereas Althusser chooses a policeman to underline the structural quality of "the other," Lévinas opts for a transcendental quantity. Jean-François Lyotard admirably and tactfully highlights this problem when he represents Lévinas by drawing on the figure of the angel: "I hear: *Hail*, and I am the angel's obligee, the you of the other" (1988: 111, Lévinas note).

7. Again, Edkins contrasts the two nicely with Žižek, when she shows how he "makes contrasts with the [Derridean] deconstructionist view of identity. Deconstruction sees identity or 'presence' as impossible in the case of opposites, which are constituted by an 'outside,' a supplement. These dichotomies are viewed within deconstruction, Žižek claims, as a paradoxical sort of identity. For Lacan, identity itself is nothing but a name for this 'supplementary feature which "sticks out" and suspends the essential quality of the domain whose identity it constitutes" (1996: 7).

8. See Neumann 1997 for a poststructurally informed critique of this and a number of the other points raised here.

9. This insistence on the need for coherence in order to live is reiterated by most constructivists: "To have some sense of social being in the world requires that lives be more than different series of isolated events or combined variables and attributes; ontological narratives thus process events into episodes" (Somers and Gibson 1994: 61). I should like to be very explicit on this point: I do *not* share this view that humans "need" a narrative of self for ontological reasons. My argument is only that given the state of discourse as it stands in Europe today, in order for a discursive move to be politically effective in a situation in which stories of selves are in circulation, an "as if" story of self needs to be fielded. This situation could, and hopefully will, change, but for the time being, this seems to be a consequence of how discourse is formatted.

10. There may be two, if one adds the idea of articulation. Jutta Weldes has shown, with reference to Stuart Hall, how "to articulate" may mean both to utter—that is, to fasten an utterance onto a conversation—but also to connect the front and the back of a lorry in order to construct what in British English is known as an articulated lorry. Thus, "The term 'articulation' refers to the process through which meaning is produced out of extant cultural raw materials or linguistic resources. Meaning is created and temporarily fixed by establishing chains of connotations among different linguistic elements. In this way, different terms and ideas come to connote one another and thereby to be welded into associative chains. Most of these terms and ideas—what I am calling linguistic elements or linguistic resources—are ones already extant within a culture. . . . With their successful repeated articulation, these linguistic elements come to seem as though they are inherently

or necessarily connected and the meanings they produce come to seem natural" (1996: 284–285). Weldes specifically takes issue with poststructuralist privileging of the signifier over the signified—and hence also with the poststructural take on identification in the form of the concept of quilting—when she insists that the notion of articulation "refuses the complete arbitrariness of the connection between linguistic elements," that it is the specific product of specific people (307–308, note 24).

References

Adenauer, Konrad. 1983. *Briefe, 1945–1947*. Edited by Hans Peter Mensing. Berlin: Siedler.

Adomeit, Hannes. 1990. "The Impact of Perestroika on Soviet European Policy." In *Perestroika: Soviet Domestic and Foreign Policies,* edited by Tsuyoshi Hasegawa and Alex Pravda, 242–266. London: SAGE, Royal Institute of International Affairs.

Ágh, Attila. 1991. "After the Revolution: A Return to Europe." In *Towards a Future European Peace Order?,* edited by Karl E. Birnbaum, Josef B. Binter, and Stephen K. Badzik, 83–97. London: Macmillan.

Agrell, Wilhelm. 1985. *Alliansfrihet och atombomber: Kontinuitet och förändring i den svenska försvarsdoktrinen, 1945–1982*. Stockholm: Liber.

Algarotti, Count Francesco. [1769] 1971. "Impressions of St Petersburg (1739)." In *Russia under Western Eyes, 1517–1825,* edited by Anthony Cross, 183–188. London: Elek.

Alker, Hayward R. 1992. "The Humanistic Moment: Thucydides and Las Casas." *International Studies Quarterly* 36 (4): 347–371.

Althusser, Louis. 1971. *Lenin and Philosophy and Other Essays*. London: New Left Books.

Anderson, Benedict. 1983. *Imagined Communities: Reflections on the Origin and Spread of Nationalism*. London: Verso.

Anderson, Matthew Smith. 1958. *Britain's Discovery of Russia, 1553–1815*. London: Macmillan.

———. 1966. *The Eastern Question, 1774–1923: A Study in International Relations*. London: Macmillan.

Andrén, Nils. 1991. "Norden and a New European Security Order." In *Towards a New Security Order: The 1990–91 Yearbook,* edited by Bo Huldt and Gunilla Herlof, 279–292. Stockholm: Swedish Institute of International Affairs.

Arendt, Hannah. [1951] 1973. *The Origins of Totalitarianism.* New York: Harcourt Brace Jovanovich.

Aron, Raymond. 1965. *Démocratie et totalitarisme.* Paris: Gallimard.

Åselius, Gunnar. 1994. *The "Russian Menace" to Sweden: The Belief System of a Small Power Security Elite in the Age of Imperialism, 1880–1914.* Stockholm: Almquist and Wiksell, Acta Universitatis Stockholmiensis, no. 51.

Ash, Timothy Garton. [1986] 1989a. "Does Central Europe Exist?" In *The Uses of Adversity: Essays on the Fate of Central Europe,* 179–213. New York: Random House.

———. [1986] 1989b. "Reform or Revolution?" In *The Uses of Adversity: Essays on the Fate of Central Europe,* 242–303. New York: Random House.

———. 1990. "Mitteleuropa?" *Daedalus* 119: 1–21.

Ash, Timothy Garton, Michael Mertes, and Dominique Moïsi. 1991. "Let the East Europeans In!" *The New York Review of Books,* 24 October, p. 19.

Ashley, Richard. 1987. "The Geopolitics of Geopolitical Space: Toward a Critical Social Theory of International Politics." *Alternatives* 12 (4): 403–434.

———. 1989. "Living on Border Lines: Man, Poststructuralism, and War." In *International/Intertextual Relations: Postmodern Readings of World Politics,* edited by James Der Derian and Michael J. Shapiro, 259–321. Lexington, Mass.: Lexington.

Ashley, Richard, and R. B. J. Walker. 1990. "Reading Dissidence/Writing the Discipline: Crisis and the Question of Sovereignty in International Studies." *International Studies Quarterly,* Special Issue: *Speaking the Language of Exile,* 24 (3): 367–416.

Bakhtin, Mikhail M. 1990. "Author and Hero in Aesthetic Activity." In *Art and Answerability: Early Philosophical Essays,* edited by Michael Holquist and Vadim Liapunov, 4–256. Austin: University of Texas Press.

Balfour, Lady Frances Campbell. 1922. *The Life of George, Fourth Earl of Aberdeen, K.G., K.T.* Vol. 1. London: Hodder and Stoughton.

Banać, Ivo. 1987. "Milan Kundera i povratak Srednje Evrope." *Gordogan* 9 (1): 39–46.

Banks, Michael. 1969. "Systems Analysis and the Study of Regions." *International Studies Quarterly,* 4 (13): 335–360.

Barbaro, Josafa [Giosofat]. [1487?] 1873. "Travels of Josafa Barbaro." In

Travels to Tana and Persia by Josafa Barbaro, Ambrogio Contadini, et al., edited by Lord Stanley of Alderley, 1–101. London: Hakluyt Society.

Bartelson, Jens. 1995. *A Genealogy of Sovereignty.* Cambridge: Cambridge University Press.

Barth, Fredrik. 1969a. Introduction to *Ethnic Groups and Boundaries*, 9–38. Oslo: Norwegian University Press.

———, ed. 1969b. *Ethnic Groups and Boundaries.* Oslo: Norwegian University Press.

———. 1994. "Enduring and Emerging Issues in the Analysis of Ethnicity." In *Anthropology of Ethnicity: Beyond "Ethnic Groups and Boundaries,"* 11–32. Amsterdam: Het Spinhuis.

Baudrillard, Jean. [1976] 1993. *Symbolic Exchange and Death.* Theory, Culture, and Society. London: Sage.

Bauman, Zygmunt. 1992. *Postmodern Ethics.* Oxford: Blackwell.

———. 1996. "From Pilgrim to Tourist; or, A Short History of Identity." In *Questions of Cultural Identity*, edited by Stuart Hall and Paul du Gay, 18–36. London: Sage.

Baumer, Franklin L. 1944. "England, the Turk, and the Common Corps of Christendom." *American Historical Review* 50 (1): 26–48.

Behnke, Andreas. 1995. "Re-Presenting the West: Nato's Security Discourse after the End of the Cold War." Paper presented to the Second Pan-European Conference on International Relations, 13–16 September, Paris.

Bell, P. M. H. 1990. *John Bull and the Bear: British Public Opinion, Foreign Policy, and the Soviet Union, 1941–1945.* London: Edward Arnold.

Berkes, Niyazi. 1964. *The Development of Secularism in Turkey.* Montreal: McGill University Press.

Berner, Örjan. 1992. *Soviet Policies toward the Nordic Countries.* Lanham, Md.: University Press of America.

Bernstein, Richard J. 1991. *The New Constellation: The Ethical-Political Horizons of Modernity/Postmodernity.* Cambridge: Polity.

Berry, Lloyd E., and Robert O. Crummey, eds. 1968. *Rude and Barbarous Kingdom: Russia in the Accounts of Sixteenth-Century English Travel Voyagers.* Madison: University of Wisconsin Press.

Bingen, Jon. 1991. *Norden, Europa og nordisk samarbeide i et historisk perspektiv.* Oslo: Norwegian Institute of International Affairs.

Bischof, Guenter, and Emil Brix. 1991. "The Central European Perspective." In *Europe and the Superpowers: Essays on European International Politics*, edited by Robert S. Jordan, 217–234. New York: St. Martin's Press.

Bloom, William. 1990. *Personal Identity, National Identity, and International Relations.* Cambridge: Cambridge University Press.

Bojtár, Endre. 1988. "Eastern or Central Europe?" *Cross Currents: A Yearbook of Central European Culture* 7: 253–269.

Bonsdorff, Göran von. 1991. "Östersjöregionens framtid." In *Att välja väg: Finlands roll i Europa*, edited by Marianne Carlsson et al., 103–108. Helsinki: Söderström.

Borisov, Vadim. [1974] 1975. "Personality and National Awareness." In *From under the Rubble*, edited by Alexander Solzhenitsyn et al., 194–228. London: Collins and Harvill.

Børresen, Beate. 1991. *Enhetstanken i Norden—fra Kalmar-unionen til Napoleonskrigene*. Oslo: Norwegian Institute of International Affairs.

Botero, Giovanni. [1589] 1956. *The Reason of State*. London: Routledge.

Bovin, A. E. and V. P. Lukin. 1989. "Perestroyka mezhdunarodnykh otnosheniy—puti i podkhody." *MEiMO*, 33 (1): 58–70.

Brennan, Edward. 1992. "Praviteli i upravlyaemye: Poryadki v Rossii v predstavlenii Zapada." Lecture given at the Kennan Institute, Washington, D.C., April 1988 and published in *Nezavisimaya gazeta*, 14 April.

Brodsky, Joseph. 1986. "Why Milan Kundera Is Wrong about Dostoyevsky." Reprinted in *Cross Currents: A Yearbook of Central European Culture* 5: 477–483.

Bronfenbrenner, Urie. 1961. "The Mirror Image in Soviet-American Relations: A Social Psychologist's Report." *Journal of Social Issues* 17 (1): 45–56.

Brown, Archie. 1990. "Perestroika and the Political System." In *Perestroika: Soviet Domestic and Foreign Policies*, edited by Tsuyoshi Hasegawa and Alex Pravda, 56–87. London: Sage, Royal Institute of International Affairs.

Brundtland, Arne Olav. 1966. "The Nordic Balance: Past and Present." *Cooperation and Conflict* 1 (1): 30–63.

———. 1992. "Østersjøpolitikk sett fra Norge." *Nordisk kontakt* 37: 44–47.

Bull, Hedley. 1977. *The Anarchical Society: A Study of Order in World Politics*. London: Macmillan.

———. 1990. "The Importance of Grotius in the Study of International Relations." In *Hugo Grotius and International Relations*, edited by Hedley Bull, Benedict Kingsbury, and Adam Roberts, 65–93. Oxford: Clarendon.

Bull, Hedley, Benedict Kingsbury, and Adam Roberts, eds. 1990. *Hugo Grotius and International Relations*. Oxford: Clarendon.

Bull, Hedley, and Adam Watson, eds. 1984. *The Expansion of International Society*. Oxford: Clarendon.

Bungs, Dzintra. 1988. "Joint Political Initiatives by Estonians, Latvians, and Lithuanians as Reflected in Samizdat Materials, 1969–1987." *Journal of Baltic Studies* 19 (3): 267–271.

Burbank, Jane. 1986. *Intelligentsia and Revolution: Russian Views of Bolshevism, 1917–1922*. New York: Oxford University Press.

Burke, Edmund. 1907. *The Works of the Right Honourable Edmund Burke.* Vol. 6. London: Oxford University Press.

Burmeister, H.-P., F. Boldt, and Gy. Mészáros, eds. 1988. *Mitteleuropa: Traum oder Trauma? Überlegungen zum Selbstbild einer Region.* Bremen: Temmen.

Buzan, Barry. 1991. *People, States, and Fear: An Agenda for International Security Studies in the Post–Cold War Era.* 2nd ed. Hemel Hempstead, Eng.: Harvester Wheatsheaf.

Cadot, Michel. 1967. *L'image de la Russie dans la vie intellectuelle française (1839–1856).* Paris: Fayard.

Campbell, David. 1992. *Writing Security: United States Foreign Policy and the Politics of Identity.* [Rev. ed., 1998.] Minneapolis: University of Minnesota Press.

———. 1993. *Politics without Principle: Sovereignty, Ethics, and the Narratives of the Gulf War.* Boulder, Colo.: Lynne Rienner.

———. 1994. "The Deterritorialization of Responsibility: Lévinas, Derrida, and Ethics after the End of Philosophy." *Alternatives* 19 (4): 455–484.

———. 1996. "The Politics of Radical Interdependence: A Rejoinder to Daniel Warner." *Millennium* 25 (1): 129-145.

Campbell, David, and Michael Dillon, eds. 1993. *The Political Subject of Violence.* Manchester, Eng.: Manchester University Press.

Cantori, Louis J., and Steven L. Spiegel. 1970. *The International Politics of Regions: A Comparative Framework.* Englewood Cliffs, N.J., Prentice-Hall.

Carr, E. H. 1958. *Socialism in One Country, 1924–1926.* Vol. 1. London: Macmillan.

Caute, David. 1973. *Les Compagnons de route, 1917–1968.* Paris: Robert Laffont.

Chancen einer stärkeren Einbindung Schleswig-Holsteins in den Ostseeraum. 1990. Kiel: Denkfabrik Schleswig-Holstein.

Charlton, Michael. 1984. *The Eagle and the Small Birds: Crisis in the Soviet Empire. From Yalta to Solidarity.* Chicago: University of Chicago Press.

Chatterjee, Partha. 1986. *Nationalist Thought and the Colonial World: A Derivative Discourse?* London: Zed.

———. 1993. *The Nation and Its Fragments: Colonial and Postcolonial Histories.* Princeton: Princeton University Press.

Cherniavsky, Michael. 1958. "'Holy Russia': A Study in the History of an Idea." *American History Review* 63 (3): 617–637.

Cohen, Stephen F. 1974. *Bukharin and the Bolshevik Revolution: A Political Biography, 1888–1938.* London: Wildwood.

Confino, Michael. 1994. "Re-Inventing the Enlightenment: Western Images of Eastern Realities in the Eighteenth Century." *Canadian Slavonic Papers* 36 (3–4): 505–522.

Connolly, William E. 1985. "Taylor, Foucault, and Otherness." *Political Theory* 13 (3): 365–376.

———. 1991. *Identity/Difference: Democratic Negotiations of Political Paradox*. Ithaca, N.Y.: Cornell University Press.

Connor, Walker. 1984. *The National Question in Marxist-Leninist Theory and Strategy*. Princeton: Princeton University Press.

Contarini, Ambrogio. 1873. "The Travels of the Magnificent M. Ambrogio Contarini, Ambassador of the Illustrious Signory of Venice to the Great Lord Ussuncassan, King of Persia, in the Year 1473." In *Travels to Tana and Persia by Josafa Barbaro, Ambrogio Contadini, et al.,* edited by Lord Stanley of Alderley, 105–173. London: Hakluyt Society.

Critchley, Simon. 1992. *The Ethics of Deconstruction: Derrida and Levinas*. Oxford: Blackwell.

Cross, Anthony, ed. 1971. *Russia under Western Eyes 1517–1825*. London: Elek.

Cross, S. H. 1933. "Mediaeval Russian Contacts with the West." *Speculum* 10: 137–144.

Custine, Marquis de. [1843] 1975. *Lettres de Russie: La Russie en 1839*. Paris: Gallimard.

Dahl, Hans Fredrik. 1994. "Fram mot det ukjente: Nansen-ekspedisjonen i historisk lys." *Nytt norsk tidsskrift* 11 (1): 24–37.

Dalby, Simon. 1988. "Geopolitical Discourse: The Soviet Union as Other." *Alternatives* 13 (4): 415–442.

———. 1990. *Creating the Second Cold War*. London: Pinter.

Dallmayr, Fred R. 1981. *Twilight of Subjectivity: Contributions to a Post-Individualist Theory of Politics*. Amherst: University of Massachusetts Press.

Danilevsky, Nikolay Yakovlevich. [1869] 1888. *Rossiya i Evropa: Vzglyad na kul'turnyya i politicheskiya otnosheniya Slavyanskago mira k Germano-Romanskomy.* 3rd ed. St. Petersburg: Strakhov.

Davies, Merryl Wyn, Ashis Nandy, and Ziauddin Sardar. 1993. *Barbaric Others: A Manifesto on Western Racism*. London: Pluto.

Delanty, Gerard. 1995. *Inventing Europe: Idea, Identity, Reality*. Houndsmills, Eng.: Macmillan.

Deletant, Dennis, and Harry Hanak, eds. 1988. *Historians as Nation-Builders: Central and South-East Europe*. London: Macmillan.

deMause, Lloyd. 1991. "The Gentle Revolution: The Childhood Origins of Soviet and East European Democratic Movements." In *Politics and Psychology: Contemporary Psychodynamic Perspectives,* edited by Joan Offerman-Zuckerberg, 177–184. New York: Plenum.

den Boer, Pim. 1995. "Europe to 1914: The Making of an Idea." In *What Is Europe?* Vol. 1: *The History of the Idea of Europe*, by Pim den Boer, Peter Bugge, and Ole Wæver (series editors Kevin Wilson and Jan van der Dussen), 13–82. London: Routledge.

Der Derian, James. 1987. *On Diplomacy: A Genealogy of Western Estrangement.* Oxford: Blackwell.

———. 1991. "Genealogy, Security, and the Gulf War: A Case for a Poststructural Approach." Paper presented to the annual British International Studies Association Conference, 16–18 December, Warwick, England.

———. 1994. "Fathers (and Sons), Mother Courage (and Her Children), and the Dog, the Cave, and the Beef." In *Global Voice*, edited by James N. Rosenau, 83–97. Boulder, Colo.: Westview Press.

Der Derian, James, and Michael J. Shapiro, eds. 1989. *International/ Intertextual Relations: Postmodern Readings of World Politics.* Lexington, Mass.: Lexington.

Derrida, Jacques. 1974. *Of Grammatology.* Baltimore: Johns Hopkins University Press.

———. 1978. "Violence and Metaphysics: An Essay on the Thought of Emmanuel Lévinas." In *Writing and Difference*, 79–153. London: Routledge.

———. 1981. "Plato's Pharmacy." In *Dissemination*, 61–171. London: Athlone.

———. 1992. *The Other Heading: Reflections on Today's Europe.* Bloomington: Indiana University Press.

Desjardins, Robert. 1988. *The Soviet Union through French Eyes, 1945–85.* Basingstoke, Eng.: Macmillan/St. Antony's College.

Deutsch, Karl W. 1957. *Political Community and the North Atlantic Area.* Princeton: Princeton University Press.

Dostoyevsky, Fyodor Mikhaylovich. [1876–1881] 1954. *The Diary of a Writer.* New York: George Braziller.

Doty, Roxanne Lynn. 1993. "Foreign Policy as Social Construction: A Post-Positivist Analysis of US Insurgency Policy in the Philippines." *International Studies Quarterly* 37 (3): 297–320.

———. 1996. *Imperial Encounters.* Minneapolis: University of Minnesota Press.

Douglas, Mary. [1957] 1975. "Animals in Lele Religious Symbolism." In *Implicit Meaning: Essays in Anthropology*, 27–46. London: Routledge and Kegan Paul.

———. [1966] 1984. *Purity and Danger: An Analysis of the Concepts of Pollution and Taboo.* London: Ark.

Duncan, Peter John Stuart. 1989. "Russian Messianism: A Historical and Political Analysis." Ph.D. diss., University of Glasgow.

Dunne, Timothy. 1995. "The Social Construction of International Society." *European Journal of International Relations* 1 (3): 367–389.

Durkheim, Emile. 1964. *The Division of Labour in Society.* New York: Free Press.

Duroselle, Jean-Baptiste. 1965. *L'idée d'Europe dans l'histoire.* Paris: Denoël.

Edkins, Jenny. 1996. "Facing Hunger: 'International Community,' Desire, and the Real in Responses to Humanitarian Disaster." Paper presented to the annual British International Studies Association Conference, 16–18 December, Durham, England.

Eisenstadt, Shmuel, and Bernd Giessen. 1996. "Analytical Frameworks for the Research Programme." Manuscript, Jerusalem University.

Engels, Friedrich. [1890] 1952. "The Foreign Policy of Russian Czarism." In *The Russian Menace to Europe: Karl Marx and Friedrich Engels,* edited by Paul W. Blackstone and Bert F. Hoselitz, 25–55. Glencoe, Ill.: Free Press.

Epstein, Arnold L. 1978. *Ethnos and Identity: Three Studies in Ethnicity.* London: Tavistock.

Eriksen, Thomas Hylland. 1993. *Ethnicity and Nationalism.* London: Pluto.

Etzioni, Amitai. 1965. *Political Unification: A Comparative Study of Leaders and Forces.* New York: Holt, Rinehart, and Winston.

Fabian, Johannes. 1983. *Time and the Other: How Anthropology Makes Its Object.* New York: Columbia University Press.

Fichte, Johann. [1800] 1979. *Der geschlossene Handelsstaat.* Hamburg: Felix Meiner.

Foucault, Michel. 1972. *The Archeology of Knowledge.* London: Tavistock.

———. 1974. *The Archaeology of Knowledge.* London: Tavistock.

———. 1977a. "Nietzsche, Genealogy, History." In *Language, Counter-Memory, Practice: Selected Essays and Interviews,* by Michel Foucault, edited by David Bouchard, 137–164. Oxford: Basil Blackwell.

———. 1977b. *Discipline and Punish: The Birth of the Prison.* London: Allen Lane.

———. 1980. Interviewed by the editors of the journal *Hérodote,* "Questions of Geography." In *Michel Foucault: Power/Knowledge. Selected Interviews and Other Writings 1972–1977,* edited by Colin Gordon, 137–164. Brighton, Eng.: Harvester.

Friedman, Jonathan. 1991. "Further Notes on the Advents of Phallus in Blunderland." In *Constructing Knowledge: Authority and Critique in Social Sciences,* edited by Lorraine Nencel and Peter Pels, 95–113. Inquiries in Social Construction. London: Sage.

Gallie, W. B. 1978. *Philosophers of Peace and War.* Cambridge: Cambridge University Press.

Garipov, Talmas Magsumovich. 1988. *Russkiy jazyk v Bashkirii i ego vzaimodeystvie s bashkirskim jazykom.* Ufa: Bashkirsky Filial Akademii Nauk.

Gasché, Rodolphe. 1986. *The Tain and the Mirror: Derrida and the Philosophy of Reflection*. Cambridge: Harvard University Press.

Geertz, Clifford. 1979. "From the Native's Point of View: On the Nature of Anthropological Understanding." In *Interpretive Social Science*, 225–241. Berkeley: University of California Press.

Gefter, Mikhail. 1989. In conversation with Gleb Pavlovskiy. "Dom Evraziya." *Vek XX i mir* 32 (6): 22–27.

Gellner, Ernest. 1983. *Nations and Nationalism*. Oxford, Blackwell.

George, Alexander L., and Gordon A. Craig. [1983] 1990. *Force and Statecraft: Diplomatic Problems of Our Time*. 2nd ed. New York: Oxford University Press.

Gerner, Kristian. 1991. *Centraleuropas återkomst*. Stockholm: Norstedts.

Gerschenkron, Alexander. 1962. "Economic Development in Russian Intellectual History of the Nineteenth Century." In *Economic Backwardness in Historical Perspective: A Book of Essays*. Cambridge: Harvard University Press.

Giddens, Anthony. 1984. *The Constitution of Society: Outline of the Theory of Structuration*. Cambridge: Polity.

———. 1991. *Modernity and Self-Identity: Self and Society in the Late Modern Age*. Cambridge: Polity.

Gleason, John Howes. 1950. *The Genesis of Russophobia in Great Britain: A Study of the Interaction of Policy and Opinion [1815–1841]*. Cambridge: Harvard University Press.

Gleason, Philip. 1983. "Identifying Identity: A Semantic History." *Journal of American History* 69 (4): 910–931.

Gleditsch, Nils Petter, et al. 1990. *Svaner på vildveie? Nordens sikkerhed mellem supermagtsflåder og europæisk opbrud*. Copenhagen: Vindrose.

Goldberg, A. L. 1963. "Diter Gro otluchaet Rossiyu ot Evropy." *Itoriya SSSR* 5: 208–212.

Gollwitzer, Heinz. 1964. *Europa bild und Europagedanke: Beiträge zur deutschen Geistesgeschichte des 18. und 19. Jahrhunderts*. Munich: C. H. Beck.

Gong, Gerrit W. 1984. *The Standard of "Civilization" in International Society*. Oxford: Clarendon.

Gorbachev, Mikhail. [1987] 1988. *Perestroika: New Thinking for Our Country and the World*. 2nd ed. London: Fontana.

Gorer, Geoffrey, and John Rickman. 1949. *The Peoples of Great Russia: A Psychological Study*. London: Cresset.

Gornicki, Grzegory. 1991. "Is Poland Really in Central Europe?" *East European Reporter* 4 (2): 57–58.

Gourevitch, Peter. 1978. "The Second Image Reversed: The International Sources of Domestic Politics." *International Organization* 32 (4): 881–911.

Groh, Dieter. 1961. *Russland und das Selbstverständnis Europas: Ein Beitrag zur europäischen Geistesgeschichte.* Neuwied: Hermann Luchterhand.

Grotius, Hugo. [1625] 1979. *The Rights of War and Peace: Including the Law of Nature and Nations.* Westport, Conn.: Hyperion.

Guboglo, Mikhail Nikolaevich, ed. 1992. *Etnopoliticheskaya mozaika Bashkortostana.* 2 vols. Moscow: RAN.

Gulick, Edward Vose. [1955] 1967. *Europe's Classical Balance of Power: A Case History of the Theory and Practice of One of the Great Concepts of European Statecraft.* 2nd ed. New York: Norton.

Gullestad, Marianne. 1996. "Home, Local Community, and Nation: Connections between Everyday Life Practices and Constructions of National Identity in Contemporary Norway." Paper presented to the European Anthropological Association Fourth Conference, 12–15 July, Barcelona, Spain.

Habermas, Jürgen. 1992. "Further Reflections on the Public Sphere." In *Habermas and the Public Sphere,* edited by Craig Calhoun, 421–461. Cambridge: MIT Press.

Halecki, Oscar. 1950. *The Limits and Divisions of European History.* New York: Sheed and Ward.

Hall, Stuart. 1996. "Introduction: Who Needs 'Identity'?" In *Questions of Cultural Identity,* edited by Stuart Hall and Paul du Gay, 1–17. London: Sage.

Hammen, Oscar J. 1952. "Free Europe versus Russia, 1830–1854." *American Slavic and East European Review* 11 (February): 17–41.

Hannaford, Ivan. 1996. *Race: The History of an Idea in the West.* Baltimore: Johns Hopkins University Press.

Hansard. 1816. *The Parliamentary History of England.* Vol. 28. London: T.C. Hansard.

Hansen, Lene. 1996. "Slovenian Identity: State-Building on the Balkan Border." *Alternatives* 21 (4): 473–496.

———. 1997a. "R. B. J. Walker: Deconstructing a Discipline." In *The Future of International Relations: Masters in the Making?,* edited by Iver B. Neumann and Ole Wæver, 316–336. London: Routledge.

———. 1997b. "Western Villains or Balkan Barbarism? Representations and Responsibility in the Debate over Bosnia." Ph.D. diss., Copenhagen University.

Harbsmeier, Michael. 1985. "Early Travels to Europe: Some Remarks on the Magic of Writing." In *Europe and Its Others,* edited by Francis Barker et al., 72–88. Colchester: University of Essex.

———. 1987. "Elementary Structures of Otherness: An Analysis of Sixteenth-Century German Travel Accounts." In *Voyager à la renaissance: Actes de colloque de Tours,* 337–356. Paris: Editions Maisonneuve et Larose.

Hartog, François. 1988. *The Mirror of Herodotus: The Representation of the Other in the Writing of History.* Berkeley: University of California Press.

Hauner, Milan. 1990. *What Is Asia to Us? Russia's Asian Heartland Yesterday and Today.* Boston: Unwin Hyman.

Havel, Václav. 1990. "President Václav Havel's Speech to the Polish Sejm and Senate, January 21, 1990." *East European Reporter* 4 (2): 55–57.

Hay, Denys. [1957] 1966. *Europe: The Emergence of an Idea.* 2nd ed. Edinburgh: Edinburgh University Press.

Hegel, Georg Wilhelm Friedrich. 1977. *Phenomenology of Spirit.* Oxford: Oxford University Press.

Heller, Mikhail, and Aleksandr M. Nekrich. 1986. *Utopia in Power: The History of the Soviet Union from 1917 to the Present.* New York: Summit.

Herberstein, Sigismund Baron [Freiherr] von. [1551] 1851, 1852. *Notes upon Russia: Being a translation of the Earliest Account of That Country Entitled "Rerum moscoviticarum commentarii."* London: Hakluyt Society.

Herzen, Aleksandr. 1968. "Ends and Beginnings: Letters to I. S. Turgenev (1862–1863)." In *My Past and Thoughts: The Memoirs of Alexander Herzen, 1680–1749.* London: Chatto and Windus.

Hinsley, F. H. 1963. *Power and the Pursuit of Peace: Theory and Practice in the History of Relations between States.* Cambridge: Cambridge University Press.

Hirst, Paul. 1979. *On Law and Ideology.* Basingstoke, Eng.: Macmillan.

Hogg, Michael A., and Dominic Abrams. 1988. *Social Identifications: A Social Psychology of Intergroup Relations and Group Processes.* London: Routledge.

Hollis, Martin. 1985. "Of Masks and Men." In *The Category of the Person: Anthropology, Philosophy, History,* edited by Michael Carrithers, Steven Collins, and Steven Lukes, 217–233. Cambridge: Cambridge University Press.

Holm, Ulla. 1993. *Det franske Europa.* Aarhus: Aarhus Universitetsforlag.

Holquist, Michael. 1990. *Dialogism: Bakhtin and His World.* London: Routledge.

Holst, Johan Jørgen. 1973. "Five Roads to Nordic Security." In *Five Roads to Nordic Security,* edited by Johan Jørgen Holst, 1–5. Oslo: Norwegian University Press.

———. 1990. Foreword to *The Nordic Region: Changing Perspectives in International Relations,* edited by Martin O. Heisler, 8–15. Annals of the American Academy of Political and Social Science. Vol. 512. Newbury Park, Calif.: Sage.

Hóly, Ladislav, and Michael Stuchlik. 1981. "The Structure of Folk Models." In *The Structure of Folk Models,* edited by Ladislav Hóly and Michael Stuchlik, 1–34. London: Academic Press.

Horsey, Sir Jerome. 1968. "Travels." In *Rude and Barbarous Kingdom: Russia in the Accounts of Sixteenth-Century English Travel Voyagers*, edited by Lloyd E. Berry and Robert O. Crummey, 202–369. Madison: University of Wisconsin Press.

Huntington, Samuel P. 1993. "The Clash of Civilizations?" *Foreign Affairs* 72 (3): 22–49.

Hurrell, Andrew. 1996. "Vitoria and the Universalist Conception of International Relations." In *Classical Theories in International Relations*, edited by Ian Clark and Iver B. Neumann, 99–119. Houndsmills, Eng.: Macmillan.

Ionescu, Eugene. 1985. "The Austro-Hungarian Empire: Forerunner of a Central European Confederation?" *Cross Currents* 4: 3–8.

Jæger, Øyvind. 1997. *Securitizing Russia: Discursive Practices of the Baltic States*. Working paper, no. 10. Copenhagen: Copenhagen Peace Research Institute.

Jameson, Fredric. 1972. *The Prison-House of Language: A Critical Account of Structuralism and Russian Formalism*. Princeton: Princeton University Press.

Järve, Priit. 1991. "The Soviet Union and the Prospects of Baltic Cooperation: An Estonian View." In *The Changing Soviet Union in the New Europe*, edited by Jyrki Iivonen, 211–224. Aldershot, Eng.: Edward Elgar.

Jervell, Sverre. 1991a. "Elementer i en ny nordisk arkitektur." In *Norden i det nye Europa: En rapport fra de fire nordiske utenrikspolitiske instituttene og universitetet i Reykjavik*, 185-222. Oslo: Norsk Utenrikspolitisk Institutt, Prosjekt Norden i Europa.

———. 1991b. "Organizing Europe's Northern Periphery: The Nordic Countries Facing the New Europe." Informal draft paper submitted to the conference The Baltic Sea Region: Cooperation or Conflict? 6–8 December, Kiel.

Joenniemi, Pertti. 1991. "A Blueprint for Baltic Sea Region Politics." Paper presented to a workshop at the European Nuclear Disarmament Convention, 15 August, Moscow.

Judt, Tony. 1992. *Past Imperfect: French Intellectuals, 1944–1956*. Berkeley: University of California Press.

Katzenstein, Peter J., ed. 1996. *The Culture of National Security: Norms and Identity in World Politics*. New York: Columbia University Press.

Kemp, Peter. 1992. *Emmanuel Lévinas. En introduktion*. Gothenberg, Sweden: Daidalos.

Khairullin F. 1992. "Natsional'noe dvizhenie ili bor'ba za prezidentskoe kreslo?" In *Etnopoliticheskaya mozaika Bashkortostana*, edited by Mikhail Nikolaevich Guboglo, vol. 2. Moscow: RAN.

Kindersley, Richard. 1962. *The First Russian Revisionists: A Study of "Legal Marxism" in Russia*. Oxford: Clarendon.

Kingsbury, Ben, and Adam Roberts. 1990. "Introduction: Grotian Thought in International Relations." In *Hugo Grotius and International Relations*, edited by Hedley Bull, Ben Kingsbury, and Adam Roberts, 1–64. Oxford: Clarendon.

Kingsley, Martin, B. 1924. *The Triumph of Lord Palmerston: A Study of Public Opinion in England before the Crimean War*. London: George Allen and Unwin.

Kinyapina, Nina Stepanovna. 1963. *Vneshnyaya politika Rossii pervoy poloviny XIX v.* Moscow: Vyshaya shkola.

Kiš, Danilo. 1987. "Variations on the Theme of Central Europe." *Cross Currents: A Yearbook of Central European Culture* 6: 1–14.

Kiss, Csaba G. 1989. "Central European Writers about Central Europe: Introduction to a Non-Existent Book of Reading." In *In Search of Central Europe*, edited by George Schöpflin and Nancy Wood, 125–136. Cambridge: Polity.

Kiss, László J. 1989. "European Security: Hungarian Interpretations, Perceptions, and Foreign Policy." In *European Polyphony: Perspectives beyond East-West Cooperation*, edited by Ole Wæver, Pierre Lemaitre, and Elzbieta Tromer, 141–153. London: Macmillan.

Knothe, Thomas. 1992. "Polen och Östesjösamarbetet." *Nordisk kontakt* 37: 35–36.

Kolstoe, Paul. 1994. *The New Russian Diaspora*. London: Hearst.

Konrád, György. 1984. *Antipolitics: An Essay*. San Diego, Calif.: Harcourt Brace Jovanovich.

———. 1985. "Is the Dream of Central Europe Still Alive?" *Cross Currents: A Yearbook of Central European Culture* 5: 109–121.

———. 1991. *Drømmen om Mellom-Europa*. Oslo: Cappelen.

Kristeva, Julia. [1966] 1986. "Word, Discourse, and Novel." In *The Kristeva Reader*, by Julia Kristeva, edited by Toril Moi, 34–61. Oxford: Blackwell.

———. 1991. *Strangers to Ourselves*. New York: Columbia University Press.

Kundera, Milan. 1984. "The Tragedy of Central Europe." *New York Review of Books*, 26 April, pp. 33–38.

———. 1991. *Žert* [A joke]. Brno: Atlantis.

Kuzeev, Rail Gumerovich, ed. 1987. *Etnicheskie protsessy v Bashkirii v novoe i noveyshee vremya*. Ufa: Bashkirsky Filial Akademiy Nauk.

Laclau, Ernesto, and Chantal Mouffe. 1985. *Hegemony and Socialist Strategy: Towards a Radical Democratic Politics*. London: Verso.

Laffey, Mark, and Jutta Weldes. 1997. "Beyond Belief: Ideas and Symbolic Technologies in the Study of International Relations." *European Journal of International Relations* 3 (2): 193–237.

Lapid, Yosef, and Friedrich Kratochwil, eds. 1996, *The Return of Culture and Identity in IR Theory*. London: Lynne Rienner.

Laue, Theodore H. von. 1963. *Sergei Witte and the Industrialization of Russia*. New York: Columbia University Press.

Lemberg, Hans. 1985. "Zur Entstehung des Osteuropabegriffs im Jahrhundert vom 'Norden' zum 'Osten' Europas." *Jahrbücher für Geschichte Osteuropas* 33: 48–91.

Lemert, Charles. 1994. "Dark Thoughts about the Self." In *Social Theory and the Politics of Identity*, edited by Craig Calhoun, 100–129. Oxford: Blackwell.

Lenin, Vladimir Ilich. [1914] 1975. "The Right of Nations to Self-Determination." In *The Lenin Anthology*, edited by Robert C. Tucker, 153–180. New York: Norton.

Lévinas, Emmanuel. 1989. *The Levinas Reader*, edited by Seàn Hand. Oxford: Blackwell.

Lévi-Strauss, Claude. [1973] 1978. "Race and History." In *Structural Anthropology*, 2: 323–362. Harmondsworth, Eng.: Penguin.

Lewis, Bernard. 1995. *The Middle East: 200 Years of History from the Rise of Christianity to the Present Day*. London: Weidenfeld and Nicolson.

Likhachev, Dmitriy S. 1980. "Zametki o russkom: Priroda, rodnik, prosto dobrota." *Novy mir* 56 (3): 10–38.

Lindquist, Åke, and Nils Lundgren. 1974. *Integrationen i Västeuropa*. Stockholm: AWE/Gebers.

Linklater, Andrew. [1982] 1990. *Men and Citizens in the Theory of International Relations*. 2nd ed. Basingstoke, Eng.: Macmillan.

Lipschutz, Ronnie D., ed. 1995. *On Security*. New York: Columbia University Press.

List, Friedrich. [1841] 1904. *The National System of Political Economy*. New York: Longman.

Lortholary, Albert. 1951. *Les "philosophes" du XVIIIe siècle et la Russie: Le mirage russe en France au XVIIIe siècle*. Paris: Boivin.

Lotman, Yuri M. 1990. *Universe of the Mind: A Semiotic Theory of Culture*. London: I. B. Tauris.

Lyotard, Jean-François. 1988. *The Differend: Phrases in Dispute*. Minneapolis: University of Minnesota Press.

M. L. [Lesur, Charles Louis]. 1812. *Des progrès de la puissance russe, depuis son origine jusqu'au commencement du XIXe siècle*. Paris: Fantin.

Maalouf, Amin. 1984. *The Crusades through Arab Eyes*. New York: Schocken.

Magris, Claudio, et al. 1991. "The Budapest Roundtable." *Cross Currents: A Yearbook of Central European Affairs* 10: 17–31.

Marx, Karl. 1994. "From the Paris Notebooks." In *Early Political Writings*, by Karl Marx, edited by Joseph O'Malley, 71–96. Cambridge: Cambridge University Press.

Matejka, Ladislav. 1990. "Milan Kundera's Central Europe." *Cross Currents: A Yearbook of Central European Culture* 9: 127–134.

Matvejević, Predrag. 1989. "Central Europe from the East of Europe." In *In Search of Central Europe*, edited by George Schöpflin and Nancy Wood, 183–190. Cambridge: Polity.

Mauss, Marcel. [1938] 1985. "A Category of the Human Mind: The Notion of Person; the Notion of Self." in *The Category of the Person: Anthropology, Philosophy, History,* edited by Michael Carrithers, Steven Collins, and Steven Lukes, 1–25. Cambridge: Cambridge University Press.

Mazzini, Giuseppe. 1912. "The Duties of Man." In *The Duties of Man and Other Essays.* London: J. P. Dent.

McCormick, John P. 1993. "Introduction to Schmitt's 'The Age of Neutralizations and Depoliticizations.'" *Telos* 26 (2): 119–129.

McKay, Derek, and H. M. Scott. 1983. *The Rise of the Great Powers: 1648–1815.* London: Longman.

McNally, Raymond T. 1958. "The Origins of Russophobia in France 1812–1830." In *American Slavic and East European Review* 17 (April): 173–189.

Meinecke, Friedrich. [1924] 1957. *Machiavellism: The Doctrine of Raison d'Etat and Its Place in Modern History.* London: Routledge and Kegan Paul.

Meyer, Henry Cord. 1955. *Mitteleuropa in German Thought and Action, 1815–1945.* The Hague: Nijhoff.

Milliken, Jennifer, and David Sylvan. 1996. "Soft Bodies, Hard Targets, and Chic Theories: US Bombing Policy in Indochina." *Millennium* 25 (2): 321–361.

Mirdzanova, S. 1989. *Yuzhnoe narechie Bashkirskogo yazyka.* Moscow: Nauka.

Møller, Peter Ulf. 1993. "Hvordan russerne er: Et stykke dansk mentalitetshistorie." In *Danmark og Rusland i 500 år,* edited by Svend Aage Christensen and Henning Gottlieb, 104–131. Copenhagen: Det Sikkerheds- og Nedrustningspolitiske Udvalg.

Montesquieu, Charles de. [1748] 1989. *The Spirit of the Laws.* Edited by Anne M. Cohler, Basia Carolyn Miller, and Harold Samuel Stone. Cambridge: Cambridge University Press.

Mortimer, Edward. 1988. "The Promise of a New Era." *Financial Times, Centenary Sunday Issue,* 15 February.

Mouffe, Chantal. 1994. "For a Politics of Nomadic Identity." In *Travellers' Tales: Narratives of Home and Displacement,* edited by George Robertson et al., 105–113. London: Routledge.

Mouritsen, Per. 1995. "Liberty, Solidarity, and Patriotism: A Republican Idea of Political Identity." Mimeo, European University Institute.

Mutton, Alice. 1961. *Central Europe: A Regional and Human Geography.* London: Longman.

Naarden, Bruno. 1992. *Socialist Europe and Revolutionary Russia: Perception and Prejudice, 1848–1923.* Cambridge: Cambridge University Press.

Naff, Thomas. 1985. "The Ottoman Empire and the European States System." In *The Expansion of International Society,* edited by Hedley Bull and Adam Watson, 143–170. Oxford: Claredon.

Nansen, Fridtjof. 1923. *Rusland og freden.* Kristiania, Norway: Jacob Dybwad.

Nathanson, Charles E. 1988. "The Social Construction of the Soviet Threat: A Study in the Politics of Representation." *Alternatives* 13 (4): 443–483.

Neuhold, Hanspeter. 1991. "From the 'Mitteleuropa' Debate to the Pentagonale." In *The Pentagonal/Hexagonal Experiment: New Forms of Cooperation in a Changing Europe,* edited by Hanspeter Neuhold, 113–125. Laxenburg, Austria: Austrian Institute of International Affairs.

Neumann, Iver B. 1992. "Poland as a Regional Great Power: The Interwar Heritage." In *Regional Great Powers in International Politics,* edited by Iver B. Neumann, 141–159. Basingstoke, Eng.: Macmillan.

———. 1996. *Russia and the Idea of Europe: A Study in Identity and International Relations.* London: Routledge.

———. 1997a. Conclusion to *The Future of International Relations: Masters in the Making?,* edited by Iver B. Neumann and Ole Wæver, 359–370. London: Routledge.

———. 1997b. "Book Review Essay: Ringmar on Identity and War." *Cooperation and Conflict* 32 (3): 309–30.

———. Forthcoming. "This Little Piggy Stayed at Home: Norwegian Negotiations of State, Nation, and European Integration." In *State, Nation, Europe: The Nordic Countries Face the European Union,* edited by Lene Hansen and Ole Wæver. London: Routledge.

Nielsson, Gunnar. 1989. "The Parallel National Action Process." In *Frameworks for International Cooperation,* edited by Paul Taylor and A. J. P. Groom, 78–108. London: Pinter.

Nietzsche, Friedrich. [1908] 1992. *Ecce Homo.* Harmondsworth, Eng.: Penguin.

Nilsen, Jens Petter. 1991. "Ønsket tsaren seg en isfri havn i nord?" *Historisk Tidsskrift* 70 (4): 604–621.

Nonnenmacher, Günther. 1987. "Gorbachev's Message for Europe a Dangerous, Phoney Metaphor." *The German Tribune,* 15 March. Translated from *Frankfurter Allgemeine Zeitung,* 9 March.

Norden i det nye Europa. En rapport fra de fire nordiske utenrikspolitiske instituttene og universitetet i Reykjavik. 1991. Oslo: Norsk Utenriks-politisk Institutt, Prosjekt Norden i Europa.

Norton, Anne. 1988. *Reflections on Political Identity*. Baltimore: Johns Hopkins University Press.

Novikov, Andrey. 1991. "Ya—rusofob." *Vek XX i mir* 33 (7): 12–14.

Nye, Joseph S., ed. 1968. *International Regionalism*. Boston: Little, Brown.

Olesen, Virginia. 1994. "Feminisms and Models of Qualitative Research." In *Handbook of Qualitative Research*, edited by Norman K. Denzin and Yvonna S. Lincoln, 158–174. London: Sage.

Özdalga, Elisabeth. 1989. *Turkiet väg in i Europa*. Världspolitikens dagsfrågor 7. Stockholm: The Swedish Institute of International Affairs.

Paleologu, Alexandru. 1991. *Minunatele amintiri ale unui ambassador al golanilor*. Bucharest: Humanitas.

Palmer, Alan 1974. *Alexander I: Tsar of War and Peace*. London: Weidenfeld and Nicolson.

Petrovich, Michael Boro. 1956. *The Emergence of Russian Panslavism, 1856–1870*. New York: Columbia University Press.

Pipes, Richard. 1964. *The Formation of the Soviet Union: Communism and Nationalism, 1917–1923*. Cambridge: Harvard University Press.

Platonov, Sergej Fedorovic. [1925] 1972. *Moscow and the West*. Edited by Joseph L. Wieczynski. Hattiesburg, Miss.: Academic International.

Polovtsoff, A. 1902. *Correspondence diplomatique des ambassadeurs et ministres de Russie en France et de France en Russie avec leurs gouvernements de 1814 à 1830*. Vols. 1, 2. St. Petersburg: Ed. de la Société Imperiale d'Histoire de Russie.

Pozdnyakov, Elgiz. 1991. "The Soviet Union: The Problem of Coming Back to European Civilisation." *Paradigms* 5 (1, 2): 45–57.

Purnell, Robert. 1973. *The Society of States*. London: Weidenfeld and Nicolson.

Rebas, Hain. 1988. "'Baltic Regionalism'?" *Journal of Baltic Studies* 19 (2): 101–116.

Reynold, Gonzague de. 1950. *Le monde Russe*. La formation de l'Europe, vol. 6. Paris: Librairie Plon.

Ricoeur, Paul. [1988] 1991. "Narrative Identity." In *On Paul Ricoeur: Narrative and Interpretation*, edited by David Wood, 188–199. London: Routledge.

———. [1990] 1992. *Oneself as Another*. Chicago: University of Chicago Press.

Riha, Thomas. 1969. *A Russian European: Paul Miliukov in Russian Politics*. Notre Dame, Ind.: University of Notre Dame Press.

Ringmar, Erik. 1995. "The Relevance of International Law: A Hegelian

Interpretation of a Peculiar Seventeenth-Century Preoccupation." *Review of International Studies* 21 (1): 87–103.

———. 1996a. *Identity, Interest, and Action: A Cultural Explanation of Sweden's Intervention in the Thirty Years War.* Cambridge: Cambridge University Press.

———. 1996b. "On the Ontological Status of the State" *European Journal of International Affairs* 2 (4): 439–466.

Roberts, Henry L. 1964a. "Reply." In *The Development of the USSR: An Exchange of Views,* edited by Donald W. Treadgold, 386–388. Seattle: University of Washington Press.

———. 1964b. "Russia and the West: A Comparison and Contrast." In *The Development of the USSR: An Exchange of Views,* edited by Donald W. Treadgold, 359–370. Seattle: University of Washington Press.

Robertson, Roland. 1992. *Globalization: Social Theory and Global Culture.* Theory, Culture, and Society. London: Sage.

Rodinson, Maxime. 1987. *Europe and the Mystique of Islam.* London: I. B. Tauris.

Ron, Ger van. 1989. "Great Britain and the Oslo States." *Journal of Contemporary History* 24 (4): 657–664.

Rougemont, Denis de. 1966. *The Idea of Europe.* New York: Macmillan.

Rousseau, Jean-Jacques. [1762] 1973. *The Social Contract.* London: Dent.

Rupnik, Jacques. 1990. "Central Europe or Mitteleuropa?" *Daedalus* 119: 249–278.

Russett, Bruce M. 1967. *International Regions and the International System.* Chicago: Rand McNally.

Safiullina, Flera Sadrievna, and Kamil Rakhimovich Galiullin, eds. 1986. *Russko-tatarskiy razgovornik.* Kazan', Russia: Kazanskoe knizhnoe izdatel'stvo.

Said, Edward W. [1978] 1985. *Orientalism.* Harmondsworth, Eng.: Penguin.

———. 1983. *The World, the Text, and the Critic.* Cambridge: Harvard University Press.

Sakharov, Andrey. [1974] 1977. "On Alexander Solzhenitsyn's *Letter to the Soviet Leaders.*" In *The Political, Social, and Religious Thought of Russian "Samizdat": An Anthology,* edited by Michael Meerson-Aksenov and Boris Shragin, 291–301. Belmont, Mass.: Nordland.

Sampson, Edward E. 1989. "The Deconstruction of the Self." In *Texts of Identity,* edited by John Shotter and Kenneth J. Gergen, 1–19. Inquiries in Social Construction. London: Sage.

Sartre, Jean-Paul. 1957. *Being and Nothingness: An Essay on Phenomenological Ontology.* London: Methuen.

Schelting, Alexander von. 1948. *Russland und Europa in Russischen Geschichtsdenken.* Berne: A. Francke.

Schmitt, Carl. 1963. *Der Begriff des Politischen: Text von 1932 mit einem Vorwort und drei Collarien*. Berlin: Duncker and Humblot.

Schöpflin, George. 1989. "Central Europe: Definitions Old and New." In *In Search of Central Europe*, edited by George Schöpflin and Nancy Wood, 7–29. Cambridge: Polity.

Schöpflin, George, and Nancy Wood, eds. 1989. *In Search of Central Europe*. Cambridge: Polity.

Schwartz, Lee. 1990. "Regional Population Distribution and National Homelands in the USSR." In *Soviet Nationality Policies: Ruling Ethnic Groups in the USSR*, edited by Henry R. Huttenbach, 121–161. London: Mansell.

Schwarz, Egon. 1989. "Central Europe: What It Is and What It Is Not." In *In Search of Central Europe*, edited by George Schöpflin and Nancy Wood, 143–156. Cambridge: Polity.

Schwoebel, Robert. 1967. *The Shadow of the Crescent: The Renaissance Image of the Turk*. Nieuwkoop: B. De Graaf.

Shafarevich, Igor. 1989. "Rusofobiya." *Nash sovremennik* 57 (6): 167–192.

Shapiro, Michael J. 1981. *Language and Political Understanding: The Politics of Discursive Practice*. New Haven, Conn.: Yale University Press.

———. 1988. *The Politics of Representation*. Madison: University of Wisconsin Press.

———. 1992. *Reading the Postmodern Polity: Political Theory as Textual Practice*. Minneapolis: University of Minnesota Press.

———. 1993. *Reading "Adam Smith": Desire, History, and Value*. Modernity and Political Thought. London: Sage.

Shevtsova, Lilia. 1990. "The Chances of Democracy." *New Times* 52: 4–6.

Short Course. [1938] 1948. *History of the Communist Party of the Soviet Union (Bolsheviks): Short Course*, edited by a Commission of the Central Committee of the CPSU (b), authorized by the CC of the CPSU (b) Moscow: Foreign Languages Publishing House.

Šimečka, Milan. 1989. "Another Civilization? An Other Civilization?" In *In Search of Central Europe*, edited by George Schöpflin and Nancy Wood, 157–162. Cambridge: Polity.

Simmel, Georg. 1970. "The Stranger." In *On Individuality and Social Forces: Selected Writings*, edited by David N. Levine, 143–149. Chicago: University of Chicago Press.

Simon, Gerhard. [1986] 1991. *Nationalism and Policy toward the Nationalities in the Soviet Union: From Totalitarian Dictatorship to Post-Stalinist Society*. Boulder, Colo.: Westview.

Skubiszewski, Krzysztof. 1992. "The Challenge to Western Policy of Change in Eastern Europe." Paper presented to the Conference on Britain and the Future of Eastern Europe and the Former Soviet Union, All Souls College, 10–12 April, Oxford.

Sodaro, Michael J. 1990. *Moscow, Germany, and the West: From Khrushchev to Gorbachev.* Ithaca, N.Y.: Cornell University Press.

Solov'ev, Vladimir Sergeevich. [1888/1891] n.d., probably 1905. "Natsional'nyy vopros v Rossii." In *Sobranie sochineniy,* 5: 1–368. St. Petersburg: Obshchestvennaya pol'za.

Solzhenitsyn, Aleksandr. [1974] 1975. "Repentance and Self-Limitation in the Life of the Nations." In *From under the Rubble,* edited by Aleksandr Solzhenitsyn et al., 105–143. London: Collins and Harvill.

———. 1990. "Kak nam obustroit' Rossiyu. Posil'nye soobrazheniya." Enclosure to *Literaturnaya gazeta* (Moscow), 19 September.

Solzhenitsyn, Aleksandr, et al., eds. [1974] 1975. *From under the Rubble.* London: Collins and Harvill.

Somers, Margaret R., and Gloria D. Gibson. 1994. "Reclaiming the Epistemological 'Other': Narrative and the Social Construction of Identity." In *Social Theory and the Politics of Identity,* edited by Craig Calhoun, 37–99. Oxford: Blackwell.

Southern, Richard W. 1962. *Western Views of Islam in the Middle Ages.* Cambridge: Harvard University Press.

Spivak, Gayatri Chakravorty. 1987a. "Reading the World: Literary Studies in the Eighties." In *In Other Worlds: Essays in Cultural Politics,* 95–102. New York: Methuen.

———. 1987b. "Subaltern Studies: Deconstructing Historiography." In *In Other Worlds: Essays in Cultural Politics,* 197–221. New York: Methuen.

Stalin, Iosif Vissarionovich. 1951. "O zadachakh kozyastvennikov: Rech' na Vsesoyuznoy konferentsii rabotnikov sotsialisticheskoy promyshlennosti 4 fevralya 1931 g." In *Sochineniya,* 13: 29–42. Moscow: Gosudarstvennoe izdatel'stvo politicheskoy literatury, 1946–1951.

Starikov, Evgeniy. 1989. "Marginaly, ili razmyshleniya na staruyu temu: 'Chto s nami proiskhodit?'" *Znamya* 59 (10): 133–162.

Steger, H.-A. and R. Morell, eds. 1987. *Ein Gespenst geht um . . . : Mitteleuropa.* Munich: Eberhard.

Strémooukhoff, Dimitri. 1953. "Moscow and the Third Rome: Sources of the Doctrine." *Speculum* 28 (1): 84–101.

Strong, Tracy B. 1992a. "Introduction: The Self and the Political Order." In *The Self and the Political Order,* edited by Tracy B. Strong, 1–21. Oxford: Blackwell.

———. 1992b. "Text and Pretexts: Reflections on Perspectivism in Nietzsche." In *The Self and the Political Order,* edited by Tracy B. Strong, 161–180. Oxford: Blackwell.

Sundelius, Bengt. 1982. "The Nordic Model of Neighborly Cooperation." In *Foreign Policies of Northern Europe,* edited by Bengt Sundelius, 177–196. Boulder, Colo.: Westview.

Svanberg, Ingvar. 1992. "Basjkirien eller Basjkortistan." In *Gamla folk och nya stater. Det upplöste sovjetimperiet*, edited by Ingvar Svanberg and Sven Gustavsson, 93–98. Stockholm: Gidlund.

Swiderski, Bronislaw. 1988. "Østeuropæernes Europa." In *Europas opdagelse: Historien om en idé*, edited by Hans Boll-Johansen and Michael Harbs-meier, 140–155. Copenhagen: Christian Eilers' Forlag.

Szücs, Jenö. 1988. "Three Historical Regions in Europe." In *Civil Society and the State: New European Perspectives*, edited by John Keane, 291–332. London: Verso.

Taylor, Charles. 1989. *Sources of the Self: The Making of the Modern Identity*. Cambridge: Cambridge University Press.

Timmermann, Heinz. 1992. "Opening to the West: Crucial Points in Soviet Policy toward Europe." In *The Soviet Union, 1990/91: Crisis—Disintegration—New Orientation*, edited by Gerhard Simon, 48–63. Cologne: Bundesinstitut für ostwissenschaftliche und internationale Studien.

Todorov, Tzvetan. [1981] 1984. *Mikhail Bakhtin: The Dialogical Principle*. Minneapolis: University of Minnesota Press.

———. [1982] 1992. *The Conquest of America: The Question of the Other*. New York: Harper Perennial.

———. 1989. *Nous et les autres: La réflexion française sur la diversité humaine*. Paris: Seuil.

Tökés, Rudolf L. 1991. "From Visegrád to Kraków: Cooperation, Competition, and Coexistence in Central Europe." *Problems of Communism* 40 (November–December): 100–114.

Tønnesson, Stein. 1991. "History and National Identity in Scandinavia: The Contemporary Debate." First lecture presented at the University of Oslo, in partial fulfillment of the Ph.D. degree, 25 October.

Trubetskoy, Nikolay Sergeevich. 1920. *Evropa i chelovechestvo*. Sofia: Rossiysko-bolgarskoe knigoizdatel'stvo.

Tunander, Ola. 1995. "A New Ottoman Empire? The Choice for Turkey: Euro-Asian Centre vs. National Fortress." *Security Dialogue* 26 (4): 413–426.

Turgenev, I. S. [1862] 1963. Letter to A. I. Herzen of 23 October/4 November. Reprinted in *Polnoe sobranie sochineniy i pisem v dvadtsati vos'mi tomakh: Pis'ma v trinadtsati tomakh*, 5: 64–65. Moscow: Akademiya nauk.

Ullock, Christoph J. 1996. "Imagining Community: A Metaphysics of Being or Becoming?" *Millennium* 25 (2): 425–441.

Vajda, Mihály. [1985] 1988a. "Central Eastern European Perspectives." In *Civil Society and the State: New European Perspectives*, edited by John Keane, 333–360. London: Verso.

———. 1988b. "Wer hat Russland aus Europa ausgeschlossen? Reflexionen über Milan Šimečkas Artikel 'Noch eine Zivilisation? Eine andere

Zivilisation?'" In *Mitteleuropa: Traum oder Trauma? Überlegungen zum Selbstbild einer Region,* edited by H.-P. Burmeister, F. Boldt, and Gy. Mészáros, 73–84. Bremen: Temmen.

———. 1989. "Who Excluded Russia from Europe? (A Reply to Simecka)." In *In Search of Central Europe,* edited by George Schöpflin and Nancy Wood, 168–175. Cambridge: Polity.

Vernadsky, George, et al. 1972. *A Source Book for Russian History from Early Times to 1917.* Vol. 2. New Haven, Conn.: Yale University Press.

Wæver, Ole. 1991. "Culture and Identity in the Baltic Sea Region." In *Co-operation in the Baltic Sea Region: Needs and Prospects,* edited by Pertti Joenniemi, 79–111. Report 42. Tampere: Tampere Peace Research Institute.

———. 1992. "Three Competing "Europes": French, German, Russian." *International Affairs* 44 (2): 477–493.

———. 1995. "Resisting the Temptations of Post Foreign Policy Analysis." In *The European Community and Changing Foreign Policy Perspectives in Europe,* edited by Walter Carlsnaes and Steve Smith, 238–273. London: Sage.

———. Forthcoming. "Beyond the Beyond of Critical International Relations Theory: Richard Ashley." In *Beyond the Interparadigm Debate,* edited by Mark Hoffmann and Nich Rengger. Hemel Hempstead, Eng.: Harvester.

Wæver, Ole, Barry Buzan, Morten Kelstrup, and Pierre Lemaitre. 1993. *Identity, Migration, and the New Security Agenda in Europe.* London: Pinter.

Wæver, Ole, Ulla Holm, and Henrik Larsen. Forthcoming. *The Struggle for "Europe": French and German Concepts of State, Nation, and European Union.* Cambridge: Cambridge University Press.

Walicki, Andrzej. 1969. *The Controversy over Capitalism: Studies in the Social Philosophy of the Russian Populists.* Oxford: Clarendon.

———. 1975. *The Slavophile Controversy: History of a Conservative Utopia in Nineteenth-Century Thought.* Oxford: Clarendon.

Walker, R. B. J. 1993. *Inside/Outside: International Relations as Political Theory.* Cambridge: Cambridge University Press.

Warner, Daniel. 1996. "Buber, Lévinas, and the Concept of the Otherness in International Relations: A Reply to David Campbell." *Millennium* 25 (1): 111–129.

Watson, Adam. 1984. "Russia and the European States System." In *The Expansion of International Society,* edited by Hedley Bull and Adam Watson, 61–74. Oxford: Clarendon.

———. 1987. "Hedley Bull, States Systems, and International Societies." *Review of International Studies* 13: 147–153.

Weisensel, Peter R. 1990. "Russian Self-Identification and Travelers' Descriptions of the Ottoman Empire in the First Half of the Nineteenth

Century." Paper presented to the Fourth World Congress for Soviet and East European Studies, 21–26 July, Harrogate, England.

Weldes, Jutta. 1996. "Constructing National Interest." *European Journal of International Relations* 2 (3): 275–318.

Welsh, Jennifer. 1995. *Edmund Burke and International Relations: The Commonwealth of Europe and the Crusade against the French Revolution.* London: Macmillan/St. Antony's College.

Wendt, Alexander. 1992. "Anarchy Is What States Make of It." *International Organization* 46 (2): 391–425.

———. 1994. "Collective Identity Formation and the International State." *American Political Science Review* 88 (2): 384–396.

White, Stephen. 1985. *The Origins of Détente: The Genoa Conference and Soviet Western Relations, 1921–1922.* Cambridge: Cambridge University Press.

Wiberg, Håkan and Ole Wæver. 1992. "Norden in the Cold War Reality." In *Nordic Security in the 1990s: Options in the Changing Europe,* edited by Jan Öberg, 13–34. London: Pinter.

Wight, Martin. 1977. *Systems of States.* Edited by Hedley Bull. Leicester, Eng.: Leicester University Press.

———. 1991. *International Theory: The Three Traditions.* Edited by Gabriele Wight and Brian Porter. Leicester, Eng.: Leicester University Press for the Royal Institute of International Affairs.

Winch, Peter. [1964] 1987. "Understanding a Primitive Society." In *Interpreting Politics,* edited by Michael T. Gibbons, 32–63. Oxford: Basil Blackwell.

Wind, Marlene. 1992. "Eksisterer Europa? Refleksioner over forsvar, identitet og borgerdyd i et nyt Europa." In *Europa: Nation—union—efter Minsk og Maastricht,* edited by Christen Sørensen, 23–81. Copenhagen: Fremad.

Wittram, Reinhard. 1973. *Russia and Europe.* London: Thanes and Hudson.

Wolff, Larry. 1994. *Inventing Eastern Europe: The Map of Civilization on the Mind of the Enlightenment.* Stanford, Calif.: Stanford University Press.

Yag'ya, V. S. 1992. "Baltiyskiy region i Sankt-Peterburg v novom izmerenii." Paper presented to the second parliamentary conference on co-operation in the Baltic Sea area, 22–24 April, Oslo.

Yapp, M. E. 1992. "Europe in the Turkish Mirror." *Past and Present* 137 (2): 134–155.

Yuldashbaev, B. 1972. *Istoriya formirovaniya Bashkirskoy natsional'nosti.* Ufa: Bashkirsky Filial Akademiy Nauk.

Zenkovsky, Serge A. 1960. *Pan-Turkism and Islam in Russia.* Cambridge: Harvard University Press.

———. 1972. Introduction to *Moscow and the West,* by S. F. Platonov, edited by Joseph L. Wieczynski, vii–xvii. Hattiesburg, Miss.: Academic International.

Žižek, Slavoj. 1989. *The Sublime Object of Ideology.* London: Verso.

Zorgbibe, Charles. 1968. *Les Etats-Unis Scandinaves.* Paris: Pédone.

Zyuganov, Gennadiy. 1994. *Derzhava.* Moscow: Informpechat'.

———. 1996. *Rossiya—rodina moya: Ideologiya gosudarstvennogo patriotizma.* Moscow: Informpechat'.

Index

CREATED BY EILEEN QUAM AND THERESA WOLNER

IVER B. NEUMANN heads the Russian Research Centre at the Norwegian Institute of International Affairs, Oslo. Among his many publications are *Russia and the Idea of Europe: A Study in Identity and International Relations* (1996) and *The Future of International Relations: Masters in the Making?* (1997), coedited with Ole Wæver.